Ruella Frank has given us a great gift. Keenly observed and richly considered, she connects us to the current of contact that underlies human experience. Her insights into the body's role in both obstructing and facilitating entry into the present moment are invaluable.

Mark Epstein is author of *Thoughts without a Thinker and The Zen of Therapy: Uncovering a Hidden Kindness in Life*

Ruella Frank's book explores a new paradigm for psychotherapy theory and practice explained with great simplicity and depth. It describes with experiential immediacy, and through sensitive case studies, the phenomenology of relational movements that build our being in the world and sets the ground for each unique therapeutic encounter. *The Bodily Roots of Experience in Psychotherapy* is an excellent tool for psychotherapists of all modalities, and for those who want to orient themselves in the relational use of the body for healing relationships.

Margherita Spagnuolo Lobb is director Istituto di Gestalt HCC Italy and author of *The Now for Next in Psychotherapy: Gestalt Therapy Recounted in Post-Modern Society*

Given her background and experience as a practising Gestalt psychotherapist, Ruella Frank's detailed specifications and case studies of the psychophysical features of the "Six Fundamental Movements" that ground human interrelationships and human-world relationships are particularly edifying. Those psychophysical features document the integral relationship of movement and feelings, showing how that relationship is experientially evident from the very beginning, that is, in infancy and from infancy onward.

Maxine Sheets-Johnstone is author of *The Primacy of Movement* and *Insides and Outsides: Interdisciplinary Perspectives on Animate Nature*

The Bodily Roots of Experience in Psychotherapy

This book explores the significance of movement processes as they shape one's experience through life. It provides a comprehensive, practical understanding of how we lose the wonder and curiosity we move with as children, and how we can reclaim that.

A new paradigm is presented in the making of experience through a radical and thorough investigation into the basics of animated life. The book utilizes a precise phenomenological language for those subverbal interactions that form the foundation of lived experience. The centrality of those interactions to the therapeutic encounter is set forth through richly detailed therapy vignettes. The building of experience is meticulously explored via the bridging of infant-parent dyads and the functional similarity of those dyads to the unfolding patient-therapist relationship. Readers learn to acknowledge routine inhibitions developed in early life, appreciate their former usefulness, and discover how to restore the lively flow of moving-feeling responses.

This book is essential for all psychotherapists who wish to integrate the dynamics of movement into their work; educators who work with babies and young children; and all those wishing to understand better their psychophysical selves.

Ruella Frank photographed by Michael Mitchell

Ruella Frank brings many years of experience to her work as a gestalt psychotherapist: professional dancer/choreographer, yoga practitioner, student of various movement theories, and student of Laura Perls, co-founder of gestalt therapy. Founder and director of the Center for Somatic Studies, Dr. Frank is faculty at the New York Institute for Gestalt Therapy, Gestalt Associates for Psychotherapy, adjunct faculty at Gestalt Institute of Toronto. She teaches throughout the United States, Europe, Eurasia, Mexico, South America, and Canada. She has written articles and book chapters, authored *Body of Awareness: A Somatic and Developmental Approach to Psychotherapy* (2001, GestaltPress, available in four languages), and co-coauthored *The First Year and the Rest of Your Life: Movement, Development and Psychotherapeutic Change* (2010, Routledge, available in three languages). Her video, *Introduction to Developmental Somatic Psychotherapy,* is available in three languages.

The Bodily Roots of Experience in Psychotherapy

Ruella Frank

Routledge
Taylor & Francis Group

LONDON AND NEW YORK

Cover image: Photo by Chris Man, Unsplash

First published 2023
by Routledge
4 Park Square, Milton Park, Abingdon, Oxon OX14 4RN

and by Routledge
605 Third Avenue, New York, NY 10158

Routledge is an imprint of the Taylor & Francis Group, an informa business

British Library Cataloguing-in-Publication Data
A catalogue record for this book is available from the British Library

Library of Congress Cataloging-in-Publication Data
Names: Frank, Ruella, author.
Title: The bodily roots of experience in psychotherapy : moving self / Ruella Frank.
Description: Milton Park, Abingdon, Oxon ; New York, NY : Routledge,
2023. | Includes bibliographical references and index. |
Identifiers: LCCN 2022007434 (print) | LCCN 2022007435 (ebook) |
ISBN 9781032210070 (hardback) | ISBN 9781032210087 (paperback) |
ISBN 9781003266341 (ebook)
Subjects: LCSH: Experience in children. | Motor ability in infants. |
Infants--Development. | Parent and infant.
Classification: LCC BF723.E95 F73 2023 (print) | LCC BF723.E95 (ebook) |
DDC 155.4--dc23/eng/20220217
LC record available at https://lccn.loc.gov/2022007434
LC ebook record available at https://lccn.loc.gov/2022007435

ISBN: 978-1-032-21007-0 (hbk)
ISBN: 978-1-032-21008-7 (pbk)
ISBN: 978-1-003-26634-1 (ebk)

DOI: 10.4324/9781003266341

Typeset in Times New Roman
by MPS Limited, Dehradun

In loving memory of
My mother, Jean Walters Frank
My teacher, Laura Perls
My friend, Dorette Mayer

Contents

Acknowledgements

I am most grateful to my colleagues at the New York Institute for Gestalt Therapy for many years of fruitful, ongoing discussions of gestalt therapy theory and practice. I especially want to thank members Dan Bloom, Lynne Jacobs, Michael Vincent Miller, Carmen Vázquez Bandín, Jean-Marie Robine, and Margherita Spagnuolo-Lobb, all of whom I have taught alongside and learned from.

I want to gratefully acknowledge those students from various classes, workshops, Developmental Somatic Psychotherapy training programs, Teacher Trainer programs, and supervision groups. It is from their ongoing interest and curiosity that my work has found and continues to find its form. I thank students of the Developmental Somatic Psychotherapy Training programs in New York City, Mexico City, Stockholm, Paris, Madrid, and Manchester. I also thank: Gary Yontef, Lynne Jacobs and students of Pacific Gestalt Institute, Los Angeles; Carolina Edwards, Jay Tropianskaia, and students of Gestalt Institute of Toronto; Gro Skottun, Daan Van Balen and students of Norsk Gestaltinstitutt, Oslo; Carmen Vázquez Bandín and students of Centro de Terapia y Psicologia, Madrid; Jean-Marie Robine, Pierre Yves Goriaux and students of Institut Français de Gestalt-therapie, Paris/Bordeaux; Peter Philipson and students of Manchester Gestalt Center; Margherita Spagnuolo-Lobb and students of Istituto di Gestalt H.C.C., Siracusa/Palermo/Milan; Lynda Osborn and students of Metanoia, London; Myriam Muñoz and students of Instituto Humanista de Psicoterapia Gestalt, Mexico City; Laura Romero and students of Instituto Humanista Psicoterapia Gestalt de Puebla; María Trinidad Cardena and students of Universidad Nexum de Mexico, Sinaloa; Guadalupe Amescua Villela and students of Centro de Estudios e Investigación Guestalticos, Veracruz; Rezeda Popova and students of Volga Region Institute of Gestalt Therapy, Kazan; Julia Filatova, Sveta Remizova, and students of Youcanlive, Moscow; Albina Martynova, Olga Yvtushenko, and students of Ukrainian Institute for Contemporary Gestalt Therapy, Kyiv; Graham Colbourne and students of

Edinburgh Gestalt Institute; Mônica Alvim and participants from Universidade Federal do Rio de Janeiro, Brazil; Lidija Pecotic and students of Gestalt Psychotherapy Training Institute, Malta; Inna Didkovska and students of Kyiv Gestalt University.

I am most grateful for all those Developmental Somatic Psychotherapy (DSP) trainers who supervise students, assist trainings, and/or teach workshops in their various countries: Billy Desmond, Miguel Islas, Jennifer Bury, Michael Mitchell, Rezeda Popova, Jacek Panster, Ruth Nightingale, Fabiola Maggio, Severine Pluvinage, Karen Ginsberg, Valeria Kulberi, Anton Savin, David Picó, Zachary Model, Caroline Dower, Claire Kaplan, Jennifer Griesbach, Chrys Kim, Line Jonsborg, and Mark Gawlinski. Much appreciation to Helena Kallner, friend, colleague, and DSP Senior Teacher. Helena has been an avid promoter of this work through her writing, supervising, teaching workshops and trainings across Europe and Eurasia. Moreover, she has been an invaluable consulting partner in the development of training programs, webinars, and workshops, providing insight and support.

I am indebted to my patients, who have been a source of inspiration to me for the almost forty years I have been in practice. This work would not have been possible without their courage and a developing trust in themselves and our therapy process. I am especially thankful to the students and patients who have permitted me to share their therapy experiences within the chapters of this book.

Thank you to dear friends and well-respected colleagues who read specific chapters of the book, and provided welcome feedback and support: Donna Orange, Michael Vincent Miller, Toby Kline, Dan Bloom, and Helena Kallner.

I am especially appreciative of my good friend and respected colleague Joe Lay, with whom I could share my ideas throughout the writing process. He skillfully read every chapter, and his comments were wonderfully useful. It was a privilege to have Joe by my side with his confirmations and challenges.

I am grateful to my editor, Susan Fischer, for her critical reading and thorough attention to detail in every chapter. Her well-developed love of language was an asset to help make my writing as clear and effective as possible. Working with Susan in the final stage of this process was a rewarding experience.

Many thanks to Kate Hawes of Routledge Press for her assistance in bringing this book to publication.

Much appreciation for the staff members of Center for Somatic Studies, who offer the necessary and substantial assistance to keep our center well-functioning: Sebastian Kaupert, webmaster, and technical support; Hilke Kaupert, graphic design; Fabian Kaupert, website maintenance; Chris Panzica and Zachary Model, administration. I value their talent, expertise, and abundance of goodwill that keeps us afloat.

This book is in memory of three generous women from whom I have learned much. My mother, Jean, who with beauty, charm, and grace traversed the health difficulties she lived with throughout most all her existence. My teacher, Laura, who offered insight and knowledge for work and life. My close confidant, Dorette, who demonstrated courage and wisdom throughout the process of living and dying. Above all, these women showed me love and taught me compassion.

A Tribute to My Teachers

There is no such thing as a new idea. We stand on the shoulders of those creators who came before us and attempt to synthesize, respectfully, what we have learned from them. The teachers acknowledged here have influenced my work and my life in profound ways, and I wish to pay homage to them.

Ada Pourmel

When I was a seven-year-old, Ada introduced me to ballet and soon after had me dancing *en pointe*, or on the tips of my toes. Ada was a former core de ballet, Ballet Russe de Monte Carlo, and I felt I was learning from one of the best. Not only did my friends and I take weekly classes, but Ada had us performing the original choreography to *Les Sylphides*, *Swan Lake*, as well as Russian folk dance. My discipline and commitment to the art of dance came from a love of ballet, and my love of Ada.

Don Farnworth

Don was known for rehabilitating dancers with his unique Farnworth Technique, and he did as much for me after back surgery. He had overcome polio as a child and went on to perform in the ballet and on Broadway. Eventually, Don opened a school of dance in New York and earned the title of "Ballet Master," teaching many prominent dancers from a variety of ballet and modern dance companies. I became a teacher at his school and passed on his brilliant understandings of movement as best I could.

Bonnie Bainbridge-Cohen

Bonnie is the founder of the School for Body-Mind Centering, now with branches throughout the world. She introduced me to her original, distinctive system of movement analysis through well-described infant developmental movements, which we students observed in babies and explored in ourselves. An aspect of her extensive movement vocabulary, yield-push, reach-pull, intrigued me and provided the ground for further development. I expanded Bonnie's four movements to become *Six Fundamental Movements*, which I have long taught. I integrated these movements into gestalt theory and practice, as primary sensorimotor supports for contacting, and I conceived their inherent psychological functions. They are the centerpiece of my work. I want to recognize several fine teachers of Body-Mind Centering with whom I also studied: Genny Kapuler, Sandy Jamrog, Gail Stern, and Kim McKeever.

Laura Perls

Laura was one of the founders of gestalt therapy along with Frederick Perls and Paul Goodman. She brought her background as a classical pianist and a student of eurythmics to her practice of gestalt and beautifully demonstrated her aesthetic approach. Laura focused acute attention on the details of bodily expression and its meaning. Observing her work, I learned to go beyond the tracking of movement to uncover its accompanying existential theme. Moreover, Laura taught me how to wait or stay with what is happening in the moment-to-moment of therapy. In the process of doing, she taught me the experience of being.

Richard Kitzler

Richard was a serious influence in my learning foundational gestalt theory. Our weekly individual sessions were dedicated to the precise understanding of the original gestalt text, and always from Richard's innovative point of view. He emphasized the synthetic unity of experience in his teaching, always crucial to my work, and supported the development of my ideas. Richard was generous with his brilliance, and I learned to think more rigorously under his tutelage.

Esther Thelen

Esther was a developmental motor theorist and explored infant development through the conceptual framework of dynamic systems theory. She greatly influenced the study of human development and radically altered the field with her emphasis on the whole of experience. Her research and theorizing demonstrated how infants' view of the world is influenced by movement. Although I never studied with Esther directly, her writings have indelibly influenced my thinking.

Maxine Sheets Johnstone

Maxine has been a dancer/choreographer, dance scholar, and professor of dance. Her ongoing research and writing remain grounded in an understanding of the tactile-kinetic-kinesthetic body. Maxine possesses considerable knowledge in the areas of philosophical biology/anthropology, phenomenology, the phenomenology of dance, aesthetics, and more. Her capacity to articulate the philosophy of the body and the phenomenon of self-movement brought the long-neglected topic of animation and its significance to the foreground. In so doing, Maxine has made a notable impact upon the world of philosophy. I have been an ardent student of Maxine's work through her many books and articles. Her continued thinking and writing is a source of heartfelt encouragement to me.

Iyengar Yoga Association of Greater New York

I discovered Iyengar yoga in 1993 and have been a regular practitioner since. Iyengar focuses on physical alignment in most precise ways and encourages students to execute each yoga pose with careful, detailed attention. It is the most profound form of healing through movement that I have encountered. I am indebted to the following teachers for sharing their love and respect for the art and science of yoga with me: Mary Dunn, James Murphy, Genny Kapuler, Brooke Meyers, Tzahi Moskovitz, Matt Dreyfus, Michelle LaRue, Tori Milner, Lara Warren, Hugh Millard, and Carolyn Christie. I especially thank Bobby Clennell, whose twice weekly online classes have been so valuable during this time of sequestering-at-home.

Note to the Reader

I began writing this book at the beginning of the Covid-19 pandemic as New York City literally shut down, and we therapists entered the world of practicing and teaching online. The case vignettes, interspersed within each chapter, were done before the pandemic and in-person, or after sequestering and online. The work took place either during training programs or in workshops, or with private patients.

Working with movement online is different from working in-person, and if we therapists are open to the difference, without making an evaluation of "better" or "worse," there are myriad possibilities for finding oneself and the other through moving-feeling explorations. Pushed out of our familiar, well-worn perspectives, we are left to wonder at the novel situation we are now entering. As we stay with the unique experience of what is, we can discover and invent what next can be.

Whereas sequestering-in-place and the need for social distance made it necessary for we therapists to work online, working this way has had many benefits. During this time, it has been possible for me to teach groups of students who either could not afford the costs of attending workshops and trainings in New York or in other major cities in Europe and the Americas or, who for a variety of reasons, were not able to travel. The possibility of learning online gave students greater access to this work, as well as to other therapy training programs that were and continue to be taught online. Greater accessibility also has been a gift for teachers, who hope to share their theory and practice with a variety of communities regardless of their socio-economic status. I hope this way of teaching/learning will continue well-past the current crisis.

When you read the case vignettes, as well as the additional scenarios included in every chapter, I invite you to imagine and experience yourself alternately as patient and therapist or baby and parent. This will assist you in knowing how theory lives within practice, and how practice lives within theory.

I have been given permission from each patient and student included in this text to share their therapy experience. The studies were based on transcripts of recorded material, or on my detailed notations taken directly after the session. Each case vignette was chosen to best illuminate the theoretical concepts proposed in the chapter in which it is contained. Although individuals have been disguised in a variety of ways such that their identities remain hidden, the unfolding therapy material remains authentic.

Foreword

The Irish poet, W.B. Yeats, left us with an intriguing question in the final couplet of his great poem "Among Schoolchildren": "O body swayed to music, O brightening glance, / How can we know the dancer from the dance?" Ruella Frank, who comes to gestalt therapy from an earlier career in professional dance, has written a book that may be the fullest answer yet to this question.

In his poem, Yeats depicts himself—or his protagonist—at age sixty walking among a class of children, seeking to think his way, via Greek mythology and philosophy, notions of love and passion, ideas of birth and old age, to a unity of experience so profound that the self cannot be easily separated from its movements through life. The dancer dancing is his metaphor for this ideal of action and form as inseparable wholeness of being. It is, of course, an aesthetic ideal.

This is not so far away from Frank's continuing exploration, set forth in this book, into how the body and its movements shape one's experience. She understands very well, as do all phenomenologists and gestalt therapists—and she is both—that experience is never just given; it has to be made. What, in her analysis of movement, does she envision being made? Nothing less than ourselves in a world of others, which is to say both our subjectivity and our relationships. Not unlike Yeats, her ideal here is an integration of movement and self. And this also is an aesthetic ideal.

Dance for her, however, is less a metaphor than an important background from which she has evolved a rich, valuable theory that tells us how our very nature unfolds itself and grows, first through its ways of moving in relation to parents or caretakers during early childhood, and from then through forming relationships in adulthood. A keyword here is "forming," which precisely means not already formed and thus complete because she insists on the dynamic nature of this process. For her, the self is a process, always in a state of becoming through its exchanges with its world.

Adult life, then, is by no means the end of human development in Frank's outlook, but its continuation via the same kinds of movements that the baby makes. Naturally, such movements in adulthood have grown into more elaborate, complex, and fluid structures. It strikes me that this way of understanding the development of how we move is analogous to how we learn and make use of our native language—simple words at first, then phrases and sentences, and eventually more and more complex modes of self-expression handled with ease. Most psychotherapy has been a cognitive affair of analysis and interpretation through language, a "talking cure," as one of Freud's early patients described it. But although Frank by no means rejects language or speech, she insists that the moving body produces a crucial language of its own, because, as she puts it, "The brain does not do all the 'thinking'; the body also does its share."

As a practicing psychotherapist and as a teacher and trainer of psychotherapists, Ruella Frank is also concerned, as a therapist must be, with those turns in the road over which human development travels that can block, fixate, or otherwise prevent the integration of movement and the self, the dancer and the dance, from taking place. Ideally, the give-and-take between a child and its parent supports the child self-regulating development of an expressive dance of life amid relationships from then on into adulthood. But when parents' own movements impinge too heavily, or with insufficient response, or in other wounding ways on the child, the result is likely to convert the child's capacity for spontaneous, increasingly self-regulating movements into habitually rigid, repetitive ones. Both children and adults will recoil or armor themselves, for flight or fight, as psychology puts it, when the need is for self-protection, and usually what the child learns by way of self-protection is passed on to the adult. This is where therapy can play a crucial role.

*****

I had a friend who went to a famous teacher of dancers many years ago. This teacher was an unusually sharp observer of how people carried themselves and moved as dancers. Eyeing my friend carefully, he put on a recording of Afro-Cuban music and told my friend to dance to it. My friend did so with ease, grace, and impressive steps. Then the teacher turned off this recording and put on a Chopin nocturne, saying now dance to this. My friend nearly fell apart on the dance floor. The teacher had noticed, with rather sublime accuracy, that my friend was quite comfortable, even expert, at moving to upbeat, fast-paced, syncopated rhythms. Those were safe for him. But awkwardness inspired by anxiety sprang up for him around moving with tenderness. That is an important piece of diagnostic information, although this dance teacher was not a therapist.

In her work as a therapist, and articulated through the elegant case vignettes within this book, Ruella Frank has brought this kind of acute observational skill at capturing how people's emotional inner lives, including their anxieties, manifest themselves in their movement *vis-à-vis* one another. And like my friend's teacher, she is good at cooking up experiments that can bring new awareness, and thereby an enlarged sense of choice to patients who feel helplessly in the grip of compulsions. Through long habituation, they may have lost the feeling that they are the makers of their own experience. Awareness that one has choice is a necessary ingredient for the restoration of a person's lost sense of agency. Only then, as a rule, do people free themselves from the constrictions and inhibitions that diminish what they can accomplish and how much they can continue to change and grow.

In order to understand how all this comes about, Frank has found and formulated through her careful observations of infants' and young children's behavior, especially in relation to and response to their parents during the first years of life, what you could call a "deep grammar" of all human movement (to borrow a term from Noam Chomsky's theory of the underpinnings of all language) from the earliest period of infantile life to adulthood. She calls these the six fundamental movements, which she explicates and elaborates in Chapters 3 and 4. She shows us how virtually all the moves we make toward and away from others, are combinations of these six fundamental movements.

It is also an essential dimension of Frank's outlook, as it is in gestalt therapy generally, to view the defensive maneuvers invented by a child who does not feel safe in the hands of its family as creative acts, sometimes ingenious ones, given the child's relative powerlessness. The subsequent rigidities come about because, unfortunately, defensive habits have a way of sticking to the forming self until they seem to become embedded in one's character or identity. Then they often become dysfunctional or even self-defeating in adulthood since they can displace an adult individual's awareness that he or she now have new creative powers for keeping safe. When old movement formations, useful for self-protection in childhood, displace the creative making of new ones appropriate to a new situation, they tend to make symptoms or neurotic character. "Such neurotic symptoms," Frank writes from her clinical standpoint, "are the results of well-learned, overly familiar behaviors that prevent the patient from responding to or even noticing the novelty of the moment and its inherent possibilities."

Another fundamental assumption of gestalt therapy is that all human activity takes place by connecting with a world beyond the self. The crucial thing is the connection itself. In the work Paul Goodman did with Laura and Frederick Perls, that connection was called "contact." Some later schools call it "relational." The most recent tendency in gestalt therapy circles is toward constructing a field theory, such that contact between people emerges from a field that contains and supports their moving together or away from one another. As Frank points out to make this principle clear in terms of movement: "There is always something or someone from which we move toward or away. A verb does not exist without an object. For this reason, all the verbs of the fundamental language I present here are attended by their intrinsic prepositions that describe not only moving but moving always in relation to the other. We move *with, against, for, onto, toward, from*; the other is implicit in every move we make, always already there" (emphasis in original).

Frank's consistency in taking movement to be always relational enables her to illuminate the development of childhood trauma in terms of what goes on between people. She makes this a foreground principle in her excellent chapter on trauma, which is the book's final chapter. She examines there how anxious movement, especially between a parent and an infant or young child, can bring about traumatic ways of relating that continue to stay around. It is all too easy, as she points out, to place all the blame on the parent for inadequacies in response to the child or imposing his or her own need, such that the child does not feel recognized or met, which is a major factor in early trauma. There is, however, a long history of blaming the mother for all the child's mental struggles: the inadequate mother, the anxious mother, the depressed mother, the borderline mother, the schizophrenic-making, double-binding mother, the pre-Oedipal mother who delivers a narcissistic wound to the child—these are among the pathological descriptions that have been leveled at mothers from various schools of psychotherapy. Not until much later did fathers really earn their way into this diagnostic picture first as the famous "absent father," then as the physically or sexually abusive one.

But Frank is nothing if not dialectical throughout her analysis of movement and its implications for the health and well-being—or their opposite—in the ongoing formation of personality. The emergence of early trauma, she argues, is already a two-way street. Her view is singularly free of simple notions of cause and effect and therefore of placing blame. We live in a world in which it is hard to avoid trauma, whether you are a child or a parent. And parent and child are inevitably shaping each other. When mothers or fathers with newborns or infants are still carrying around their own traumas, it is very difficult for them to background their own unfulfilled neediness in order to give full attention to the needs of the baby. They become far too demanding, and the baby turns away, or they are not really there, and the baby knows it.

Frank's sensitivity to the smallest clues in movement, gesture, and posture allows her to show us in acute detail, even in the prelinguistic situation of the baby, whether the parent speaks or not, how the baby becomes traumatized and the parent re-traumatized in a terrible, forlorn *pas de deux* that leaves both suffering. And the consequences are long-lasting. "The child," Frank writes, "loses an aspect of core intelligence: a bodily knowing how to orient clearly and how to maneuver freely through the world. It is a loss of bodily agency; the power to do." And the re-traumatized parent "experiences a similar fate" along with the theme "*Something is wrong with us. I cannot find you and you cannot find me*" (emphasis in original). As she does in every chapter, she presents here case histories concerning early trauma that show vividly and touchingly how this sort of situation can unfold in an escalating way.

*****

Because Ruella Frank started out as a dancer, then due to certain life events that she describes in her prologue, turned to a new career as a psychotherapist, it is no surprise that she was drawn to gestalt therapy among the many schools of therapy currently available in our times. She is treading a path in this respect that was paved by the founders of Gestalt therapy and continues to this day. Frederick (Fritz) Perls fell in love with the theater in his early youth in Germany and studied with the famous director Max Reinhardt. He went on to become a psychiatrist, but he preserved his attachment to the theater in the very way that he brought dramatic methods of practice into the gestalt therapy that he helped create with his wife, Laura Perls. Laura was a psychologist who had preceded her clinical career with a devotion to music and dance, and she introduced themes from both into gestalt therapy. Paul Goodman, who joined the Perls in creating gestalt therapy when they first came to New York, became its leading theorist and writer. He was also on his way to becoming an important radical social and cultural critic for the 1960s; and in addition, he was an accomplished poet and novelist. He greatly enriched the way that gestalt therapy understands and works with the function of language in making or failing to make contact.

All three central founders of gestalt therapy were enthusiastic devotees to artistic pursuits. And this trend has often continued to be the case well after these three figures. In the next generation of influential teachers and trainers of gestalt therapists, Miriam Polster had been a serious classical vocalist before she became a practicing and teaching psychologist. Joseph Zinker is a painter and sculptor as well as a clinical psychologist. Many of the gestalt therapists who have come along still later have arrived there because gestalt therapy held out the promise that they could combine the skills they had learned and practiced in a given art form into this innovative mode of psychotherapy. The significant consequence of the trajectory from art to psychotherapy deeply influenced and nourished the very roots of gestalt therapy, making it unique among therapies in the degree that it is grounded in aesthetic principles, viewing both health and pathology through the lens of artistic values, rather than attempting to place itself among the sciences.

The psychological study of human nature, ranging from Freud's initial neurological interests to recent efforts to unify psychology and brain research, has longed for its theories of human mental health and pathology to be understood as numbering among the sciences. So do the psychotherapeutic views and methods that take their cue from these theories wish to be considered based on science. There is a good deal of talk these days about the desirability of "evidence-based therapy," although there is much ambiguity about what sort of evidence accurately describes or predicts something so subjective as a person's quality of life. Psychotherapies that take their lead from science do not generally raise questions about what rhythm and form, economy and grace have to do with whether a person lives his or her life in the full bloom of well-being or in a neurotically diminished form. Yet this is exactly the focus of gestalt therapy's emphasis on exploring, in collaboration with its patients, whether they are managing to make good or bad art out of their daily lives.

The same creative energies go into the creation of symptoms as into a fulfilling life; but in the former case, they have gotten stuck there. In making this distinction, there is nothing in it that says people suffering from their symptoms are somehow at fault. Gestalt therapy views symptoms as creative acts of children or of people trying to stay in contact with their situations when the situations themselves are oppressive or otherwise untenable, and there is no other place to go. This is characteristic of Ruella Frank's thinking as well. She writes that "the symptoms brought to therapy are the best way individuals can adjust to the ongoing difficulties developing in their varied environments.... They are a person's most efficient, practical endeavors to meet and be met by the other, to find and make contact. Symptoms, or routine behaviors lacking spontaneity, are *attempts to cohere*; to achieve some sense of completeness within the arduous and often incomprehensible situations in which patients repeatedly find themselves" (emphasis in original).

To implement this kind of aesthetic outlook, a central premise of gestalt therapy practice is that it is necessary for the therapist to give full attention and respect to the experience of the patient and how he or she creates it, rather than the therapist taking on the role of being an expert interpreter of it, as in most psychotherapy since Freud, including psychoanalysis and behaviorism. But in the light of such respect, the therapeutic work becomes less a diagnosis of pathology than a focus on the patient's creative strengths, which have become too much tied up in old, outworn defensive postures from childhood. Helping patients restore a sense of agency that became lost in the habituation of such defenses is, therefore, a major goal of psychotherapy. Such an outlook serves to support patients in discovering that they can reframe and reshape their experience to fit it more satisfyingly to present circumstances. A particular kind of transformation then becomes a real possibility—to use one's resources, talents, skills, life experience to make good art out of one's daily life rather than bad.

Ruella Frank's fundamental movements, when they are well-coordinated and integrated, are among our best possibilities, along with the give and take of our speaking, for supporting our making good contact in our experiencing ourselves and our world. John Dewey (1980) wrote in *Art and Experience*, "Experience is the result, the sign, and the reward of that interaction of organism and environment which, when it is carried to the full, is a transformation of interaction into participation and communication" (22). And he added that space and time are "the organized and organizing medium of the rhythmic ebb and flow of expectant impulse, forward and retracted movement, resistance and suspense, with fulfillment and consummation" (23). It would be hard to find a better characterization of the general sense in which Frank brings into both her therapeutic and teaching practice the making and shaping of experience as creative transactions between ourselves and our world, between ourselves and others, through our purposeful movement through time and space.

Michael Vincent Miller,
New York City,
November 25, 2021

Prologue

Personal Reflection: When I was a young child, and in preparation for an exam, I would take out a small chalk board and begin to go over the information on which I was to be tested, as if I were teaching a class. It was through teaching imaginary others that I taught myself. This book has been a similar kind of venture.

The joy of movement in its various forms has been the most prominent aspect of my life. Perhaps I could say I was born to it as my parents were glorious ballroom dancers and would stop whatever they were doing, as if by magically cueing each other, to spontaneously dance around the room.

At age seven, I began to study ballet and was blessed to find Ada Pourmel, former corps de ballet of Ballet Russe de Monte Carlo, who taught in the small farming community in which we lived. I continued my ballet studies into adulthood, adding other forms of dance that included acrobatics and jazz. This led to a career as a professional dancer and choreographer, unexpectedly cut short by discovering a congenital problem in my lower spine. An operation followed, and although I did dance for some years after, to continue this path became impossible. The loss of my ability to dance as I once had was life changing. Apparently, the operation made the situation worse rather than better, and I was left with debilitating pain and constrictions. Movement became my conduit to healing, and I studied all forms of rehabilitation including Body-Mind Centering, Alexander Technique, Feldenkrais, Ideokinesis, Sensory Awareness, breath rehabilitation, yoga, and pursued a Masters in Movement Education. Throughout this time, I worked with individuals as a movement therapist and taught dance and movement to professional dancers, actors, and to anyone who wanted to experience the beauty of moving.

In the early 1980s, I became interested in becoming a practitioner of gestalt, not only from having been a patient but also from having taught developmental movement explorations to a group of gestalt therapists and trainers. Responding to the elegance of gestalt theory with its focus on present-centered experience and the power of dialogue, a desire to further investigate movement within the practice of therapy leapt forward. To begin my formal studies in gestalt, I attended a four-year training program at the Gestalt Associates for Psychotherapy, after which I joined their faculty. Upon graduation, I began weekly classes with Laura Perls, founder of gestalt therapy along with Frederick Perls and Paul Goodman, and remained for the four years prior to her death. Studying with Laura was a revelation; her attention to gesture, posture, breathing, and gait assured me that I had found a home. I was further inspired to begin what became a long-term tutelage (seventeen years to be exact) with her colleague, and a most revered presence at the New York Institute for Gestalt Therapy, Richard Kitzler. Richard encouraged the developing of the nonverbal vocabulary that is further explored within this text. He became a significant ally in the process, and especially during the time of my doctoral studies. Both Laura and Richard carried the core of gestalt theory, and their teachings made certain that its crucial significance would not be lost.

As a psychotherapeutic modality, gestalt therapy became popularized in the 1960s, and then was known for a succession of techniques alone rather than its substantive theorizing. The earlier experiments, such as talking to empty chairs or smashing bataka bats into pillows, emphasized emotional outpour and catharsis, which was thought to be a primary aspect of practice. This left the discovery of deeper meaning, seemingly, in the background. Gestalt therapy theory, however, is and always has been a present centered, dialogic, and, importantly, a clinical phenomenological approach to therapy conversant with post-modern ideas of intersubjectivity. Although the founders of gestalt therapy did not emphasize phenomenology, our therapy is a philosophical understanding that holds a clinical phenomenological attitude; uncovering that which appears, unfolds, and emerges. That is, we attend to what we see, what we feel, what we touch, what we hear; the original state of what is given before us, and that precedes our thinking about it.

Within the past several decades, many gestalt theoreticians have been delving into foundational gestalt theory and, from their individual and unique changing perspectives, have originated advances in its theory and practice. Their innovations have supported risk-taking in others, who also come forward with their own ideas. In my attempt to integrate seamlessly a development and somatic perspective within its frame, I have taken up the invitation to explore the richness inherent in gestalt therapy theory. As is true of the abundance of any well-conceived theory, from what has been said there is much left to say. Continuing to explore what is left to say has been the driving force behind my work, and the reason for this most recent book.

Gestalt theoretical concepts, as can be true for all theories describing experience, can become reified and fixed, risking the loss of the creativity of their original meanings. This text, therefore, is written solely through the language of movement. It has a dual purpose. First, it invites non-gestalt practitioners to directly apprehend how experience forms without importing language from a particular therapy modality. This enables practitioners to integrate the approach more readily, and as is appropriate to their particular methodology. Second, it describes difficult theoretical constructs using an aesthetic approach, a moving-feeling knowing. This encourages practitioners to experience themselves more clearly in the process of learning theory. In other words, to feel what they learn and to learn what they feel.

The case vignettes within each chapter invite the reader into the world of the patient and demonstrate what, how, and why I did what I did. Not all therapists will be comfortable working with movement explorations, and not all patients will be comfortable moving, nor should they be. Through understanding the theoretical underpinnings of the work, and developing an appreciation for the profundity of movement dynamics, I believe practitioners will find their own distinctive ways of using this approach in therapy with individuals, couples, families, and children.

Laura Perls eloquently stated: "Gestalt therapy is gestalt therapists." That is, we all work from our unique, individual backgrounds. This is mine.

Chapter 1

Developing Presence

The Give and Take of Therapy

It is now common knowledge among therapy practitioners that the primary indicator of successful psychotherapeutic outcome is the therapy relationship (Fiedler 1950). The degree to which therapists can be with (give to and receive from) their patients and to which their patients can be with their therapist remain at the heart of our therapy practice. This process of giving to and receiving from the other, both active and receptive, is our "capacity to meet and interpenetrate our surrounding world and to gain something new from it" (Miller 2011, 26). Despite this fundamental agreement, it has not always been clear as to the basic elements that constitute a well-developing and satisfying therapeutic relationship and, for that matter, any relationship.

Carl Rogers, one of the founders of Humanist Psychology, believed that a necessary pre-requisite for a person to grow and change is an environment that provides genuineness (openness and self-disclosure), acceptance (being seen with positive regard), and empathy (being listened to and understood). These "necessary conditions," as Rogers referred to them, assisted in his therapeutic goal, which was to support patients to be free to follow their inclinations (Wachtel 2007). In other words, the goal was for patients to discover their nascent desires and allow them to move towards realization, a satisfactory completion. What is missing from Rogers's early and illuminating conceptions regarding the ground upon which beneficial therapy stands is, however, the phenomenal aspects of a positive and constructive patient-therapist relationship. That is, what happens in immediate experience that enables the co-creation of fluid presence within the therapy situation, and what happens when the fluidity of presence becomes diminished.

Rogers's original thinking echoes the principles of gestalt therapy theory; the therapist helps to facilitate awareness of patients' movements, feelings, perceptions, emotions, and thoughts that are being choked down by habitual shame, anxiety, self-criticality, and so on. What differs between the two is the clinically phenomenological stance of gestalt practitioners with a focus on *how* the symptom is being organized in the here-and-now of the session.

DOI: 10.4324/9781003266341-1

When there are striking modifications in our patients' capacities to find and make contact with the other, the effortless building of excitation that constitutes experience and its expression falters. The sense of synthetic unity is lost, a sense of completeness absent. Such neurotic symptoms are the result of well-learned, overly familiar behaviors that now prevent patients from responding to or even noticing the novelty of the moment and its inherent possibilities. These behaviors were necessary and useful adaptations within an earlier and persistently difficult environment from which patients could not find and make stable, supportive enough ground with others. They served as forms of protection. Within the unfolding therapy session, what had been of assistance to patients in the past is no longer sufficient now. In analyzing the symptom that emerges within the therapy relationship, the therapist guides patients first to recognize *that*, *when*, *where*, and *how* they block their experience; by doing so, they disallow the greater range of self. In discovering the value of having denied and hindered their experience, and in developing a new respect for these kinds of obstructions, patients can move toward more gratifying ways of being and behaving. In time, the free flow of spontaneous and creative adjusting within the situation can be restored.

Autonomous Criteria

The working through of obstructed to fluid states of experience is situated in the nucleus of the patient-therapist relationship and can be seen and felt through the autonomous criteria that are an inseparable part of any interaction and aesthetic by nature. But what do we mean by the word aesthetic, as it has held assorted meanings due to cultural shifts throughout the centuries? Originally, an early form of the word was a combination of Greek words *aistheta*, meaning perceptible things, and *aisthesthai,* meaning perceive. The later Greek *aisthētikos* was defined as relating to perception by the senses. This was taken to mean sensibility or responsiveness to sensory stimulation. Further developing this idea, German philosopher Alexander Baumgarten, writing between 1735 and 1758, appropriated the word aesthetics to mean taste or sense of beauty, whether good or bad, according to the individual. Taste in its broader meaning referred to an individual's ability to evaluate according to what is felt rather than what is thought. And so, bodily experience was privileged over intellectual ponderings.

Aesthetics, Baumgarten (1988) concurred, is fundamentally subjective by nature and the ability to judge beauty through the expressive form it takes is based on individual bodily feelings of pleasure or displeasure. Such feelings are experienced through varied qualities, feeling tones, or affects, that are essential or naturally belonging to the immediacy of all human experience. The flow of these affective happenings is part of the structure/function from which lived experience comes into being. Qualities are pre-reflective in nature and form a pre-cognitive kind of understanding, not yet made distinct; this says far more than when we make it distinct by interpreting or intellectualizing.

Perceiving the flow of human experience is similar to how we kinetically and kinesthetically involve ourselves within the arts, for example, painting, sculpture, music, dance. Being moved by and moving with any work of art as well as the artistry of everyday life, we experience a variety of qualities of feeling ranging from bound and constrained to free and unimpeded. They all constitute myriad rhythms of existence and are an essential part in the forming of contact, of experience. For example, take the qualities of hard and shaky that can underlie an awkward experience, abrupt and sharp that can accompany a sudden revelation, free and light at the aftermath of accomplishing something difficult, compact and solid that are part of a sense of rightness, heavy and blunted alongside a deep loss. These are the qualities through which we know the individual authentic truths of our responses as we meet and are met by the world in a variety of ways that span from lively animation to the dullness of fixation. The knowing of qualities informs us as to how we live the situation that we are living.

The intrinsic qualities inherent in the creativity of all human acts are the essentials that organize the experience of presence. Rather than define presence with words alone, it can be useful to find descriptors and/or metaphors that will illuminate the unique feelings that presence demands. Certain ideas of Walter Benjamin, art, social critic, and philosopher in 1930s Germany, are relevant here. Benjamin (2010) wrote of presence in terms of objects of art. He was concerned with the mechanical reproduction of art and, in particular, photography and film. It was his contention that reproduction, even the most perfect, lack in one element: its presence in time and space, its unique existence at the place where it comes into being (13). Benjamin states that the presence of the original is the prerequisite for authenticity. Authenticity is not reproducible, and that which fades in the age of mechanical reproduction is the aura of the work of art. He goes on to say that it is an aura, the distinctive atmosphere or qualities that seem to surround and be generated by a person or thing, that "envelopes an object as we experience wonder not at this or that aspect of it, but at the simple fact that *it is* and that *we*, observing it, *are*" (17). This process goes well beyond the realm of art alone. It is the experience of surrendering to the other, object or person, in order to give to and receive from that other. "To perceive the aura of an object we look at the means to invest it with the ability to look at us in return" (17). The experience of presence is both active and receptive.

Losing and Finding the Experience of Presence in Therapy

The capacity of openly giving to and receiving from the other is the hallmark of fluid contacting. It is the wonder of finding *me* with *you* as we dissolve into a *we* or an *I/You*. Let us imagine that the therapist feels himself to be disconnected from his patient, who is reporting stories about her life in what appears to be an endless monologue. With no apparent conclusion in sight, the therapist impulsively cuts himself off in an anxious withdrawing not knowing what to do next. To intervene and interrupt the patient would be seen as intrusive, he imagines, but to say nothing would be seen as powerless and ineffectual. For some moments the therapist freezes, then catching himself, he begins to wonder about his experience and attend to the qualities of feeling, his ragged breathing pattern, hardened abdomen, narrowed and clenched eyebrows, and pinched mouth. These are familiar signals, and he recognizes how he can diminish himself, literally and figuratively, when he is confused and feels the pressure to "do something!" In this moment, the therapist endures a habitual and all too recognizable way of being, a mechanical reproduction of how he thinks he *should* be to satisfy some assumed "art critic" that is all too ready with a harsh opinion of his work.

Once he fully realizes what he is doing to himself, he can find a deeper breath: he exhales. In valuing the verity of his experience, he begins to wonder what is happening between himself and his patient that elicits this reaction; and how he might have contributed to what he feels to be the patient's experience of disconnect. Attending to the aesthetics of his experience with his patient, he appreciates that the felt distance between them is not threatening, but quite benign and something to be explored rather than overcome. He feels himself more clearly and is now better in touch with his patient, whom he understands is doing the best she can in her ambivalent approach to being seen, heard, felt, and understood.

From here, the therapist can enquire as to what the patient may be experiencing at this moment. Might it be similar to the feeling of the therapist: a sense of disconnect, or something quite different? Or the patient might be feeling nothing, which still provides valuable information as nothing is the beginning of something. What do the patient's stories reveal about her, which are important for her therapist to know? What do they say about how she lives in her world? Finally, how do her stories, no matter what the content, include her therapist? After all, her story is being said to him and shaped for him. This wondering is always done with attention to the aesthetics of the moment. The quality of feeling is part and parcel of all that is happening and is crucial to the creation of the sense of synthetic unity or the experience of completeness. Sometimes it can be more obvious to find oneself, as the therapist does in this scenario, and sometimes less so. But when therapists slow down and move "inside" themselves, they find they are "inside" the unfolding relational field. As the exploration continues, the patient begins to feel understood not only cognitively but on a bodily level: "I see you seeing me seeing you, I feel you feeling me feeling you." To paraphrase Benjamin: it is the simple fact that *you are* and *I am*. Once the pervading psychological distance can be explored through open dialogue, while attending to the arising, varied qualities of feeling, a sense of presence develops. The authenticity of relationship has replaced mechanical re-production.

Conversely, the diminishing of aura, a pre-requisite for presence, is a loss of the capacity to respond fully to the other; the active and receptive qualities of self are not easily available. It is a diminishment of the capacity to wonder in the situation. For example, when surrendering is confused with subjugating oneself to that other, the risk of finding and making an *I/You* is too great to entertain. Neurotic functioning is the outcome. The person may be able cognitively to reflect upon their ability to respond, but still not be able to feel the immediacy of experience, to "wonder the situation." In such moments of damaged presence, the person exists but cannot clearly feel with the other. What is missed are the felt qualities that constitute the uniqueness and authenticity of the moment, the genuineness and uniqueness we find and make together.

Patients as the Artist of Their Experience

Taking this formulation of presence further, let us look at the work of therapy itself as a work of art and the patient as the artist of her/his/their own existence (Rank 1932). Otto Rank first talked about neurotics as artists of their neurosis: *artistes manqués*, failed or perhaps frustrated artists. At the very least, these are not artists who get much or any satisfaction from their creations. Rank suggests that any work of art presents an accord between its effect and the recipient of its creation; a "spiritual harmony" between artist and beneficiary is intrinsic (Rank 1932). Both art and therapy "share underlying features which point to their common source in a peculiarly human tendency to form and transform one's given relation to the world" (Miller 2011, 24). Looking at one's patient as artist, it is possible to see the habitual and enduring symptom as an attempt to create a form that is fluid, graceful, bright, and efficient in the hope of being well-met by the therapist. This, of course, is with a lack of sufficient materials to make something satisfying enough for the patient and for the recipient of the work. All is lost if the patient's artistic creation is neither appreciated nor understood. Hope, once more, crumbles into dread.

The therapist can analyze the patient's primary and habitually fixed symptom by exploring how she (the patient) lives the world she is co-producing, either with or without awareness. To realize and acknowledge *how* this patient is organizing the materials she chooses for her art making, she must move "inside" to discover what is pleasing or displeasing to herself. The patient needs to be able to feel the qualities that underlie and funda-mentally shape her experience to discern more clearly what attracts her, what is attracted by her, and what repels, and is repelled by her. In other words, she needs to be able to touch that which moves with and through her, as she moves with and through that other, in a variety of lived situations. The work of therapy, then, is to facilitate kinesthetic attentiveness to the qualities that are defining her emerging experience, while discovering relational support. Wondering through bodily affects, the patient becomes the arbiter of the truth of experience and learns to distinguish her own truth from her "inner art critic" who invites her into a mechanically reproduced and inauthentic version of herself.

As simple as this may sound, it is often difficult for the patient (and therapist) to take the risk of feeling an emerging nascent desire in the present moment of the session. This is so when the person was repeatedly met by significant others in an earlier environment that was frequently both frustrating and dangerous. Frustrating because the desire to be seen, heard, felt, held, and therefore understood and accepted, was so beyond the person's reach that she learned either to give up as no one was reaching back, "You will never be with me. Why bother to even try?" or doggedly to push forward in the eventuality that somehow, someday she would be met: "Whatever it takes, I will get you to reach back." The ongoing and frustrating lack and emptiness that these encounters produce must be shut down and can be a danger in the long run. This is because the essentials necessary to feel a sense of completeness are missing and can neither be made nor found. On the other hand, a dangerous environment frightens in a different way; the possibility of being invaded, injured, destroyed for what the person desires is always already on the horizon and must be shut out. With this is also the accompanying frustration of having to shut down desiring impulses to save oneself from the panic of the chronic threat of obliteration (Perls et al. 1990, 160–161).

To now take the risk to heal a damaged sense of presence, a surrendering of me with you, one must be able to endure and give oneself to the feelings of overwhelming loss and fear that accompany such surrendering. That is, one needs to wonder the situation one lives and with compassion, one's suffering shared with another. Experiencing what necessarily had to be shut down and shut out to adjust creatively to an earlier environment, the patient now is invited to suffer with the therapist that which had been insufferable alone. The wondering becomes bi-directional.

The Developing Experience of Presence and its Loss

Let us explore the loss of presence from a developmental and somatic perspective.

> *Five-year-old Donny sits on his bedroom floor and under a large window streaked with sunshine. He is playing with his favorite toy car, a special gift from his father. Sometimes Donny gets these gifts when father must stay late at work for many nights. Those evenings father does come home,*

he walks through the door and goes straight up to Donny and tosses him in the air. This is a special game between them. Remembering this, Donny smiles and a "jiggling" feeling arises from his belly. He pictures his father's big hands holding him in such a way that he fits perfectly between them. During the game, Donny and father laugh a lot. But it seems to Donny that father spends more time with his "private" computer than with him or with his mother. Donny already has learned not to bother father when he is with the computer. He has learned from experience that disturbing father can bring trouble not only for him, but also trouble between his father and mother. The trouble feeling is like a heavy stone sitting on Donny's chest, and sometimes his eyes feel wet.

Donny pushes his orange truck forward and back, in circles, and in figure eights. He knows he is the best racing car driver in the world. Donny is just about to go into the living room to share this fact with his mother and father, when he hears them raising their voices to one another. Donny does not know what they are talking about, but as he listens, there is a spikey feeling in his throat, as if there is something there he cannot swallow down. Suddenly, father bursts into Donny's room, holding both their jackets in his hands, "Come on," father says somewhat briskly, "we're going for a walk to the park." Donny bounces up, puts on his jacket, and out they go. It feels like a long while since they have gone for a walk to the park, just the two of them, and Donny is delighted. During other similar excursions, Donny grasps onto father's hand once they walk down the cobblestone path leading from house to sidewalk. Grasping onto and being enveloped by father's large and warm hand gives Donny a sense of real pleasure, like that of being tossed up in the air and then grasped between father's steady hands. Now Donny feels warm and squiggly in his abdomen, his experience of joy. Being firmly held by his father is important to him and offers the sense of belonging in his world, a sense of home. Those excursions also have provided his father a feeling of warmth that spreads throughout his chest. At those times, father too feels home.

This day, however, father is distracted by his ambitions regarding work. He is trying to figure out something that he cannot quite manage to think through. He wishes he could stay home and deliberate more on these work matters, but mother insists that he go out with Donny. For one thing, mother says she needs a "well-deserved break" from caring for Donny and, for another, she says father does not "spend enough time" with his son. This has become a litany, an oft-repeated narrative that emerges between them.

On the sidewalk, Donny reaches for his father's hand to grasp onto it. But father, feeling somewhat resentful that he must interrupt his work to be with Donny, pulls his hand away and adjusts his hat. Donny again tries to reach for and grasp onto father's hand. But once more, father abruptly moves his hand away and distractedly fusses with his jacket. Donny well remembers when father and he have walked together. He recalls the moment of reaching-for and grasping-onto father's hand, and the pleasing squiggling feelings that accompany this. These have become part of their parent-son relational dialogue, just like the tossing-in-the-air game. When he gives his hand to father and father now refuses it, Donny's hoped for world falls to pieces for that moment. What was joyfully anticipated, the gathering of me with you in this simple hand-holding gesture, is suddenly doubted.

Donny expresses this loss with a litany of angry muffled sobs. There are no more attempts on Donny's part to grasp his father's hand. Instead, he grasps his own jacket. Donny's muted cries, which father thinks appear to "go on forever and sound like whining," are finally met as father abruptly, and all too firmly, pulls Donny's hand from his jacket and grasps it. Without the comfort of his father to help him navigate this breach of confidence, Donny's crying comes to a jagged halt. Rather than the more soothing full exhalations that accompany a completed cry, Donny clenches his chest and holds his breath on inhalation. The feeling of warmth and squiggly joy is no longer part of Donny's experience and is replaced with a rock in his belly and a clutched ache in his heart. Donny is scared and sad. Fearful that father's hand will once again disappear, Donny firmly clings onto it. It is as if he will lose his place of belonging in the world if he does not cling so tightly. Paradoxically, the more he clings, the less he feels himself with father. The unique and unrepeatability of earlier moments of holding and feeling held in the warm container of his father's hand are no longer there. In this moment, Donny does not trust that father will not leave again, nor does he trust that his father wants to be with him at all. For father's part, there are myriad thoughts regarding his son's "unnecessary expressions of over dependency," as well as his own feelings of having disappointed Donny. He experiences a familiar sense of guilt that includes a residue of resentment for both Donny and his wife, thinking, "they make me feel like I'm a bad father." There is not the touch of warmth spreading throughout his chest as in earlier excursions. This has been replaced with the hard chill of emptiness; something he has experienced before in similar family situations, and all too often.

Donny now must diminish the qualities of feeling, as they are too much for him to bear alone. He is no longer the arbiter of the truth of his experience, as he cannot trust his diminished bodily responses. Father now continues to distract himself from what he feels, as he reasons through the situation. The art of wondering, for both, withers away. Neither Donny nor father can find nor make a fluid and satisfying contact where I am here and with you. A bodily narrative develops on both sides of this equation and, if oft repeated, one that will habitually supplant the authenticity and ongoing effortlessness of being that presence demands.

Learning the Experience of Wonder

The experience of wonder is a primary possession of babies and children and is fundamental to how they live and learn the world. As children move through their world, they are in touch with how they feel as they move, that is, the smooth solid surface of the table as they bang their hands upon it, the squishy texture of a wet sponge when it is squeezed, the hard scratchy impression of bared feet on a dry lawn, the jumpy rumbling in the chest upon seeing an elephant at the zoo. Infants and children are naturally led to the wonderings of their own moving bodies; they feel the world move through them as they move through the world. Attuning to the qualities of their experience, the newness of an unfamiliar world also has its familiarity. A primary and fundamental moving-feeling link to this world is found and made.

To wonder is not in the least cognitive, as shown by the youngest of babies, the neonates or those less than four-weeks-old. In a landmark study conducted by infant researchers Meltzoff and Moore (1977), babies forty-five minutes after birth were observed having the capacity to imitate several actions of other people, specifically, tongue protrusion. Seated directly in front of the baby, a researcher extended his tongue repeatedly and the baby, after a while, could imitate the movement and extend the tongue as well. In time, the babies who took part in this experiment had learned to execute their moves with greater precision and efficiency through practice. In addition, they were able to imitate other movements made by the researchers, such as opening their mouths and pursing their lips in direct response to them. Those movements made were also behaviors the babies spontaneously could do without having been invited to do so (Maratos 1998). It was concluded that neonates could understand the difference between changes of the other's body they could see and the changes of their own bodies that they could generate (Meltzoff 1985, 15).

To wonder about the feel of their own moving bodies, babies develop a sense of orienting: the body I move and feel moving is *here,* and the body you move is *there*. This is the earliest matching of one to another and forms the ground for a later developing sense of differentiation. The feel of contingency arises as each partner predicts a forthcoming response from the other. The expectation of the reaching back of the other, as one is reaching for that other, is primal acknowledgement. Daniel Stern (1985) refers to this same process as "consequential relationships"; Lois Bloom (1993) describes it as "relational concepts"; and Alan Fogel (1993) calls it "co-regulation." All are based on the preverbal premise: moving/feeling here is somehow connected to seeing/moving there, which becomes the very basis of bodily agency. The qualities of experience do not disappear as development proceeds; rather they expand and refine along with an elaboration of the baby's, child's, adult's growing repertoire of movement. That is, as the baby learns to move in relation to the other, person or object, the range of movement potentialities expand, and with them, the varying qualities of experience. Throughout development, baby, child, and later adult learn to apprehend progressively in synthetic unity, a feel of completeness as they form *I/You* or *We*. This is an achievement.

It is thought that the neonates' capacity to respond to visual stimulation is based on the earlier experiences of the fetus in the womb (Richardson 2000). It can experience its mouth, tongue, lips, its whole body moving and being moved, as it changes shape within the amniotic fluid of the uterine environment. Although not having an idea that it is the one that perceives, perceiving exists nonetheless and begins at eight weeks of uterine life (Bornemark 2016). From a background of intermodal relations organized in fetal life—the sensation or percept in one sense modality simultaneously is experienced in the other—neonates are now incrementally capable of seeing what they feel and feeling what they see. As posited by James Gibson (1979), to perceive the world is to co-perceive oneself in the world. Kinetic-kinesthetic process in connection with sensory capacities specify "own-body" as differentiated, situated, and an agent among other agents in the world (Rochat 2011).

Happenings or events are perceived through their dynamic properties; the earlier experience of an individual constitutes and is constituted within the now situation. A baby, then, has prior experience of these acts with his tongue, lips, mouth, and jaw from the fetal period and brings that into the budding relationship with the researcher. Neonates enter the world with minimal bodily awareness. These interactions become a response-response dialogue similar to the fetus' response-response within the womb: fluids that push against it as it pushes back, the touching/hearing rhythm of the mother's heartbeat, the touching/tasting of the uterine wall, the tasting/feeling/smelling of the surrounding amniotic fluid, and so forth. Thus, the infant comes into the world having always and already responded to this first environment. The qualities of touching and being touched, moving and being moved, form the foundation for wondering and is the fundamental origin of learning. The experiences of the baby are not merely recorded somewhere in the brain, nervous system, or muscles. Instead, moving achievements, and along with them the varied qualities generated as one moves, are a building-up of faculties in animated response to the inviting situation. These responses have a logic all their own, a moving-feeling intelligence grown through wondering.

Wondering about the world, however, often gets lost as we age and grow to be taken up with everyday matters of our practical existence. The things we used to wonder about are now taken for granted and overlooked. When we cannot find how to return to a sense of wonder, we lose something crucial in our discovering ourselves in relation to our world. Rather than feel the situation through the reality of our bodies, we must rely on our intellect, a secondary process of apprehension. The capacity for contacting oneself and the other, a sensuous process of bodily knowing, is greatly depleted.

Wondering: A Philosophical Act

The sense of wonder is the mark of the philosopher (Plato Theaetetus). Even after philosophers have wondered, they continue to wonder what they have wondered about (Sheets-Johnstone 1999, 323). The philosophical school of phenomenology, in its attempt to describe the details of lived human experience, is more similar to gestalt therapy than to other therapy modalities, as it focuses on how we come to be and maintain who we are. To wonder, then, is an inherent ingredient and illustrates the very nature of our human existence—the nature of being. Wondering is the direct knowing of our situation, whereby we put that process in motion.

Eugene Fink, a German philosopher writing in the 1940s, stated "Wonder dislodges man from the prejudice of everyday, publicly pregiven, traditional and worn-out familiarity... drives him from the already authorized and expressly explicated interpretation of the sense of the world and into the poverty of not knowing" (cited in Sheets-Johnstone 1999, 327). In the very moment of wonder, we attend to the *how* of experience that forms through bodily happenings rather than cogitate the circumstances of our situation. We do not know what we will discover of ourselves and how we live in our world as we begin our search, often a disquieting and disturbing experience. To surrender to and suffer *the poverty of not knowing* opens us to a mixture of feelings including hope and desire as well as dread. The former comes with suggestions of longing and the latter with suggestions of fear (Sheets-Johnstone 329). In daring to move away from the familiar, in the novelty of this wondering moment, one imagines that these discoveries will lead to a powerful, unmitigated disillusionment, and one will feel once more betrayed.

To not allow oneself to wonder, therefore, is an attempt to hold fast to some familiar and fixed idea about oneself and the world. This firmly held belief is often discomforting to the person, yet familiar enough that it does not threaten the long-held certainty of one's existence. There is no disappointment on the horizon as one already lives prepared for its eventuality, thus staving off a deeper kind of anxiety that crashes into despair. In grasping onto the routine of daily life, a mechanized reproduction of our existence, we are spared from the uncertainty and mystery that is part of any authentic relationship. "Who am I with you, and who are you with me? Will there be enough familiar in the novelty of our exchange that I can enter into it with as much of the recognizable as necessary, and with enough unusual that I am ready to risk what yet cannot be known?" What reveals itself in wondering about the human condition is not a puzzle to be solved, but a mystery to be unfolded. Moving out of the constraints of our fixities, we find freedom and with freedom come both anxiety and excitement. How could it be otherwise?

The pre-requisite for wondering is to be open to the background qualities of all experience—the affective nature of being. The patient and therapist are invited to notice what happens "inside" to touch the feelings that express the circumstances in which they are living. Although attention may be drawn to various locations in the body, it is often useful to invite the patient to notice the area of chest and/or abdomen, the primary containers of sensitivity and sensibility. For example, the therapist might inquire at different times, "Do you have a sense of open or closed, hard or soft, full or empty, held or free, in either area?" There are as many varied qualities as there are unique individual experiences. If patients have trouble finding a quality to describe their experience, there are always metaphors, such as a grey and stormy night in my abdomen, or a light wind over a grassy field in my chest, or a brewing tornado. And the response of "nothing" or "not much feeling at all," can lead to the exploration of what the meaning of the nothing might be. What could be useful about not feeling much, or not at all? The therapist always must remember that the successful diminishment of feeling is also an accomplishment for this patient, and a necessary assistance that had proved valuable and sometimes lifesaving, at an earlier time. Though not beneficial now, the capacity to shut down one's feelings while cutting out the threatening environment needs to be appreciated and understood, not by intellectual interpretations but by an openness to the strength and purpose of the original act.

Case Vignette

The following vignette is taken from a therapy demonstration and was recorded during an Open Workshop in New York. The session is not so much to show how to do therapy, since therapists must work from their own background, as to illustrate how to work attending to the moving-feeling processes that organize experience or contacting. Mark, who volunteered for this session, was a student at a gestalt training institute in the mid-west and came to New York for this weekend in furtherance of his studies. He and I had met at a workshop I had taught in his home state the year before.

Prior to the therapy illustration below, the workshop group had concluded a dyadic experiment whose purpose was to heighten kinesthetic awareness in relation to setting the distance between partners. One partner (A) stood in front of the other (B) and about four to five feet apart. I facilitated the experiment, at first, by giving specific directions. The structure was rather inflexible, although participants could always choose not to follow these directions.

Participants were asked to experience their feet on the floor by bending their knees and then slowly straightening their legs as they pushed against the floor from the souls of their feet. After executing this move several times to note any changes that might have occurred in their relationship with the floor, each participant then explored shifting body weight from balls to heels of their feet, and shifting body weight by moving side to side, using their feet to initiate the move. Participants next were asked slowly to notice their experience as they brought attention from feet upward to legs, thighs, and pelvis, moving upward until they discovered their head subtly reaching-for the ceiling. Once done, particular attention was given to what participants felt inside their chest and abdomen, such as empty or full, open or closed, or images like the lightness of air, or the heaviness of concrete. These qualities, produced by subtle internal movements, had been the focus of several different workshop experiments that weekend.

Once participants were able to feel themselves more distinctly, I invited them to notice the partner standing in front of them. They never were asked to look into the other's eyes, as contacting the other visually could diminish their kinesthesia. Rather, it was suggested for them to cast their eyes slightly downward. Privileging feelings rather than seeing can harvest a different kind of information.

When partner A felt ready to begin, this person was invited to take one step only toward, away, or to the side of B but not without first having been aware of feelings arising in chest, abdomen, or wherever they predominately emerged. The newly arising feelings would guide them as to *where, when,* and *how* to move rather than using their intellect to direct them. That is, A was encouraged to feel her/his/their body with the other before, during, and after they moved. "How do I feel myself move toward or away from you?" B was invited to notice how he/she/they felt in response to A's movements. "How do I feel when you move toward or away from me?"

Next, B was invited to do something similar, that is, not to move until he/she/they felt as clear an impulse as possible to step either toward, away, or to the side. Once A and B understood the structure of the experiment, they continued moving toward and away from the other and, for some time, without my guidance. The experiment was performed with a great deal of attention as participants slowed themselves down to wait until they knew *when, how, where* they wanted to move.

When they completed their moving-feeling dialogue, each dyad sat down to make explicit what had happened between them. What had they come to understand about themselves? What had they come to imagine about their partner? After processing their experience, the discussion was developed further as participants gathered to form a larger group.

After the group discussion and a twenty-minute break to refresh themselves, I asked the group if anyone would like to work with what had emerged in their experiment. From the periphery of my vision, I could see that Mark slowly had raised his arm holding it close to his body with elbow bent, fingers somewhat curled. When I directed my gaze towards him, Mark extended his hand more fully, but not quite straightened at the elbow, his fingers this time opening and then quickly lowering to their original position. I invited Mark to join me as I sat on the floor in the center of the room, as did he. Participants have the choice to sit either on the floor, where we generally find ourselves after these experiments, or on a chair.

The session already had begun with my request for a volunteer and Mark's response, which I imagined to be a "maybe, yes, maybe." This gesture was formed in response to not only me but also to the surrounding group, as we were part of the material he had used to create that gesture along with all its psychological relevance. This, and his performance in the earlier experiment, formed the background for our working together now.

The session below is written in the present tense, as if happening in the moment, so that readers can more easily place themselves into the experience.

Mark pulls up several cushions, crossing his legs in front of him. He is a small, thin man in his early thirties with the well-defined muscles of his athletic frame appearing to hug his bones. I notice now that Mark's chest is slightly hollowing (concave), the area of his collarbones narrowing, all contribute to making a minimal but noticeable shortening of his upper spine. With his whole upper torso he reaches for me, yet his head and eyes are cast downward. His arms lie across his thighs, elbows push backward, and his hands, with palms up, appear to droop. "Yes, maybe, yes," I imagine he is saying to himself and to me. These imaginings I keep to myself.

I feel an almost imperceptible holding in my abdomen and, staying with that experience, I enquire, "How is this distance between us?" Mark responds by shifting his body from side to side, as if attempting to find a place to be. A few moments later, he lifts his head but maintains his eyes looking slightly downward: "I'm much more with myself right now and I have some excitement and energy. I don't know yet about us." Mark now looks directly at me. "When I just said that I noticed that I am leaning forward." I respond: "Yes, you are. You are leaning toward me. I wonder what you might be feeling now as you lean?" Saying this, I notice a subtle sense of also being pulled forward, as if by a magnet, and I am beginning to lean toward Mark. I do not wish to change the distance between us as I lack enough information as to what he experiences. My continuing to lean forward could feel intrusive to him. Mark must explore his reaching, a measuring of the distance between us, and find how close or far *he* wishes to be. I center myself, finding my buttock bones on the floor beneath me and attend to my exhalations. I notice the slight holding that I experienced as we began the session now is diminished.

Mark continues to reach both for and away from me simultaneously; his upper torso is without a solid base of support for his reaching move. Without this support, I surmise that Mark cannot distinctly feel himself and me. "I'm excited," Mark says as his chest incrementally unfolds, and he lengthens his spine. His reaching is now more upright (vertical), rather than his prior posture of advancing toward me (sagittal) in an almost precarious way. His eyes look at me, although I am uncertain as to whether he is seeing/feeling me with him. Feeling my own uprightness, I say, "I would be interested in knowing how you feel your excitement." Again, Mark glances downward and pauses. He seems to be taking the time to consider himself. He sets the pace for our interactions, which I appreciate and hope to follow, giving him and me the necessary time to wonder our experience.

Still looking downward, he says, "I mostly feel a kind of trembling in my arms, and I also notice some holding in my chest." I enter again: "Is there a way that I influence your holding and your trembling? Am I part of those experiences of excitement?" I ask this knowing that I am as responsible for these events as is Mark. We influence and are influenced by each other and co-create the happening transpiring between us, a trans-corporeal encounter.

Mark smiles, his face widens, and he looks directly at me: "I have a story in my head. I am wondering what it would be like to show my excitement to you." Now Mark lengthens his spine even more, appearing fuller as he opens and widens his chest such that it almost bulges out (convex). "Oh, here it is," I say. "I can see your excitement." Upon hearing me, Mark almost imperceptibly folds himself in and looks down. His face reddens a bit: "Yes, I let it out more."

I pause and allow some moments to pass, respecting Mark's need to fold inward, while I notice a vague feeling of heaviness in my chest, the edge of sadness. From this place I ask: "Yes, you let yourself out more. How is it to show me more of your excitement?" Mark responds, this time immediately: "I feel some vulnerability and a kind of freeing... and some water in my eyes... some shaking in my voice." Mark's expression of vulnerability, which is an indication of his receptivity, invites me to soften more in my chest and abdomen. I feel both touched and sad.

Placing my hand on my chest, I ask: "What happened to the held feeling here—the feeling in your chest?" Mark reports: "I still feel it in my chest." He places his hand toward his chest firmly pressing upon it.

"But I feel more sensation in my arms." He brings his arms chest high, softly, smoothly, and gradually waving them around. I touch both my arms and ask: "What are you saying to me here?" I choose to experiment with the animation of his arms rather than the holding in his chest as it shows where we will go. The next step is indicated by the freedom of these movements, his shaky feeling of vulnerability, and the rising lightness in my own chest. I go with what I feel is a novel experience for him, rather than with the habitual.

Mark begins to move his arms with greater intensity and more rapidly, yet with softness to the motion. "I want to be with you. I want to play with you." Saying this, Mark takes a long pause and sighs several times. "I do," he says, with a poignant intensity to his voice: "I do want to play with you." At this moment, I no longer hear/feel the "maybe," only a clear "yes."

Warmth spreads throughout the area of my open chest and my eyes grow moist. I feel moved. Wondering how Mark is taking me in right now, I ask: "How do I look to you when you say that?" Now Mark is fully unfolded and reaches his torso forward. His hands are placed in the middle of his thighs with a slight pressing upon them, which lengthens his spine even more, as he declares: "Invited. I feel you invite me with the nodding of your head, your eyes, your smile." I ask: "How much of my invitation—my smile and my nod—do you take in?" Suddenly and subtly, Mark shrinks himself. He incrementally narrows and hollows his upper chest and shortens his spine. He sighs several times, and each sigh settles at the bottom of his exhalation. From here, the next inhalation takes some effort, as now it is not so easily available. "It's hard for me to take in your eyes and your smile," he says. I question, "Is there a way I might be making it hard? Give yourself some time to feel if that is so. How might I make it hard for you to take me in?"

Soon Mark posits an answer: "There is something about your attentiveness. You become attentive and I feel you join me and then that feeling that we are together comes and goes." I ask: "What do you make of that? What does it mean to you that you feel I come and go?" Mark rapidly responds: "I think you will be with me and then not be with me and I won't know the difference." To clarify, for both of us, that what he said is what I heard, I repeat: "You won't know when I am here with you and when I'm not here. That can be confusing and even alarming." "Yes, yes," Mark declares, "That's right. And it hurts me." He goes on to say, "In the experiment that we just did (he refers to approaching and/or distancing), I found out that it's me. I'm here and then I'm not. Somehow, I'm here, but I also am not. And I'm not always sure when I'm here and when I'm not." I ask: "And what do you feel as you say that to me?" Mark responds: "The holding in my chest gets tighter and I feel a heaviness there."

Mark loosely clasps his arms as if to hug himself and breathes more deeply. He remains in the folded position and asserts: "It's important that I can be away and then come back to you and know that I'm here with you. I need to know when I come and go." I quickly respond: "And you need to know I will be here if and when you wish to return." I put forward a building hypothesis and wait to see how he responds.

Now Mark takes a long pause and slowly unfolds so that he is more vertical and has a greater width in his chest. "Yes, I believe that you will be waiting. I know something about that from this weekend and from the other workshop with you. It's about learning to trust that, to trust that you will wait for me to come back when I'm ready and when I decide that I want to be with you again. I need to trust that. That you will wait." I add: "It is also about trusting yourself. You need to know when you trust that I want to be here with you. And you need to know when you don't trust that I want to be here." Mark laughingly says: "Yes, I need to trust my distrust." "Exactly. Exactly so," I reply.

Mark's eyes reach-for me, quickly away, and just as quickly return to find mine. Our being with each other now finds a steady rhythm. He slowly and gradually expands himself and I too feel myself settle more onto the floor, widening my shoulders and lengthening my spine. My breathing feels deep and free. The feeling between us has changed; there is a softness and a kind of sweetness that cannot easily be described.

Mark says: "I'm so in the experience of you now. And my mind wants to understand it." I pursue: "Your mind wants to... " Mark cuts me off to explain: "It's as if I could get some kind of stability if I start to think about what's happening." I restate his words: "So many things are happening, and you think you have to make some kind of meaning to make stability and bring it all together." I continue: "Mark, I trust your flexibility here right now." As I say this, I notice him teetering from one side to the other. "Right now, you are wobbling in the newness of what we are making here. Your wobbling is important and necessary. The kind of stability that you speak of will come in time. It will come on its own and the meaning will naturally evolve."

Mark continues to remain open, spine long, and chest wide and looks directly at me. Soon he says: "I feel finished now, thank you." Feeling that something between us is cut short I say: "I feel something is almost finished, but not quite. I would like to stay with you a bit longer so I can remember this feeling between us. I would like to wonder more about what is happening in *my* body and, if you have the interest, you might wonder about what is happening in *yours*."

Mark pauses, but this time neither folds nor looks down. "I feel free in my belly and still have some holding in my chest. But it's different

> too. I'm not so held." Mark gestures touching the area of his heart with his hand and then reaches it toward me. He does this several times and tells me: "Maybe I feel something thick between us from here to here." "Yes, I feel this too." I repeat his gesture as I slowly touch my chest and extend my hand to Mark. My eyes now are moist, and my voice fills with feeling. Repeating the gesture, "From my heart to yours." Mark responds taking several deep breaths. "Yes. I appreciate that you remind me about my heart." I state the obvious: "I feel we are complete for now, and this we will remember."

Psychodynamics

All volunteers for group therapy demonstrations are courageous and to be admired. It is not easy to expose oneself in front of the teacher and the surrounding group. Bearing that in mind, Mark's ambivalence at being seen was evident in his gesture of volunteering, his semi-raised hand quickly ascending and immediately descending. I imagined him saying, "I neither reach-for you with all of myself, nor do I completely hold back." Clearly, he had the impulse to come forward and, at the same time, the anxiety of potentially moving toward *the poverty of not knowing*. What would he discover about himself and in front of all of us? What would he reveal that he also wishes to conceal?

The process of folding and unfolding his torso in relation to the developing situation demonstrated the hope and desire that Mark's excitement would be well-received and the dread and shame that being received may not happen. From the start of the session, Mark incrementally allowed himself to wonder about his experience as he moved from registering the surface physicality of what he was *doing* to touching the depth of what he was *feeling*. His building desire to have me acknowledge and appreciate his excitement alongside of him was paramount.

The experience of moving-feeling is always situated and never assembles in isolation. In the session, our emerging experiences belonged to the situation of which we were both a part. I could register my bodily experience of his ambiguity and diagnose our building relationship through aesthetic criteria, a phenomenological diagnosis. As I saw Mark move, I also spontaneously moved, creatively adjusting with him. This is how we experience ourselves in relation, whether it is through a felt experience of the subtle movement of the other's breathing, minimal shifts in posture, changes in vocal tone, or fine adjustments of gaze. The more I could feel myself with Mark, the more I could see him and vice-versa. A subverbal narrative was generated by our bodies as they were shaping and being shaped, a *kinesthetic pre-reflective consciousness* forming and informing us.

All babies and children wonder about themselves through their bodies and with the available presence of a significant other. Over time, with the help of the caring other, what was implicit becomes explicit. In the session, I became the significant other who could meet Mark with a steady available presence necessary to facilitate an exploration of the feelings moving through him. Attending to the changing qualities of his feelings, Mark became more able to sensitize himself to what was happening between us to support the sense of self that emerges from being recognized by the other (Spagnuolo-Lobb 2018). Our relationship grew through greater awareness of each other. It is an aesthetic subjective perspective, whereby one invests the other with the possibility of finding and making moments of reciprocity: "I see you seeing me seeing you, I feel you feeling me feeling you." Once fully integrated and assimilated, these moments will be remembered.

At the sessions' end, Mark allowed an increased vulnerability to spread within him, as was seen by his expanding torso and the softness of our direct gaze. The expression of "yes" shown by this upright posture and the flowing moving through his arms eclipsed the diminishing "no" held within the remaining compressions of his chest. Moving from a more constricted state to one of greater freedom was not reliant on interpreting Mark's behaviors from a cause-and-effect perspective. Instead, Mark was able to work through habitual patterns of being and behaving in the present of this therapy session, and with a developing presence that gradually led him from the all too familiar to a supported novelty. Staying with my kinetic-kinesthetic happenings was also a risk for me. As I allowed my vulnerability to move foreground, I felt the impact of Mark's influence on my expressions. Whether expressed subtly or overtly, the animated body, whether open or closed, is the core of felt dynamics and the fundamental nature of self-reflection.

Concluding Remarks

The capacity for presence is always already part of human experience and unfolds within the relational situation. It is our capacity to respond, fluidly giving and receiving, in order to gain something new from the environment. The prevailing distance between us is not to be conquered but rather to be cleared, the obstacles removed such that we can find each other. This is similar to what parents do when they openly wonder with their child, neither intruding nor benignly neglecting. If this happens enough throughout development, it becomes the habitual ground for intimate experience. In fact, it is a requirement for intimacy—the openness to risk moving into that clearing where *I/You* become *We*.

Chapter 2

Kinesthetic Resonance

The Sense of Situation

As clinical phenomenologists, we gestalt therapists are concerned with an understanding of *how* we live the situation we are living: how to analyze, describe, and know it. It also is the work of clinicians from other modalities, who are present-centered, dialogical, and process oriented, to explore the *philosophy of the obvious* or "what is immediately accessible to the patient's or my own awareness" (L. Perls 1992, 134). That is, to dwell in what is given, the immanent experience of appearances (Finlay 2011, 45). This, however, can be elusive and what is visible is often not yet seen. Precise and meticulous descriptions based on authentic bodily experience unfolding moment-to-moment are needed to better illustrate the flow of human experience and the foundational structures that co-organize the building of such experience.

This chapter will illuminate more fully the organizing processes that form the veritable basis of social understanding; a trans-subjective experience from which subjectivity takes form. To this end, a closer investigation will be provided, a next step into the qualitative dynamics of human movement, tactile-kinetic-kinesthetic. Movement will be dissected into its most basic elements to explore the means by which we make manifest experience before it becomes objectified in reflection. Here, as introduced in Chapter 1, we will emphasize affective experience, or what Eugene Gendlin (1992) refers to as the bodily sense of the situation, arguing that "the situation and you are not two things, as if the external things were a situation without you" (5). This embedding of body/world is similar to gestalt therapy theory, which states that the organism is decidedly inseparable from the environment (Perls et al. 1990). In action, we make sense of the world, which we both constitute and are constituted by. We are informed as we inform; we are impressed as we impress, and almost simultaneously we affect others as we ourselves are affected. The body, therefore, lives the situation it is living, and without affective experience, we would not know *that* we are, *where* we are, and *how* we are (Frank 2016, 372). The human body is not separate from the environment—whether a what or a who—since the other is always already there as part of the whole of experience. It is the lived body that expresses that relation.

DOI: 10.4324/9781003266341-2

The Lived Body

Edmund Husserl, referred to as the father of phenomenology, thought of the lived body as the lived center of experience. That is, lived bodily experience is the *zero point* of orientation (Husserl 1989), denoting and differentiating "the feeling of a potential here from a possible there" (Finlay 2011, 16). Lived bodies form an ever-shifting subjective experience; a unique and personal perspective of *how* it is to be here always already in relation to the other that is already there. It is the felt bodily presence primarily formed in kinesthetic experience (Sheets-Johnstone 2019). How we fundamentally are contacting others is based on the body's capacities of moving, and the affective experience elicited through moving, that enlighten us as to how we are situated in the world. "The lived body is indeed a basic source of knowledge: what is known and what comes to be known springs from movement: that is, from moving and having moved" (6).

A phenomenological inquiry into the lived body reveals the character of ongoing human experience and, more accurately, how we structure that experience and only with the other. As Husserl (1973) concluded, the lived body is one of affect and movement and describes bodily experience as principally receptive in nature. In agreement, Thomas Fuchs (2019) states that the phenomenal world is at the core of the lived body and, therefore, operates background to all subjective experience. In this way, lived body negotiates all relations with the world and is the foundation of all our interactions. Lived body, then, is the implicit conduit and arbiter of the perceived world. The other becomes known as one is witness to bodily performance and either consciously or unconsciously experiences and expresses one's own responses in relation to what has been seen, heard, and felt. In fact, "the body—and bodily feeling—is the starting point of every experience" (Robine 2015, 49). Myriad experiences of giving to and receiving from, most often subtly expressed as micro-movements transmitted from one to the other, form the basis of social understanding. Who each is within the interaction is always already influenced by the other. As we experience ourselves while moving through our world, we realize that lived body is the way in which our world comes to be.

Kinesthesia: The Feel of Our Moving

The word kinesthesia is derived from the Greek *cineo,* "to put in motion," and aesthesis, "sensation" or "impression." Kinesthesia, a continually co-constituted happening, is the feel of our self-movements as we impress and are impressed by the other, as we touch and are touched. Through varied kinesthetic qualities of experience, or movement in awareness, the body reveals its potentiality for affective capacity, and we immediately and directly experience the situation we are living. We listen or attend to our self-movements and feel the subtleties of our creative and spontaneous adjusting within the evolving situation. Our kinesthetic capacity allows us to attend to ourselves and to others. It is, in fact, a most unique sense that provides the subject with greater awareness of its own and the other's body. Husserl describes this process as "kinesthetic consciousness"; this is not a consciousness *of* movement but a capacity to move freely, spontaneously, and responsively. It is the experience of subjectivity. That is, a bodily disposition that enables us to apprehend the body of the other as we apprehend our own: "My feeling in the other's presence… says something about me, about the other, about the situation, about the atmosphere, about our encounter" (Robine 2015, 41).

Kinesthetic experiences, continuous internally facilitated sensitivities to moving, cannot be suppressed (Jeannerod 2006). They are always already and irrepressibly part of self-experience. We can, however, either bring them to awareness or obscure them. And when brought forth, valuable information regarding our condition and the state of our world becomes available. Conversely, when the potentiality of kinesthesia is diminished, the possibilities of the environment remain concealed. What can be decidedly obtained from the other is lost. Through affective experiences, we directly and immediately consider the situation we are living in a pre-reflective, preconscious, pre-personal way. Such evaluations are aesthetic by nature in that they enfold what we experience into aesthetic assessment (Paterson 2012). That is, the situation unveils itself to us through a variety of felt qualities and combinations of quality; aesthetic evaluations that are experienced through moving. Felt qualities are feeling-tones or affects, such as the following continuums: bound-free, gradual-abrupt, light-heavy, open-closed, soft-hard, hi-intensity-low intensity, and many more. Qualities are not relegated to parts of the body alone; instead these bodily ways of knowing indicate a *feeling through* the whole body. Affective experience plays an essential role in how we respond within our social world (Krueger 2018).

Feeling tone or affectivity is not to be confused with emotion. It is from aesthetic evaluations emerging in relation to the situation at hand—whether actual, imagined, hallucinated, dreamed—that emotional life organizes. Emotions do not spring forward without some background that precedes them. What comes first is a *setting in motion* within the body, an experience that is initially only a feeling: a "pre-experience, pre-verbal, pre-emotional, pre-significant" (Robine 2015, 54). The tacit meaning made from these qualitative experiences in relation to the environment takes the form of or coalesces into an emotion. The forming emotion, therefore, relies upon its predecessor, the background of qualities, for its clarity. When the quality of feeling, kinesthetic experience, is blotted out or distorted, the emotion will not have the support necessary for precisely "integrating the awareness of organism/environment" (Perls et al. 1990, 407–408), person/world. "If a person has crude emotions, it is that his experience as a whole is crude" (407). Gendlin (1992), too, differentiates emotion from bodily feeling and refers to the latter as felt sense; an implicit feeling-knowing sense. Flowing on the stream of movement, affective happenings are part of the structure/function from which lived experience comes into being (Frank 2016, 373). Moving-feeling bodies are central to the co-creating of one's experienced world. To be kinesthetically awake is simply the feeling of being alive.

As the situation alters, in subtle or overt ways, there are changes in the experience of affectivity, *the subjectively felt quality of movement*, as well as changes in the overall muscular tone of the body. Even a slight tilt of the head as we refocus our eyes influences the tonus of our entire body and perceptions and forms our postural dynamic. This is the readiness to respond: to do something in relation to our situation. Postural dynamic is the felt ground from which perceptions and actions emerge, and affectivity arises (Frank 2016, 373). How we move toward or away from the other, the directionality of our movements, and the quality of these movements, organizes our perceptions of the world, a subjective experience. Again, whenever there is a change in situation, there is a modification in the quality of movements, which alters affect. A concomitant shift in overall postural tone organizes our perceptions and the following action. And likewise, as affect, perceptions, and actions surface, postural tone transforms itself.

Moving, feeling, perceiving, and postural tone, then, are inextricably intertwined. They make apparent our experience of the world. As direct and immediate evaluations, such experiences do not require mediation by thoughts or concepts. This delicate interweaving, along with feedback from our external sense organs and tactility, form the basis of awareness. Kinesthetically informed, we know what we know before we know we know (Frank 2016, 373). From here, situations organize, emotion and cognition take shape, and we can further appraise the situation.

Kinesthetic Resonance: The Condition of Being Relational

> *On this warm summer day, I sit on my favorite park bench, my head presses downward, and my upper body softly folds inward as I look through the daily paper. Suddenly, I hear you call my name and feel you approach. I look up to see your smile. I sharply inhale my breath, and now feel the area of my heart expand and swell forward, as the whole of my body lengthens upward. You laugh, lean toward me and grasp my shoulders. Feeling the firmness of your hands around me, I now sense an urge to stand and face you. I slightly rock forward, feel the weight of my legs press onto the balls of my feet, and I rise. Directly meeting your gaze I feel light, and I too smile.*

The above description of interactive process is the trans-subjective dimension of subjectivity. And it is based on kinesthetic resonance, *reverberating feeling tones that are generated from one person to another* (Frank 2016, 373, emphasis mine).

It is the phenomenon brought forward most strongly in contacting experience: the sensed, the felt, and the lived. It is how we listen to ourselves with others and realize we are here (373). Kinesthetically resonating is the folding and unfolding relationship made manifest and expressed through contacting, through experience. "Contact is nothing one has, or is, or stays in or out of…. We make contact by acknowledging and tackling the other and experiencing ourselves in doing so" (L. Perls 1992, 144). Arising out of contacting processes, kinesthetic resonance is the fundamentally co-constructed condition of our being in relationship as we compose and are composed by the situation we live. This meeting of one and the other generates a combined effect greater than the totality of its separate effects; the whole being greater than the sum of its parts. Social understanding, therefore, is a co-creation, a process of interacting as well as an individual happening.

Looking at the experience of resonance from a sociological perspective, Hartmut Rosa (2019) applies his theory of resonance to varied realms of human interactions and describes the ways in which we establish our relationship with the world: "If we accept this notion of a fundamental relatedness that precedes the division of subject and object and serves as the very basis both of the presence of world and of subjective experience, then resonance appears not as something that first develops between a self-conscious subject and a 'premade' world but as the event through which both commence" (35). Rosa goes on to state that human beings are primarily and fundamentally "creatures capable of resonance" rather than "creatures capable of language, reason or sensation" (36), a concept first advanced within phenomenological tradition. We are continually responding in relation to the other who responds to us (Waldenfels 2011). Such responses are experienced through the moving-feeling or lived body, continually shaping itself in myriad situations. Kinesthetic resonance exemplifies the dynamic, situational, and relational aspects of this embedding. Precisely said by phenomenologist Maurice Merleau-Ponty (1968), "The world and I are within one another" (123).

> *You move toward me and extend your hand abruptly, directly and with hi-intensity. I immediately feel the sides of my body squeezing together, and I feel braced. The image of a large steel pipe, dark on the interior and grey on the exterior, appears as if inside me. I think you are encroaching upon me, and I must protect myself. I take a step back, and the held feeling continues. Now I feel a gnawing kind of emptiness in my chest. I convince myself that I should… I must greet you in a warm and open way, but I cannot. I worry, as always, that something is wrong with me.*

In the above illustration, the individual is in touch with kinesthetic experience, lived bodily dispositions, and a familiar and habitual interpretation immediately is made. As kinesthetic experience or potentialities spring foreground, the possibilities within the environment are perceived. And likewise, the possibilities of the environment stimulate the potentiality of the individual. Simply put, we reach toward the other and, almost simultaneously, we perceive how the other reaches back (Frank 2001; Frank and La Barre 2011; Frank 2016, Frank 2021). As we assess how available that other can be in terms of fitting our needs, desires, and interests, we either move toward or away in response. The lived body, persistently and kinesthetically resonating with potential, is interwoven within environmental possibility—a bi-directional event.

Lived bodily experience, then, is not without values that are either pleasing or displeasing to the individual. As values arise, they describe a moment of being from which doing takes shape, offering the freedom to move in whatever direction feels appropriate. When lived body experience is made too soon into analytic evaluations, such as good/bad, right/wrong, worthy/unworthy, choices of being and behaving are limited. To further understand how aesthetically assessed values emerge in pre-reflective experience, and how they become diminished and distorted, it is necessary to consider the primordial and dynamic relations continually expressed and experienced in the developing child.

Infancy: A Phenomenological Lens

We are animated from our very beginning and already always prepared to take up the world in which we are situated. This attribute of infant development is characterized by shared and familiar practices that delineate the infant's social-cultural world. In the act of picking up, placing down, carrying, feeding, playing with the child, responses of both parent and child are integrated through touching-moving-feeling, as are the social understandings that are shaped within this interplay. Continually moving through a world of other people and objects, babies learn what their world has to offer. This is discovered through a developing sequence of actions that Edmund Husserl (1989) describes as "I move," "I do," "I can" (Husserl 27). These acts resemble concepts of orientation-manipulation, and each is securely fastened to lived bodily experience. Originally, "I move," precedes "I do," which precedes "I can." That is, as we tactilely and kinetically make our way through the world, we immediately experience feedback in the form of kinesthesia from whatever it is we move with and against, whether person, object, and always in relation to the universal forces of the field—gravity, earth, space. This feeling, then, feeds forward and serves as ground for the next move. It is the continual response of the other that gives form to the "I" as subjectivity emerges. The experience of an "I" is found and made, therefore, through developing sequences of interactivity; moving and being moved. Through the ceaselessness of our responding, we come to exist.

Husserl's "I do" is acknowledged by babies once they have done, as the move completes itself. Every moving, every doing, is practiced repeatedly, and the "I can" in time becomes part of the developing potentialities of the child, which opens greater environmental possibilities. The greater possibilities, in turn, are fodder for the child's potentialities. The moving repertoire of the baby changes and grows and with it an ever-expanding affective vocabulary. As these primary patterns form, always in relation to the world, they inform the baby's growing kinesthetic experience, which in turn informs the capacity to move. Following Husserl's thinking, moving is the substratum of learning our world and is central to all our engagements with the world (Sheets-Johnstone 1999). Movement offers the experience of *being a body* and, almost simultaneously, *being a body* offers the experience of *being of the world* (Frank 2016, 375).

Each act, each "I move," "I do," "I can" organizes a new form of behavior, stable in some features but flexible in others. When the child is encouraged and enabled to respond spontaneously and creatively, the range of variability around a stable mode is greatly expanded (Thelen and Smith 1994, 73). The form that arises cannot be separated from the dynamics between the baby and the situation. This is the process of an organizing gestalt; the ongoing progression of contacting, form-forming-form. The action in relation to the other "becomes part of the dynamic history of the organism and contributes to the morphology of future actions" (Thelen and Smith 74). That is, the earlier action becomes inscribed in the experience of kinesthetic remembering; the experienced past kinesthetically resonates in each new moment. The unfolding remembering is neither in the muscles nor nervous system of the child or parent, but rather springs forward in the co-created forming of a tactilely-kinetically-kinesthetically situated sense of self. Patterns of kinetic-kinesthetic remembering are not in the least imprecise or abstract for a baby or an adult. As postural-gestural patterns are co-shaped in this now new moment, the earlier contacting experiences in relation to previous and significant others in our life and their kinesthetic values are enfolded within. That is, the well-practiced kinetic-kinesthetic experience—the newly acquired and integrated part of the infant's developing repertoire—moves background and is included in the present now and anticipated next. The earlier experience is always part/whole of the emerging sense of self. At every threshold of experience, we look for the other that is already there (Frank 2016, 380).

There is a continually evolving kinesthetic consciousness that emerges from an uncoiling dynamic kinetic experience. It is "a basic process of knowing, which sub-tends all bodily actions and synthesizes them" (Sheets-Johnstone 1999, 131). When babies directly touch the other, different parts of their own bodies, other bodies or objects, a two-fold experience is produced. They feel the other impressing upon their body, as well as their body impressing upon the other. For example, if babies touch the blanket beneath them, they might feel the palms of their hands as *lightly tickled* as they move over it, as well as qualities of the soft, scratchy blanket underneath their hands. Such bodily impressions *of* the other, as well as singular qualities *from* that other, form this two-fold experience: *touch-touching-touch*. All tactile-kinetic-kinesthetic experience involves contact with and against the other in organizing the experience of *me* and *not me* and implies a *being with* in the presence of this different other. Contacting is not possible without differentiation, and differentiation is not possible without contact (L.Perls 1992, 152). It is contact that is "the simplest and first reality" (Perls et al. 1990, 227). From here one's relationships arise, and we come to know ourselves and our world.

When we touch the other directly, skin-to-skin, it is always through a medium between one and the other. In this case, the air serves as that medium. The idea of an intermediary is made clear if we imagine one hand touching or pushing-against the other under water. There is no way that the water is not felt between the two hands, as it is the intervening substance through which the impression of one hand is conveyed to the other. Staying with this water metaphor, imagine a three-month-old baby in the bathtub. The mother holds her baby with one firm forearm and hand under his head and neck and gently moves the other through the water, such that little waves reach the baby. The mother's efforts, as she swishes the water toward her child, create vibrations that are transferred through the water medium. Feeling the waves touch his feet, legs, and belly, he laughs and wiggles his whole self in response. Mother also laughs and creates more waves for her baby to enjoy. In other words, vibrations move through the medium of water from its source, the mother's fluttering hand, to the recipient, who moves and feels his moving in response. Responsiveness is never passive in nature: but active. The vibrational channel sets a tactile, kinetic, kinesthetic process in play, and the appearance of the baby's world changes. The mother is influenced as well.

It is not only through vision, then, that mother and child are connected, but through the medium of water, each can feel the other's peripheral touching as well. So too, the medium of air carries the surface vibration between one and the other: "Through touch we are sensitive to pressure waves and vibrations, as well as other similar signals, and these stimuli are capable of travel through media just like light and sound waves" (Fulkerson 2014, 150). It only makes sense that our bodily rhythmic responses, co-created in contacting, are influenced by the other's distal touch. Tactile-kinetic-kinesthetic operations form an inseparable whole of experience in the finding and making of contact. This can be seen in the following baby-parent scenario.

Imagine that a four-month-old baby lies in the arms of her father and looks up at his face. Father, holding the baby with a firm and gentle grasp, gazes down at his child. The baby lightly squirms in response to her father's holding and his gaze. As she moves, she is kinesthetically resonating in relation to her father. The baby's movements are not something separate from the situation in which she is living but rather express that situation. The baby progressively forms the experience of I see you seeing me seeing you. I feel you feeling me feeling you.

Imagine that the baby smiles at her father. The father smiles back, and the baby wiggles and coos. We might infer for the baby: I saw-felt-found a part of myself in your face that I did not know was there until this very moment. Not until I experienced your smiling face responding to my smile did I know it was mine and that it mattered.

Now the baby softly and gradually reaches her hand toward her father's smiling face. Kinesthetically resonating within the situation, she senses and feels how her move will complete itself. Its anticipated achievement is made known through the dynamics of a presiding felt experience. (see Frank 2016, 375)

The above scenario is an example of the mutuality of contacting whereby one smoothly attunes to the other. The infant naturally responds to the direct skin-to-skin and distal touch/gaze of the parent and, likewise, the parent responds to his child. It is through the gaze and touch of the other that infants begin to experience themselves as subjects. That is, from within this kinesthetically re-sonating sphere, one's personal, unique, subjective perspective emerges. A spontaneous and creative adjusting emerges from our attentively listening for and responding to the other's response. Bodily powers, then, arise from our primitive sense of aliveness. In time, I know what I can do with you because I have done with you, and simultaneously, I know what you can do with me. The felt past is ground to the feeling present (Frank 2016, 375).

Contacting, or any interaction between the organism and its environment, is a movement of the field. Although it is seen as mutual or receptive in the above baby-parent exchange, it is not always the case. We can make contact with someone who is not making contact with us as in a remembrance of or fantasy about a person, or one can make contact through looking out a window at someone who does not even know we are looking at her. The distal touching is not reciprocated. There also are other situations of awk-ward interactions, modified contacting experiences, which indicate a lack of fluid coordination between partners. When neither partner can meet the other spontaneously or freely, frustration, disappointment, and confusion can build on one or both sides of the equation. This is illustrated in the following baby-parent scenario.

When the father reaches down to pick up his four-month-old baby, he narrows the skin along his forehead and pushes his lips together. As he lifts his daughter out of her crib, his movements are dense, hi-intensity, and abrupt. The especially sensitive baby kinesthetically resonates to both her father's facial and bodily expressions and responds. As she feels him advancing toward her and then lifting her up and away from the support of her crib, she pulls her arms and legs together, which narrows the areas of her chest and abdomen, and she holds her breath. We can infer that the baby kinesthetically registers these feelings as not safe.

While her father holds her with a condensed, hi-intensity grasp, the baby abruptly reaches her head and eyes away from him. She begins subtly yet firmly to push her pelvis and legs against the limiting resistance of her father's strong embrace. Misinterpreting his daughter's developing discomfort and desire for distance, and imagining that she is calling for a more solid container, the father abruptly pulls his daughter toward his chest as he holds his breath. The baby then whimpers, and her father begins quickly bouncing her up-and-down with an unyielding staccato rhythm. This is all he knows to do. (see Frank, 2016, 379)

In this example, both parent and baby bring a kinetic-kinesthetic history to their meeting. Perhaps the father was raised in such a way that prohibited displays of sensitivity, and his showing a gentle side of himself most assuredly would be labeled as "weak" or be dangerous for him. Here his behaviors are the result of cultural, political, social, and familial traits. Perhaps the father was not well enough supported in his infancy and throughout his childhood. The unaware and self-fulfilled expectation of awkwardness becomes apparent. As he reaches down to pick up his child, an enduring relational theme emerges (Jacobs 2009, 69): *No one held me and made me feel safe, so I don't know how to do that for you.* Or possibly an unaware expression of resentment: *Why would I make you feel safe if no one made me feel safe?* In any of these situations, the father's dynamic reaching action—gripped, abrupt, and of hi-intensity—was at one time well-practiced in reaction to the significant figures of his early upbringing. These historic experiences of reaching and being reached are now re-stimulated in the present and create a familiar kinesthetic resonance that is only peripherally sensed and felt. Although the father's behavior is not yet understood through reflection, it is already grasped in terms of pre-reflective bodily engagement.

As to the baby's experience, imagine that in her life a tenuous holding experience has already become routine. Now, even before she is touched and moved, she will predict what is coming—that the holding situation will not be supportive—and she reacts in anticipation. She has formed a generalized experience of the situation (Stern 1985). As she sees her father move toward her, she prepares by binding her muscles, holding her breath, and heightening the intensity of her movements. Kinesthetically resonating and pre-reflectively aware of her circumstance, she feels the coming next. She lives the situation at hand, contacting the full reality of her experience. These kinds of repeated occurrences become etched into the newly forming repertoire of baby-parent transactions, and the baby's patterns of breath, gesture, posture, and gait take form. Her ongoing bodily responses to her father confirm how she was received. The parent's body, too, is influenced in these ongoing nonverbal conversations: neither father nor child find their basic desires met. Thus, their capacity to respond fluidly in interactions within the social environment grows disturbed; choices of being and behaving are limited.

The experienced past kinesthetically resonates in each new moment. It is "a particular kind of affect belonging both to the body that precedes our subjectivity (narrowly construed) and the contingent, cumulative subjectivity our body allows us to build over time" (Noland 2009, 4). Postural-gestural patterns are co-shaped in the passing present. The earlier contacting experiences in relation to previous and significant others in our life, and their kinesthetic values, are enfolded within: "collective behaviors and beliefs, acquired through acculturation, are rendered individual and 'lived' at the level of the body" (Noland 2009, 9). The re-membering contains historic kinesthetic experiences included in the forming of gesture, posture, gait, and breathing pattern. These "affective dispositions," or traces of past relations with our significant others, always take shape in the present to affect and be affected (Mühlhoff 2019). Re-membering allows us to actualize our past and thereby find ourselves at home in the present. Overtime, this synergy of meaningful movements becomes interwoven with the stories we have made and continue to make of our lives. The earlier experience is always part/whole of the continuing emerging sense of self. At every threshold of engaging, we look for the other that is already there.

Building Social Understanding within Adult Therapy

Imagine the patient who, during session, slowly and delicately reaches his arms toward his therapist as he moves his upper body forward and away from the back of the chair. As his reaching pattern unfolds, familiar kinetic-kinesthetic impressions now inform and form his reaching. Feeling himself move beyond the presumed safety of his own personal expanse, and moving into a space where he may not belong, he suddenly pulls his arms inward and pushes himself back. He feels the whole of his body clutch, and he immediately lowers his head to focus his eyes on the floor in front of him. Enveloped within his reaching for and pushing away is the familiar and reliable kinesthetic, historic expectation. He imagines what he can and cannot do with his therapist, and what she can and cannot do with him. With every kinesthetically felt relational move, the sedimented past flows into the anticipated future.

The therapist, sensitizing herself to the dynamics of the situation, feels touched by her patient's ambiguous gestural pattern. Her body softens and she gently and quietly sighs. Her hands, once lying folded upon her lap, now open and spread onto the arms of her chair. As she makes herself present to the subtle yet profound transactions of this encounter, and attunes to herself and the patient, she lays the ground from which he can take support.

Hearing the softness of his therapist's sigh, the patient slowly looks up once more and observes her different posture. Affected by what he sees, he incrementally frees some of the gripping of his body, yet holds on to as much as necessary as a kind of support in this still uncertain situation. With heightened awareness on both their parts, the therapy situation reorganizes, and a novel co-creating of relationship is made possible.

In the above scenario, the therapist takes a clinical, phenomenological approach and includes her lived body as a means of diagnosing—to know thoroughly—the unfolding social situation. Her bodily disposition is not a singular experience, but rather expresses the ongoing movements of the field, an all-inclusive phenomenon. Phenomenal field is a synthesis of background feelings, bodily relations with the environment, and social interactions. It is constituted by the organizing function of kinesthetic experiences permeating not only the body but also the environment: "Persons inhabit their bodies and by mediation of the body they enact their lives, extended into space and engaged with others" who are always already included (Fuchs 2019, 69). The therapist's bodily disposition, therefore, expresses the phenomenal field as contributing to the situation and being formed by it concurrently (Mühlhoff 2019).

The patient's furtive reaching for and swiftly pushing away from his therapist indicates some confusion as to the possibilities of his "I can" repertoire: *Can I approach you and if I do, what will happen?* In that moment, he is pre-reflectively remembering the meaningful encounters with significant others who have influenced his life. The individual constitutes and is constituted by this passing present as it readily moves to an expected future horizon. The unfolding kinesthetic history, with its accompanying and enduring relational themes, announces itself in the form of the patient's stifled, interactive pattern. With an inhibition in moving and concomitant diminishment of feeling, the patient loses the capacity to resonant fluidly with the therapist before him. When resonance diminishes, there is loss of world (Rosa, 2019).

The therapist, realizing she is part of the patient's ambivalent gestures toward and away from her, attunes to the feeling tones of kinesthetic resonance generating between them, and remains open to her lived bodily experience. The coherence of the therapist's lived body, vulnerable and therefore receptive, offers an unspoken invitation to the patient: *I am here and with you.* With heightened awareness on her part, a relational shift occurs. The patient's subtle evidence of the other's lived bodily response offers him the opportunity to find a more coherent sense of self. He can recognize and own that he has a different response from that of his therapist. That difference becomes the background from which he can make another choice: that of slowly opening to her. Contacting, a meeting of one and the other, relies on "recognition of the other, the different, the new, the strange" (L. Perls 1992, 152) and becomes clarified through moments of heightened kinesthetic resonating. The basis of social understanding, then, emerges from a trans-corporeal process in which interacting plays a primary role.

Diagnosing the Situation

Rather than initially investigating patients' possible cognitive dissonance—the holding of conflicting beliefs, values, or attitudes—the clinical phenomenologist begins with first-person accounts as to *how* patients affectively experience the situation they are living; *how and when* kinesthetic experience flows well, and *how and when* it becomes disturbed. In all arising phenomena, the "body functions as a medium of experiencing the world; its overall state imbues and pervades the experiential field as a whole" (Fuchs 2013, 615). The body is simply the felt channel of our affective relation to the world. These temporal-spatial affects or qualities of movements, with their phenomenological character, shape the way the world is for us, whether remaining as background or moving into awareness. Discovering therapist and patient's individual qualities of experience gives information as to how each co-creates a shared social world. When the ground of kinesthetic aliveness grows dull and distorted, patients experience a diminished sense of situation, as well as confusion as to what they can or cannot do relative to that situation.

The first step in this process is to explore exactly what is here-and-now and to listen for what cannot be heard (Bloom 2019); that is, to discover what is elusive or hidden in what appears most obvious. Implicit in holding away from lively social engagement, the patient's dissociated state is an important, even crucial, attempt to prevent further suffering, feelings of alienation, excessive loneliness, all too familiar beliefs of not belonging are kept at bay. These are attempts to protect oneself from an uncertain and frightening future. There is also the simultaneous shrinking of experiential space to contain oneself rather than floating off into some vast expanse or being crushed by what is out there. Although experienced and expressed behaviors were once lively, spontaneous, and creative adjustments to an earlier field, now they have grown routine and dull. The varied symptoms, the very reasons that brought patients to therapy, are accomplishments in contacting as they endeavor to establish a coherent and sense-making experience. Using the resources most easily available, the patient relies on familiar, and therefore preferred, attempts to make some kind of support in a too often uncertain world. These must be acknowledged and credited as such.

The therapist facilitates an appropriate and incremental opening of the patient's kinesthetic experience by uncovering how and where he/she/they hold fast their body out of perceived necessity. Once the holding experience is noted—remnants of the distant past surviving in the forming present—therapist and patient now can explore what happens between them. What made it necessary for the patient to constrain kinesthetic/affective flow and curtail movement repertoire during the session? In other words, in what ways might the therapist be contributing to the patient's need to hold tight by inadvertently stimulating past influences presented in this here-and-now. Although every moment is made anew, earlier experiences have a great deal to do with the experience of each present moment. Held within the restricting bodily patterns are the patient's earlier formed and anxious beliefs that contain the meaning of unaware intention: to control the situation by controlling one's body.

Monitoring her effect on the patient during the therapeutic inquiries, the therapist is in touch with either the fluid, creative responses or routine reactions arising between them. It is important that the therapist know when and how her own kinesthetic enduring themes emerge and cause a routine reaction to the situation. Sensitivity to her bodily experience allows the therapist to move through her own all too familiar reactions and, in so doing, spontaneously adjust to the actuality of the moment.

From a background of lived bodily experience, meaning is found and made. Meaning, however, is not always made explicit. That is, the kinetic-kinesthetic experience can contain meanings that are lived and implicitly grasped rather than explicitly garnered. The felt meaning is not the same as the precise, symbolized, explicit meaning. Felt meanings do not hide more explicit meanings that must be unearthed from some dark place. The felt meanings, a "sensing of body life," can have myriad organized characteristics; however, they are not shaped abstractly, explicitly, and concealed (Gendlin 1997). Rather, we complete them as they take form in the present, unfolding, dynamic relationship. In other words, the organizing of explicit meaning is an emergent experience; behaviors that happen now are not a matter of what happened then-and-there. Alternately, emerging experience expresses what gestalt therapist Gary Yontef refers to as the "then-and-now." Remainders of the past are stimulated and revived in this immediate present as they both constitute and are constituted within the situation. This is analogous to the thinking of psychoanalyst Donnel Stern (2003) when he states that experience is not given but made. Its meaning is frequently a creation instead of a discovery of some prior truth. Meaning, then, is a co-creative activity found and made in the experience of contact.

Case Vignette

The following case vignette exemplifies how implicit meaning is co-created, not necessarily explicated, as the patient comes to understand her part in the organizing of her world. It is a kind of microanalysis of the moment-to-moment structure of therapy by looking at the function of tactile-kinetic-kinesthetic processes in developing social understanding. Just as babies learn their bodies and themselves first and foremost through ongoing and co-created tactile-kinetic-kinesthetic experiences, so too can the adult patient relearn her capacity to make a more coherent sense of her subjective self within the patient-therapist field. It is the therapist's intention to facilitate an expanding of patients' kinesthetic capacities and to create an environment from which they can find and make relational support; both are central to restructuring the process of social understanding.

At the time of this session, forty-two-year-old Sara and I had been working together for several months. Before coming to me, she had been a patient in gestalt therapy with a colleague for approximately five years. Sara decided to return to therapy, as she was having difficulties at work with the head of her department. All too often, she felt belittled in his presence and was not sure how to respond. Sara begins this session by relating a story about an uncomfortable situation between her and a boy she had dated when she was seventeen. The boy asked her to do something sexual with him that made Sara feel uncomfortable. Rather than say no, she complied.

As she speaks, Sara slowly hollows and narrows her chest and shortens her spine. Her head now pushes downward, and she looks at the floor. Her hands, once resting by her sides, grasp each other. Her feet, which appeared planted on the floor, now subtly push backward leaving Sara precariously balanced on each set of toes. Her thighs rotate and press inward as her knees pull together. Sara appears to be shrinking. Sitting across from and relatively close to Sara, I feel farther away than I actually am. A memory emerges, something long forgotten, and I find myself identifying with Sara's story. I now notice my held breath and the uncomfortably loose feeling of my hands, now hanging on the armrests of the chair. I take a fuller exhale, slowly inhale and bring my hands to my lap. I enjoy the heavier feeling of their resting, palms down, on my thighs.

When Sara finishes her story, we both pause. I feel a sense of emptiness around me, and a dense, murky feeling sinking downward in the area my chest. I adjust myself and find the back of my chair behind me, the seat under me, and then notice the soles of my feet directly placed on the floor. I take several slow, full breaths and wonder aloud what Sara might be feeling after telling me her story.

Sara raises her head and looks directly at me. "I feel shame," she responds, and then glances downward. I ask Sara where the feeling of shame is located in her body and, if she can find it, what she exactly notices. Sara says there is "something" in her chest, but she doesn't have words for it. I suggest she stay with the feeling that has no words.

More moments pass, and Sara looks up again and says, "I feel shame like this," circling her hand loosely in front of her chest and letting it flop from her wrist. I repeat the movement, so that I have a better sense of what she might be feeling. Sara then replies: "I feel empty. I feel shame." I wait several moments and ask: "How might I be part of your shameful experience?" Sara looks directly at me and says: "I always feel shameful when I talk about this, or even when I think about what happened. I feel like I'm bad in some way. I'm bad." As she says this, she slightly shortens her spine and narrows her chest a bit more. I pause and ask again: "How might I be part of your shameful experience?" This time, Sara waits and then sighs deeply. "Well, this kind of thing would never happen to you," she says convinced and convincingly. "What makes you think so?" I ask and Sara responds: "You sit up so straight and tall. No, this would never happen to you." Hearing Sara say this, I feel a subtle jolt run through me and realize that my upright posture is a familiar place of "home" for me. Our next exploration is constructed through the clarity of her statement and my experience of what "home" can feel like. At my invitation, Sara and I begin shrinking and growing slowly and incrementally in relation to one another. Without words, we explore the feel of our movements and in all dimensions. I shorten, narrow and hollow, while she lengthens, widens, and bulges, as we explore this continuum.

After time passes in mutual fascination, Sara and I come to mirror each other: we both have grown upright and expanded. Sara looks at me, momentarily pauses, and abruptly shrinks: "I cannot be as big as you," she exclaims. I pause to feel the swift change in her shape and a hollow forms in my chest. "I get to be big and you get to be little." Sara and I sit with this thought, and I query: "What would happen if you and I were big together?" Sara replies: "I'm not sure. That's what's scary. I'm not sure." I tell Sara: "I think the risk would be to try to be 'big' together and notice what actually would happen between us. Here is how we might begin: I would remain upright in my 'big' position, and you would stay in your 'little' position as long as you wish. Only when and if you feel ready, you can begin to stretch yourself upward. And if you start to feel some discomfort on your way to becoming 'big' like me, you can make yourself 'little' again."

As I detail the experiment for Sara, a light bubbling feeling rises from my abdomen to my throat, and I wonder if Sara feels something similar. I ask: "How do you feel after I have explained all of this?" Sara replies, giving a slight wiggling movement: "I feel excited. I want to try." I respond matching her brief wiggle: "Let's see what will be."

Sara condenses herself even more, and from there she gradually begins her upward ascent. I attend to my body and especially to my breathing, noticing the subtle rise and fall of its pattern as Sara changes shape before me. She moves steadily and with no apparent hesitation until she and I are almost at eye level. Then she pauses and condenses herself a bit. Waiting a few moments in that position, she then swiftly grows to her full height once more and faces me directly. No words are exchanged, only smiles, as we remain "big" together. The session ends.

Psychodynamics

In the experiment, Sara and I primarily reflected upon our lived bodily experience: moving-into-feeling-into-moving. We took a phenomenological approach and focused our work on emerging experience rather than placing attention on cognition, insight orientation, or historic excavation. Instead of diagnosing the "internal" life of the patient, a one-person therapy, it is the phenomenal field that provides the context for change.

Sara and I acted in concert with one another and with no pre-conceived notions of what we were doing or what we were to do. I gave as much attention to my felt experience of her movements as I did to my visual perception of them. I grasped the subtle expressions of her body and evaluated their aesthetics through the feel of my own body. In this way, I could enter her world. In the continuing process of therapy, these kinds of ongoing, animate experiences became woven into the fabric of the relationship, accumulating insights for both Sara and me.

No posture-gesture can be completely freed from its socially acquired meaning, but when we attend to arising kinesthetic resonances produced by and producing gestures of one's own and of the other, we can separate what we assume a movement means and discover the reality of the moving situation itself. Sara's familiar, stunted posture that she perennially labeled as "bad" took on new and different meaning in the moment, as its relational significance clarified. My upright posture *said* something important to Sara, as her shrinking experience *said* something important to me. In addition, with a heightening of kinesthetic awareness, Sara would have the possibility of expanding her movement repertoire over time and experience the novelty of our building relationship

In regard to the above, Jean-Marie Robine (2011) states, "When a patient sits in front of me and tells me that he is anxious, I can choose to listen to his words not only as words *in* a certain situation, but also as words *of* the situation, *as if* these words were belonging to an undifferentiated field which has to be explored, instead of to an individual, the one who tells them" (113). In agreement, Donnel Stern (2003) affirms that moment-to-moment experience emerges from our individual, unique patterns of interacting in relation to the requirements of the situation, almost always referring to other, real or imagined people. Similarly, rather than the moving-feeling experience of *shrinking* being Sara's individual symptom, it too belonged to Robine's undifferentiated field or Stern's concept of unformulated experience. As Sara and I explored, attuning to the emerging kinetic-kinesthetic resonances of the situation, we could spontaneously evaluate our relationship and together validate as real and true what was happening between us. From here, a new narrative could form, and through movement in awareness, its emerging meaning is made known.

Concluding Remarks

Experiences of kinesthetic-kinetic resonance ground our social interactions from the very beginning of our lives and are crucial in the making of meaning throughout life. Such body-to-body kinesthetically felt engagements shape the background from which the present experience becomes figural. In our everyday therapy experience, this process begins as soon as our patients press our doorbell with a certain rhythm and intensity, say hello and walk into our consulting room, and seat themselves on our couch in characteristic ways. This also applies when working on the internet, when the patient appears instantly before us shaped in a particular postural configuration and with a certain facial expression. These transactions are essential and fundamental to the opening dialogue or "starting situation" of therapy (Perls et al. 1990, 3). If we listen to our bodily resonance right from the start, we become accessible to the possibilities emerging between our patients and ourselves. We stay close to the felt qualities of a moving dialogue and remain open to whatever unfolds. We wait with utmost availability and listen for what is happening rather than make something happen. This is crucial in allowing the relationship to disclose itself rather than closing it off by interpreting the moment too soon, or at all.

Staying with our kinesthetic resonating, we re-find our lived sensuality, which enables us to find the qualities of our being with the other. We are not merely aware of how we sit in the chair or how we breathe, common and useful interventions in body-based therapies, but we are aware even more how we negotiate the felt qualities of our lived spatiality. In other words, we attend to the myriad ways micro-movements of our existence move through the other as the other moves through us. Attending to kinesthetic resonating experiences, relational patterns between patient and therapist can be re-constituted such that novel and satisfying engagements are found and made and social understandings are clarified.

Chapter 3

The Forming of Form

Six Fundamental Movements and the Building of Experience

In this chapter and throughout the book, the making of experience is articulated through a comprehensive investigation into the basic elements of animated life and through the language of movement. An exploration of human movement progressions, the continually changing particulars of experience, provides a precise phenomenological language for those sub-verbal interactions that are the foundation of lived experience, the foundations of contacting. The exploration of moving *is* an exploration of contacting, the meeting of one and the other, whether a person or an object. Breaking down movement into its constitutive elements, we more clearly understand the constructing of experience and the forming of gestalts. The tactile-kinetic-kinesthetic body—the body that moves, feels, and learns—comes to know itself in the act of experiencing. Through a deeper understanding of the ephemeral processes of moving, we see-feel how we live the situation we are living. Any situation can be analyzed by how I move in relation to you, how you move in relation to me, and the meanings we each make from this creative adjusting (Robine 2013).

To this end, let us turn our attention to an exploration of the primordial movements that originate within infant life to understand the processes by which we meet and are met by the other from its very roots. There is a functional similarity as to how movements arise always in relation to the other in the first year of life and in the moment-to-moment of the therapy session, whether individual, family, or couple. In other words, how baby and parent make meaning through their continual moving conversations throughout that first year tells us something of how children, adolescents, and adults make meaning in the passing present: the primordial now. Taking a movement-oriented and developmental lens to the contacting process deepens our discovery of how we become and continually maintain who we are. That is the primary question in development as well as in our clinical phenomenological explorations. We examine how we co-structure our

DOI: 10.4324/9781003266341-3

experience in relation to and with the other that is always already there but not yet identified, and how this process gives meaning to our situation.

The Language of Experience

We are born and readied to move through the continual emergence of the Six Fundamental Movements (Frank 2001, 2005, 2013, 2016, 2021; Frank and La Barre 2011, Frank 2021). These six movements, which appear in the infant, organize within a relational dynamic. In other words, there is no central generator on a developmental timetable that prescribes when a movement pattern will appear. And no sole aspect of the environment extracts any specific pattern from the baby. "Development does not happen because internal processes tell the system how to develop. Rather, development happens because of the activity of the system itself" (Thelen and Smith 1994, 305). That is, how each partner finds and makes contact with the other is the basis for development, whether in the longer timeline of the first year of life, or in real-time moment-to-moment experience. Movements are co-created and emerge as spontaneous and original adaptations within the context of the relational field; solutions to ongoing and developing challenges.

In the process of finding and making themselves in the world, babies use this moving vocabulary of micro-movements. They experience themselves *yielding-with, pushing-against, reaching-for, grasping-onto, pulling-toward, releasing-from* the other. Co-constructed within the early relational field, these interactions are primitive responses to the responses of the other in ongoing rapport. They organize an experience that is spatial as well as social and give the baby a sense of being with while separating from others. Moving through their world, babies develop a pre-reflective tactile-kinesthetic orienting that lets them know their experience of that other; one whose space is not mine yet, at the same time, is forming mine (Hermans and Hermans-Konopka 2010).

The six fundamental movement patterns continue to be essential to all our interactions throughout life, supporting the most basic elements of animated psychological functioning. Although they are continually perceived to some degree, they remain peripheral to perception. Later, patterns of animated being are founded on earlier ones, which then influence the next to come. In addition, later emerging patterns feedback to the earlier ones, influencing those patterns as well. This feed-forward and feedback process happens throughout the longer timeline of development, as well as in the real-time of moment-to-moment experience. In other words, the corporeal foundations of movement do not disappear over time, but remain part/whole of the emerging and further elaborated processes that form the background of present adult relating. The earlier patterns, rich with their primary foundational experiences, are integrated within those newly achieved patterns and serve other functions. Although learned in the first year of life, these patterns function here-and-now and are comprising and comprised by the present situation (Frank 2001, 2005, 2013, 2016, 2021; Frank and La Barre 2011, Frank 2021).

The coordination of lips, tongue, and jaw make feasible the act of reaching with an open mouth for the nipple; the breast or bottle is grasped-onto and pulled-toward the infant all in the service of sucking. One can surmise that the infant's perceptions of taste, temperature, and texture of the milk, along with well-practiced movements of lips, tongue, and jaw, form the background to later experiences of incorporation. This background supports the subsequent reaching-for objects to grasp-onto and pull-toward the mouth and even later in development, reaching-for, and pushing objects into and out of containers (Rochat 2009, 162). In real time, the act of reaching was notably and beautifully depicted as the basketball player, Michael Jordan, pushed-against the court's floor with one leg, thereby leveraging him to leap through the air from mid-court and extend legs, arms, and head with open mouth—all reaching for the pleasure of sinking yet another ball into the enticing basket. All six fundamental movements that support the sequential contacting experience are always in relation to the attracting environment, a bi-directional happening.

Subjective experience is yoked to these moving patterns with their accompanying kinesthesia; a kinesthesia that is persistently "reconstructed after each phase of movement" (Merleau-Ponty 2012, 118). We can push-against the other freely or with a firmer quality; we can reach abruptly or gradually; we can grasp with low intensity or hi-intensity. The task to be accomplished calls forward the movements to be performed, and *how* the movement can be performed, and with what variety of qualities it can be performed. The performance, in response, calls back to the task. From the baby's and then adult's continued practice of these six movements, variations in both execution of the pattern and their attendant kinesthetic qualities spring forth and modify the emerging experience.

Six-month-old Alex sits on his high-chair and freely slaps the table in front of him with both hands and with a moderate intensity. Appearing delighted by his slapping motions, he smiles and babbles, "da-da-da-da." Mother sits facing Alex and also smiles as she watches her child's enthusiastic slapping movements. Reaching her head and torso closer to her child, she says: "Oh, you're really enjoying that. You like to slap your hands on the table, don't you? Slap, slap, slap." Her vocal intonation is crisp, matching the tone of Alex's movements and forming a kind of harmony with him. Alex looks up at mother and pauses; his hands now rest on the table. In a moment, mother picks up the slapping movement, alternately pushing one hand down upon the table and then the other but using a more gradual quality than Alex had used. Alex carefully watches his mother executing the pattern of pushing-against his table. Seeing Alex following her movements, she continues talking to him: "Oh, now you're going to let me play this game alone, huh?" Mother then changes the pattern by slowing down her slapping movements; each alternating hand rests on the table for some time as she continues talking to him. As mother's hand comes to rest, Alex reaches-for it and places his palm downward on the back of her hand. He begins gradually to explore it as he lifts and then releases her thumb and first two fingers one at a time—lift drop, lift drop, lift drop. Mother continues to follow her child's actions: "Oh, this is a different game is it? I liked the slapping game, but you like something else." Alex gazes up at mother, pushes-against the seat of his chair with his pelvis and against the table with his left hand. Both give him the feel of a pushing back support, which enables him to reach-for his mother's glasses with his free right hand. He then grasps-onto them and attempts to pull the glasses off mother's face. "Ooops," she remarks, "These are MY glasses, Alex. Mommy's glasses. Not YOURS." Mother says this gently, with a firm tone. Alex, hearing her words and, with some help from mother, releases his grasp. His two hands are now near his face, and his fingers grasp-onto the air, making two fists. Quickly, Alex again pushes his buttocks against the seat of the chair, reaches both hands upward as his spine and head lengthen. He then glances downward at the table, abruptly drops his hands to push-against its surface, and returns to his slapping movements, a wide smile on his face.

The above account illustrates the proto conversation between mother and child expressed and experienced kinetically and kinesthetically. Here, we see clearly how infants learn to move themselves always with the other; in this case with the supporting ground of both mother and table. The mother's tone, matching the sonic and rhythmic quality of her child's slapping rhythms, is an attuning or kinesthetic empathy. In this interaction, mother and Alex illustrate how all meetings of one and the other (whether object or person) require pushing-against and pushing back. This background of support enables the creative adjusting of response to response. "*I*" does not come to exist without feeling with and against "*You*." As Alex pushes-against the table with his slapping movements, he also experiences the table's push back: a *material* resistance against which he can move. There is a solidity to his experience as he explores what he has done and, therefore, what he can do. Similarly, the mother enters the conversation both with words and movements, thus giving Alex a sense of a pushing back of the *phenomenal field*. Alex also offers that pushing back experience to mother and through the movements of his body, facial expressions, and vocalizing. In this brief exposition of the ongoing dialogues that are part of their immediate interactions, they learn who they are and who they are becoming together and individually. The meanings found and made are enfolded within the emerging sequence of fundamental movements, always psycho-physical in nature and expressed as part/whole of the relational field. This example of a fluid and satisfying meeting for both parties is not always the case. Elucidating the fluid structure of contacting is most useful, however, in describing how fluidity becomes blocked, habitual, and lacks spontaneous creativity.

Supports for Contacting

Laura Perls (1992) affirmed that coordinated movement patterns serve as primary supports for contacting (84). While this concept was only briefly discussed in her book, *Living at the Boundary*, her therapy and teaching illustrated her belief that sharp awareness of the differences between oneself and another, an essential component of sensuous and lively experience, always emerges from a background of coordinated support. Whereas Perls looked at sensorimotor support systems in terms of one part of the body in coordination with the other, my work has furthered this idea by exploring the coordinating of one part of the body with the other *and* in relation to the environment. The configuring or interweaving of moving-feeling-perceiving, as primal corporeal elements of the ever-changing organism/environment situation, provides the substratum necessary for the emergence of synthetic unified experience. The body part of the environment, the kinetic-kinesthetic-perceptive, is delineated into a series of six foundational maneuvers and their particular psychological functions, thus enabling phenomenological description of the forming of direct experience and the analyzing of contact (Frank 2001, 2005, 2013, 2016, Frank 2021; Frank and La Barre 2011; Frank 2021).

The processes of contacting and their primary sensorimotor supports, the six movements, are inextricably linked—there is no contacting without sensorimotor support, nor is there sensorimotor support without contacting. One meets the other through movement, and in the meeting one moves. Dynamic, relational, and contextual, these form a synergy of meaningful movements already always in relation to the environment. Even in the less complex experiences of eating soup, or looking at the sunset, these six movements are present and available. They are potentialities that continually find their realization when invited out by the environment, no matter *with whom* or *with what*. Observing these emerging movements, we see how the invitation from the attractive and attracting other has been accepted or not, which influences the forming gestalt and its inherent meaning. The fundamental movements sketch out how the offerings and opportunities of the environment appear and can be utilized.

James Gibson (1977) refers to these environmental offerings as affordances, turning the verb "afford" into a noun. What the environment offers or affords the person is what one perceives as something one *can do with* it;

how one can utilize it in some sufficient way or not. For example, the glass filled with lemon water to the right of my keyboard offers me a shape I can reach-for, grasp-onto, and pull-toward me, anticipating that the contents will quench my thirst. That which the environment supplies, and how the person perceives what is usefully available, differs from person to person. A skating rink does not invite the baby to skate upon it, but it does invite the older child or adult to do so: "Affordances relate to not just some body shape but to skill" (Gallagher 2020, 10). The baby simply does not have the biomechanical, physiological capacities to utilize the rink, nor would he/she know what to do with it. The recordings of Miles Davis afford the jazz *aficionado* the possibility of getting lost in his playing but does not necessarily provide the lover of Barry Manilow's pop and soft rock arrangements the same likelihood. The latter individual might not be drawn to the complex progressions of Davis's trumpet, insofar as the sounds would not invite out the requisite interest or appreciative response. And the jazz enthusiast might not be attracted to the lyrical style of Manilow's melodies. Affordances are relational in that objective features of the environment are described in relation to the particularity of the individual involved (Gallagher 2020, 10). In other words, the affordance that is selected by an individual is a response to that individual's present disposition; emerging from a background of prior experience stimulated in the now.

In these above situations, the affordance is an object, a "what." In the situation with a "who," a person serving as possible affordance, it is generally a matter of how one might utilize the person's otherness to feel more clearly in relation to that other and find, for example, comfort, companionship, or the means to clarify one's contrasting beliefs. How the invitation is received is dependent upon the individual's unique patterns of coordinated supports, the six fundamental movements that form and inform every sequence of experience. These movements arise in response to that which is offered. Fuchs and Koch (2014) use the words "affective affordances" in relation to things that appear pleasing or revolting, significant or inconsequential, fascinating, or tedious, and so on. Do the kind words and soft touch of one reaching-for the other invite that other to reach back or is it all experienced as inauthentic, distrustful, and to be avoided. In that case, the invitation expressed through a gentle reaching-for is met by an abrupt pushing away of the other: "The object is different for each individual owing to his perspective and his possibility of response to the object" (Mead 1938, 6).

Working in concert, the dynamics of the six movements form an amalgam of mutually implied powers; a synthesis of what the person can or cannot do in relation to the other. The affordance, in other words, emerges from a person's individual world of moving-feeling-perceiving and the meanings made from these ongoing synergies, which lead one toward or away from the other. Every movement in this sequence, and in combination with others, undergirds each moment-to-moment of contacting. The organism moves and is moved from the emerging impulse, a response to the other's stimulating response, fueled by the excitement of interest, curiosity, and desire, building to consummation or satisfaction. The six fundamental movements give the emerging interest, curiosity, and desire the possibility of expression. Their potential availability for use in any episode of contacting shapes the flow of experience. If the individual moves toward or away from the other with the equipoise of flexibility and stability, there is a sense of animation—a feeling of aliveness in the act. When this background of support is stable enough, neither inflexible nor too malleable, the experience of contacting streams. All six movements are a flowing part of the building of experience. If the encounter lacks the appropriate and necessary moving background support, contacting grows dull and lacks the kind of spontaneity and aliveness necessary to adjust creatively within the environment. One or two patterns can be repetitively used and stuck in the foreground, while others can seem so far background that they are not easily available for use.

The Implied Other

There is always something or someone from which we move toward or away. A verb does not exist without an object. For this reason, all the verbs of this fundamental language I present here are attended by their intrinsic prepositions that describe not only moving but moving always in relation to the other. We move *with, against, for, onto, toward, and from*; the other is implicit in every move we make, always already there, albeit not always recognized. As the sequence of contacting progresses with sufficient bodily support, excitement builds as one's intentions clarify in each newly developing situation and then diminish as desires, interests, or curiosities are either met or not.

Each movement, having its own psychophysical function and working in concert with all the others, is an expression of a whole experience. The patterns are not only of the literal moving body but also of the phenomenal body—the body of awareness—or *the situation through which I experience the world moving through me and me moving through the world*. Every act supporting the building of experience is bi-directional, response to response. These six movements are invited out in varied ways and in different combinations, but all interact with one another and become foreground when organic and environmental conditions are ripe and then smoothly shift to become available background. None of these six moving elements is any more prominent than any of the others in the assembling of experience. That is, no one movement outranks the other as a support for contacting.

The Creating of Forms

The vocabulary of six fundamental movements offers a way to search the depths of experience as expressed on the surface: a comprehensive investigation into how we see, how we hear, how we touch, and how we feel. The movements provide the means by which we respond with the world and demonstrate our personal readiness to engage. They form the primordial bodily processes that create experience and its result, the meanings that are found and made. This synergy of movement dynamics forms an "intentional arc" (Merleau-Ponty 2012, 137). Intentionality is the directedness of contacting toward an object or person to satisfy ongoing emerging needs, desires, curiosities, interests. The processes of contacting, a rhythm of moving, feeling, perceiving, and emoting, form a knowing or understanding of the situation as it is lived. Expressed in the language of direct experience, these movements provide the basis for phenomenological diagnosis of the unfolding therapy relationship. Through this approach, one can describe a first step in the evolving processes of gestalt formation—form, forming, form—as soundly as possible.

Jean-Marie Robine (2015) discusses the defining of form, starting with the ancient Greeks, in terms of what is stable. The stability of form implies that it is balanced, harmonic, and in equipoise. For most disciples—biology, chemistry, mathematics, physics, linguistics, psychology, philosophy, aesthetics—Robine states, "form refers to a configuration of parts seen as a whole, and this whole is what defines the parts and renders them interdependent" (149). He continues; "This spatial organization of things in motion—parts and whole—also was referred to by another word, *rhythm*" (150). Form, then, as the fluctuation of movement that creates a rhythmic pattern, is liberated from its prior motionless static position. Rhythmic forms involve the dimensions of time and space.

Though the word "gestalt" is translated most closely as form; the word *gestaltung* refers to the process by which forms are formed; how forming achieves form. "With gestalt theory," Robine (2015) states: "the primary awareness is highlighted because the perceiving form (the phenomenal pattern) is what unifies the perceived contents" (150). From the individual interacting within the situation, many and varied forms of contacting are created in the accomplishing of some necessary task. The primary awareness is, of course, emergent of the situation: "Form comes out of the endless transformation of the facticity of the real world into the subjective reality of the 'creator,'" (Robine 138). It is the way we shape and integrate our experiences.

In the unfolding of therapy, the therapist facilitates awareness such that patients realize what composes the forming of their unique and signature forms of being and behaving. In other words, therapists look for the elements that construct the pattern brought forward in the therapy situation; a situation that includes the therapist in the process of formation. Knowing that whatever patients reveal to the therapist in their particular stories, they also are telling the therapist something of what is happening between themselves and the therapist. Patients tell their story *to* the therapist, *for* the therapist, and often *about* the therapist. The therapist, then, is part of the shaping of this story and must wonder what it has to do with the form that both together make. At the conclusion of a course of therapy or of a series of therapy sessions, patients need to have an idea of how they have created their often routine and habitual forms and how, in the exploration of these routine patterns, they can find a means for possible change. In other words, the organizing theme or themes, reoccurring patterns of co-created meaning, must be brought to light. "Development is the organizing of experience over time, and form is what renders the nature of this organizing explicit" (Robine 2015, 137). Development and form are intrinsic to one another:

Case Vignette

The following is an example of the constructing and destructing of form within therapy. This session emerged within a weekend training workshop in Europe. We were working with a large group of participants, and I asked for a volunteer to join me for a session. Illustration sessions are part of our gestalt teaching method and can illuminate the lecture material. The young man who immediately raised his hand was neither a student of gestalt theory and practice nor an instructor. In fact, he had never had a therapy session and had come to the workshop because he was curious about our approach. I did not know any of this information as we began.

Sitting across from each other and surrounded by 135 participants, I first attended to my breathing and my felt support of the chair under and behind me, and the floor beneath me: I knew that this process would give me bodily data about the starting situation between the two of us amongst the roomful of participants. Attending to myself in this way was my first intervention, in that I was creating an environment from which my volunteer, Martin, could take support when ready and interested. It also gave me a chance to experience myself more clearly with Martin, and in the middle of this large group: to feel myself, my experience of being with him and the group and, even in those early moments, what we were co-creating in the opening of this lived situation.

Martin, sitting in a vertical posture, appeared rather held or braced, especially along the length of his spine. His feet, flat on the floor, were gathered together as were his thighs, which seemed somewhat clenched. His face was chiseled and narrow, especially around the

---

area of his jawline. As I sat with him, I felt a hollow in my chest that descended toward my abdomen, now somewhat held or bound. After a few moments, Martin said: "I want to dance with you. I want us to tango." I felt myself brace. I imagined that the group had some expectation that this would happen. After all, I had been a professional dancer, and I worked with movement in therapy.

I never did tango with Martin. But I did take seriously his request to do so. His invitation included his restrained postural attitude, his yet unfelt emotions, and his thoughts in relation to me and to the group. His wish to tango was his form, a way of adjusting to a situation I imagined was difficult for him, and unfamiliar. I knew he wanted something from me, but what he wanted felt vague to me and probably to him as well. I became curious about his desire to dance, and I wondered aloud: "What would it look like if we danced tango together? What would the group see about us?" I wanted to know what his anticipation of this event might be, what he hoped to show me and the group about himself, as every behavior has an important function for the individual. Finally, I asked him: "What about me encouraged you to ask me to dance." I wanted to know how I was a part of the building of this form; how I was included. Every question was asked slowly and offered sufficient time for Martin to consider his responses, which he did. Every question was shaped by my responses in relation to and with his responses; his thoughts, as well as the tone of voice, shifts in posture, gesture, as well as the shifting of my moment-to-moment moving-feeling experiences. Within this construction of what could be considered his symptom, Martin, through this form, is trying to solve a problem (Robine 2015, 56). I wanted to discover more about this problem emerging between us and needing to be solved.

In our back-and-forth exchanges around these questions, I closely attended to Martin's gestures and noticed that several times he stretched his hands toward me with his palms up. Although his fingers were more fully extended, his arms were not. This left his reaching movements remaining fairly close to his body. Noticing his protracted reach for me, I felt a distinct yet distant sadness, as if the sad feeling surrounded me and was not yet within me. Although I might have asked Martin to become aware of his gesture, which is common enough in our therapy approach, I strongly felt that focusing on his gesture could have brought up an anxiety and shame that he would not be able to support. Thus, I asked him if he would be interested in doing an experiment with me.

I sometimes work with properties in therapy. That is the use of devices such as small or large balls, blocks, or really anything that can heighten kinetic-kinesthetic awareness on the part of my patient. In this session, I introduced a Theraband, which has a resistant property when stretched. With two people pulling at each end of the band, it is possible to feel clearly how one influences and is influenced by the other. If Martin initiated a pull-toward me from his end, it would be met by my pull-toward him at my end. I could be found by his pulling action and would be ready to respond to his nonverbal request. After explaining the experiment, he was curious and interested and agreed to try and see what would happen.

Without words, we slowly used the band to pull-toward each other. At first, Martin's pulling-toward me was tentative, but after some time he pulled-toward me with a variety of qualities and in varied directions, as the band moved up-and-down and to the sides. He smiled broadly and clearly was enjoying this improvised dance between us. "I like this playing with you," he said. I replied: "Yes, you have my full attention and I have yours." Martin smiled. After some exploration with the band in all three planes, vertical-sagittal-horizontal, I asked if Martin might want to slow himself down and be aware of what, if anything, happened around the area of his naval as he pulled-toward me. His change in tempo and shift to a softer quality of the pulling movement brought the experience of yielding-with or being-with each other to the foreground. With the shifting qualities of our movements, I felt closer to and touched by him. Martin reported that with each gentler pull, he began to feel something come together in his belly. "I feel that too," I said. "It is as if you and I are coming together as we pull-toward each other." Martin agreed: his face and the area of his jaw appeared to soften, and his eyes began to water. Now the feeling of sadness that I had experienced earlier and at a distance, moved inside me. We lingered for a while with this feeling resonating between us. The session came to a close.

Psychodynamics

Martin's request to tango with me was, I hypothesized, the only way he thought he could realize his desire. Sequestered within the original form, the invitation to dance, I imagined, was the longing to be met by me with interest and even appreciation. As I held the other end of the band while Martin pulled-toward me, I kinesthetically experienced how he was conceiving himself and me and how I was conceiving him. The forming of a bodily narrative appeared. Using the Theraband to pull-toward each other provided a kinetic-kinesthetic pathway for us to meet, to contact. His sharper experience of what he was feeling as he was doing formed the ground for incremental shifts of his muscular tone. This was illustrated by the seeming softness of his face and jaw, which indicated a softening in other bodily areas and shifted his perceptions and precipitated the co-creating of meanings. I responded as my body softened, and my breathing deepened.

Gradually, and through our back and forth pulling-toward gestures, we approached the source of Martin's longing: intentionality manifest into intention so that what was vague became clear. Together, we discovered that there was more than one way to satisfy Martin's desire, which was for him to be compelling enough to garner my interest and attention. Finding ourselves giving to and receiving from each other, we moved closer. A new form was forming and one with greater flexibility. At the session's end, a more distinct sadness between us was fashioned through the phenomenal body, the continually emerging situation through which experience flows. I felt myself move through his world as he moved through mine. I was touched that Martin and I had managed to find each other, and this feeling appeared against a background, I imagined, of his having tried so hard to be found in his earlier and significant relationships, but too much of the time he had failed. Newly discovered forms of being and behaving containing their own and different sets of rhythms evolved. They now would need practice.

The Psychological Functions of the Act

The six fundamental movement patterns described below are illustrated through the baby-mother configuration where they can be seen most readily. They are prefigured in the body of the baby, ever ready to be invited out, and continue to shape and be shaped throughout our lifespan. They grow potentially more intricate in relation to the developing possibilities of the environment.

Throughout the first year of infancy and beyond, these patterns are the means by which both infant and caregivers bi-directionally attach. The feelings that accompany these moving patterns are *how* infants experience the world moving through them. An infant's survival is based on the capacity to stay close to and in proximity of the parent and to explore the world by adventuring away. Just as the parent offers an invitation for the infant to draw close for comfort and safety, so too the infant invites the parent to move close to fulfill the parent's longing for intimacy, a significant part of the human experience.

The process of *healthy attaching* is the result of predictable, reliable, and consistent enough ways that one joins with the other, offering stability and flexibility in a relationship. *Traumatic attaching* refers to how one joins the other in such a way as to create an intractable relational rigidity with diminished flexibility. Both modes of the attaching process are reliant upon the undercarriage of moving-feeling-perceiving-emoting. Preverbal infants must come to develop clear modes of expressing themselves in relation to their significant others, just as parents also must develop a clarity of non-verbal expressions that infants can come to understand.

The following passages describe the situation of mother (indicating the significant caretaker whether it be father, sibling, grandparent, or nanny) and child in relation to the six fundamental movements. They are exemplified in situations of both fluid and modified contacting. The illustrations are for the purpose of understanding the flow of movements only, and not to evaluate good or bad relationships nor to indicate normal or abnormal functioning. The six movements are presented here in a linear fashion, although one category of movement does not occur in isolation from the others. They all work together to enable and illustrate the interactive nature of our being and becoming. More attention will be given to the first two patterns within the sequence: yielding-with and pushing-against. These are the primary and basic ingredients for contact-making, as they are essential for moving out and into the world and bringing back to oneself the fruits of contacting. A case vignette of mother and son follows this section. It illustrates how the therapist utilizes a heightening of awareness through these six movements to diagnose the unfolding therapy experience.

Through an understanding of the ongoing interchanges between mother and infant, one garners insight into a "something more" that is part of therapeutic interaction. Just as the infant is a "sub-system within a larger dyadic regulatory system" (Tronick 2007, 9), so too is the patient a "sub-system" within the unfolding therapy situation. As you read the mother-baby dialogues, imagine some similar situation between therapist and patient when communicating within the therapeutic dyad goes smoothly and culminates in satisfaction for both parties and, alternately, when each partner is misunderstood by the other and satisfaction is neither found nor made.

The Flow of Contacting

Yielding-with (allowing to-be-with): The act of giving to and almost simultaneously receiving from the presence of the other, as that other gives to and receives from us. Yielding-with is the experience of relating in the world without rational thought. When yielding-with is foreground, we begin in *otherness* as there are no clear boundaries between one and the other; no figures of interest are formed at this point, and all possibilities are open.

This phase initiates the process of kinesthetic resonance: reverberating feeling tones that are generated from one person to the other, and that enable the organizing of perceptions. *I see you seeing me seeing you. I feel you feeling me feeling you.* The quality of our receptivity is expressed and experienced through yielding-with and is dependent upon a mutual adjusting with the other, whether object or person. The lived body, the body I experience, has a gradually emerging sense of weight in relation to the situation, which is essential for orienting. We feel *that* we are, *how* we are, and *where* we are.

Yielding-with is part of the pre-personal, pre-reflective, pre-known world. It is the experience of intentionality before it clarifies into deliberate intention. This phase establishes the basis of an emerging shared affective intentionality; that which Merleau-Ponty (2012) refers to as "intercorporality." That is, yielding-with forms the ground for the ongoing, unremittingly stream of experience to continue, and offers the basis for a coherent and core sense of self to be achieved over time. In doing so, it provides the organism with the capacity to feel itself throughout the forming of experience. Yielding-with, in situations of stability, is a joining or merging with that other. It is the psychophysical aspect of trans-subjectivity. It initiates a growing excitement necessary to complete the act in its entirety. The developing psychological issues inherent in yielding-with are basic to issues of trust and may be: "Do I have faith in your predictability, reliability, and consistency?" "How safe do I feel to give myself to you and receive from you?" "If I give myself to you, will you reciprocate and give yourself to me?"

Imagine a two-month-old baby resting in the arms of his attentive mother. If the mother's arms provide enough stability, the baby is able to give the weight of his body over to the mother and receive mother's support. Both partners breathe relatively deeply and evenly in this exchange. In the moment of gazing into the eyes of her child, mother gives herself over to the experience. She melds with her baby and opens herself to receiving and being received by her child. In doing so, she feels herself as she feels her child and intuitively knows how to adjust her arms around the baby to provide the necessary sense of containing.

Imagine now that mother becomes distracted, frustrated, or anxious by an intruding thought, disturbing reoccurring memory, or some perceived danger in the environment. She now clenches her body by binding her muscles closer to the bone and limiting her breathing, which is held. The receptivity of yielding-with and the qualities that provided the prior comforting experience for both herself and her child are no longer easily available. The support of the parent does not feel safe and stabilizing enough so that the baby's breathing becomes inhibited. He muscularly holds onto himself, as mother does not provide a firm enough container for him. At this moment, neither parent nor child give to nor receive from each other in some relatively equal measure. Receptivity diminishes between them.

In this next situation, imagine a mother that is initially receptive and available as she picks up her baby from the crib, but the baby, in response to her, is now fervidly squirming in her arms. Mother becomes somewhat flustered and confused as to what her baby wants, and unsure as to whether she can provide whatever that might be. In her perplexed state, she no longer feels herself yielding-with her child; rather, she holds back. Not being intuitively in touch with herself or her child, she cannot imagine what she could do for him and with him. Instead, she grows blank.

Pushing-against: The act of separating from while including the other; discovering and making difference. There is no pushing-against without a concomitant pushing back, or the dynamic effort created as one energetic force moves against the other. It does not mean that the pressure of one and the other—pushing-against-pushing back—is equal; there is interchange, but not necessarily mutuality or a resulting benefit for both. It is only from the quality of the other's pushing back (soft-hard, abrupt-gradual, and so on) that we feel ourselves and know that we exist.

In the process of pushing-against-pushing back, we discover the qualities and subtleties of the other and come to realize there is *me* and *not me*. Being present, we provide an indispensable push-against, for the other to push back. In so doing, we feel that other is with us, and almost simultaneously yield-with their presence. How we come to know ourselves, then, is dependent on the bi-directional experience of pushing-against and pushing back.

Pushing-against narrows the possibilities within the environment and the figure of interest begins to take form. The individual deliberately chooses and approaches the other through actively aggressing or moving out and into the environment (Perls et al. 1990). One moves toward what is desirous and interesting and excludes what is not, as excitement builds. Pushing-against with the requisite pushing back is, therefore, the prime mover of experience. One moves from an undifferentiated experience to one that is more cohering as the responding other comes into sharper awareness. Excitement continues to grow in the approach either toward or away from what is welcoming or unwelcoming. The developing psychological issues inherent in pushing-against may be: "Can I be different than you and still be together with you?" "Can I be separate from you without losing myself?" "Can I be separate from you without losing you?"

Imagine the five-month-old baby lying in the arms of the mother and pushing-against her with head, chest, buttocks, and along the length of his spinal column as if to test the boundaries of where he begins and where he ends. In doing so, the baby begins to differentiate himself: "I move here and see you moving there." Pushing-against is the means by which he levers off his mother in order to discover himself in relation to the world. Through the baby's pushing-against and the pushing back of mother's containing arms, the baby comes to learn their relationship. For this pattern to appear with clarity, the arms of the parent must provide appropriate stability and leverage for the baby to push-against. Without this sufficient and necessary push back from the mother, the baby cannot feel himself distinctly. The qualities that accompany his moving body give the baby information about the kind of world that also moves with him. This is true for the mother as well, who comes to know something of her baby and herself through her continually emerging qualities. Mother provides a solid and firm push back as the baby fidgets in her holding arms, and mother's voice, just firm enough, also indicates her consistent presence.

Imagine another scenario where a five-month-old baby and his mother have very contrasting and unique movement signatures; their ways of moving through the world are very different from each other. This baby wiggles and twists in mother's arms with a firm and hi-intensity push-against mother using buttocks, chest, and legs. The baby looks for a push back with enough firmness to make these twisting, wiggling movements not only possible but pleasurable. His mother, misinterpreting these moves and assuming her son wants to be soothed, rocks him gradually while holding him gently. Her pushing back does not match his desire for a firm container such that he can be well-met and clearly feel himself and with her. Becoming frustrated, the baby pushes-against his mother now with both hands and makes growling sounds that echo the quality of his pushing-against movements. The mother now is at a loss to know how to respond, and in her state of stress, she does more of what she is accustomed to doing rather than experiment with a different way of adjusting. She rocks her child even more gradually, accompanied by a soft and low-intensity vocal tone. The baby's response is to intensify his pushing-against movements as well as his vocalizations. A clear sense of separating from the different other, while including that other in experience, is diminished.

The initial micro-movements that build contacting, the receptivity of yielding-with and the activity of pushing-against, are foundational. The organizing of an impulse, which is the orienting response slowly forming in relation to and with the invitation from the environment, is interwoven within the processes of manipulation. The progressing of yielding-with, the affective and receptive component, is always already accompanied by pushing-against, the more active aspect. The yielding-with enables the felt experience of bodily weight, and pushing-against enables the capacity to move within the environment. They shape two sides of a coin, and one does not exist without the other. Yielding-with is the kinesthetic consciousness of the act and pushing-against gives it continually changing form. There must be that other, a "what" or a "who," for one to merge with in order to feel separate from. Likewise, to feel separate from, there must be someone or something to merge with. Together, they are required for the fostering of maturation; the defining processes that underlie *me* and *not me*.

The rhythmic flow, a pulsation developed through yielding-with-pushing-against, always shapes the ongoing interaction that is contacting.

Every emerging figure is built upon these movements and their concomitant shifting affects. One moves out and into the enticing environment while almost simultaneously withdrawing, whether unconsciously or consciously. The withdrawing provides a kind of rejuvenation, an affective experience that can enable the evaluating of a situation immediately prior to reaching-for what is wanted or away from what is not. One becomes aware of the other through pushing-against that other and almost instantaneously feels the pushing back. In yielding-with, one withdraws, and in so doing, continually recreates the other in experience. In other words, what one takes in from the other is always a unique and personal subjective experience. Working in tandem, these patterns are essential to the building of contacting. They are the micro- sequences of rhythmic pulsations and are consequential in forming the substratum of the larger macro-sequence of a moving intentionality.

Reaching-for: The act of seeking, wanting, desiring; extending beyond oneself and into the environment. One reaches-for the other with eyes, ears, nose, mouth, and all the limbs, including head and tailbone. The fluidity of the reaching-for moment is dependent upon the supports from the prior yielding-with-pushing-against-pushing back experiences that form the ground for its emergence.

Reaching-for the other is either with the hope of being well-met by someone or something, or the dread of not. It is an investigation into what might be possible, and a measure of distance: "How far away is what I long for? How close is that which terrifies me?" For a moment, and without knowing how available the other is to grasp-onto, one loses balance; a naturally precarious and destabilizing situation arises.

Furthering the processes of differentiation, reaching-for is a nascent knowing of what one can and cannot do with that other. One develops a progressive feeling of apprehending; what I reach *with* is an integrated part of me, and what I reach-for is of the other. In this way, the reaching-for enhances the capacity to differentiate. The object of interest comes into greater clarity and adds excitement to the already generating anticipation. Reaching-for is the bridge from intentionality to intention as desires unfold and are clarified. As is true with all the six fundamental movements, the act of reaching is a bi-directional event. One is always simultaneously reaching and being reached, although not always with equal intensity: "Every focusing is a focusing of something that presents itself to be focused upon" (Merleau-Ponty 2012, 275). That is, the reaching-for arises due to a request by the attractive/attracting other: response to response.

The underlying foundation of yielding-with-pushing-against-pushing back serves as ground for this next reaching step. As one yields-with-pushes-against to receive the push back of the other, information is gained that shapes reaching-for. It is always implicit in these earlier sequences and is a primary recognition that the other is already there and with us. This is inherent when contacting is fluid and satisfying. But when contacting is modified, such that there are blocks in the flow, what is native to authentic experience can be denied. The developing psychological issues inherent in reaching-for may be: "How much of myself can I expose to you?" "How open and receptive can I be with you?" "How much of my desire for you do I wish you to see?" "If I want you, will you want me?"

Imagine a five-month-old baby lying in the arms of his mother and reaching-for her breast. The baby yields-with-pushes-against the mother's arms with buttocks and chest to reach his head and mouth for the breast. His arms and fingers are also part of his reaching experience as his open mouth sketches the form of the mother's nipple. The mother also reaches back as she brings the nipple toward baby's mouth. The breast needs to be drained and the baby needs to be comforted and/or nourished. The reaching-for movement shapes and is shaped by the assistance of the mother. As the mother holds her baby firmly, they are both able to reach-for each other and their mutual desire for satisfaction is consummated.

In a different scenario, imagine a similar age baby who demonstrates hi-intensity, abrupt and held qualities of movement underlying his hungry wails, asking to be fed/comforted. While continuing to cry, his narrowed eyes appear as if slammed shut. His mother, on the other hand, shows a far lower intensity and more gradually free movement signature. As she reaches-for the baby with her breast, much of his belly is exposed while he rolls outward rather than toward her. Her hands do not well-support the baby's head nor buttocks. It is the smell of the milk and his mother's soft voice that solicit the baby reaching back. But to do so, he must rotate his head almost completely toward mother's breast. This requires a greater pushing-against her arms, such that yielding-with becomes less available. The strain of this now is reflected in sucking with all his might to get the milk to stream. This ends in his coughing and choking. For her part mother, unsure of how to help her child, grasps-onto him with higher intensity but does not roll him toward her. Instead, he rolls farther outward and away from the possible comfort mother's body could afford. This ongoing and presumably habitual dialogue ends in exhaustion for both parties. How the mother reaches back, attentively, or distractedly and insufficiently, naturally influences both the baby's reaching movements, and the underlying supports of yielding-with-pushing-against. There is a feed-forward and feed-back structure in play throughout all the sequences.

Grasping-onto: The act of enclosing and containing. In grasping-onto, what was reached for can be manipulated and further explored in a more immediate way. Grasping-onto is executed with mouth, hands, and even feet as they grasp-onto the earth with every step taken. What was desired in reaching-for, moves toward greater satisfaction with the phase of grasping-onto.

Grasping-onto is already always implicit in the sub-structure of reaching-for. Reaching-for brings with it the risk of moving to the edge of and beyond one's own potential kinesphere—the personal space around us where limbs reach out while one stands still. As one extends into what is not yet known, grasping-onto can reestablish a feeling of stability and balance. We begin to learn something about our body through the body of the other: perceiving ourselves, we perceive the other and simultaneously perceiving the other, we perceive ourselves. One's perception of what one can or cannot do with the other becomes further clarified as a newly developing understanding of that other is elucidated and delineated. The developing psychological issues inherent in grasping-onto may be: "If I grasp-onto you, will I find you there and willing to grasp-onto me?" "As I grasp-onto you, will I learn something about us that I long to know, or that I will dread knowing?" "If I grasp-onto you, will you stay with me as long as I want, or will you soon leave?"

Imagine the six-month-old baby as he sits on his mother's lap faced outwards. Mother's arms are around the baby's waist with her hands placed one on top of the other and her thumbs extended upward and resting on the baby's chest. She grasps-onto her baby with firm enough pressure for the baby to feel solidly held. The baby looks at mother's hands and grasps-onto each of mother's thumbs with his fists. Feeling her baby's grasp onto her, she looks down at her child, placing her face close to the baby's face. She then begins to wiggle her thumbs, moving them this way and that, in a playful manner. The baby, now smiling and laughing, looks up at mother still grasping onto her thumbs. As they gaze at each other, mother folds the fingers of each hand around her baby's fisted hands and begins slowly rocking side-to-side. Grasping-onto his mother, the baby can evaluate how that which he has grasped-onto fits his desires, thereby eliciting the beginnings of satisfaction. Each contains and includes the other in experience, as a burgeoning sense of belonging is found and made. Imagine another six-month-old baby seated in his mother's lap facing outward. His mother places her hands around his waist, with her thumbs facing upward. Becoming curious about mother's hands, the baby looks downward and firmly grasps onto her thumbs with his fists and begins bending them this way and that. Mother, unfocused and not clearly paying attention to her child, unconsciously moves her hands away from him and refolds them with her thumbs now buried under her hands. The baby tries to grasp-onto mother's fingers instead of her thumbs, but when he does so, she holds them more stiffly and firmly together. The baby soon gives up and pops his own thumb into his mouth and grasps-onto it. Unable to find the other to surround, contain, and satisfy his desire for connection, he uses his resilience to satisfy himself.

Pulling-toward: The act of drawing what is other toward oneself with the possibility of incorporating that other into oneself. Pulling-toward the other with the necessary push back from that other enables the capacity to differentiate with even greater clarity.

Through pulling-toward, a movement of absorption and furthering the process of inclusion, we make the other *mine*. We experience *me* with *you* and the degree to which *me* and *you* are becoming *we*. The fluid act of pulling-toward, bringing the other in closer relation to oneself, creates a rhythm moving from the body's edges to the core or midline of the body, and back to the periphery. Simply put, the movement flows from periphery to core and out again and creates a solidity of experience. It is how we know we are here with the other. Pulling-toward is a crucial step in the act of assimilating and is inherent in solidifying the sense of belonging. The psychological issues inherent in pulling-toward may be: "How much of you can I take in and make mine?" "How much of me can you take in and make yours?" "What will happen if we come closer and you are mine as I am yours?"

> *Imagine a six-month-old baby lying on his back upon a changing table. Mother is going about the business of changing the baby's diaper and talking to the baby as she does so. Gazing directly at his mother, the baby reaches-for her with grasping fingers. Seeing this, mother bends to come closer and extends her fingers so that the baby can grasp onto them. The baby grasps and begins pulling-toward the mother, to bring mother even closer. This becomes a game between them, as mother pulls-toward her child and he pulls right back. The back-and-forth moving patterns demonstrate a vigor in their animation. Excitement is heightened as meaningful moments of "I am yours and you are mine" arise.*

> *Imagine a different six-month-old baby about to have her diaper changed. The mother, performing the task in a hurried fashion, does not talk to her baby. In fact, she does not realize this is something she could do that would be enjoyable for both. The baby also does not make a sound during the diaper changing task. Gazing at his mother, the baby reaches-for her with grasping fingers that appear on the cusp of pulling-toward mother as they stretch and flex yet with no partner to complete the act. Mother, accomplishing her task as efficiently as possible, does not notice this expression of her baby's desire. Without vocal communications nor the moving exchanges of pulling-toward the other, the potentially consolidating experience of that moment is lost.*

Releasing-from: Letting go of the figure of the absorbing and absorbed other, whether object or person. The now disorganizing experience, with its multiplicity of meanings, has been taken in and realized to become part of the sedimented past, thus supporting assimilation and growth.

Fluidly releasing-from is an achievement of contacting. The act of relinquishing enables one to move toward what is becoming or what next will be. The act completes itself and the figure de-structures as one moves from now to next. Releasing-from occurs in the aftermath of social contacting and marks the forming of who one knows oneself to be. Excitement diminishes. The developing psychological issues inherent in releasing-from may be: "If I will let you go, will I find you again?" "If I will let you go, will you find me again?" "How can I release you if I never fully had you with me?" "If I now let you go, what will happen next?"

> *Imagine a seven-month-old baby seated on the floor next to his mother. There are some toys in front of him. He reaches-for, grasps-onto, and pulls-toward the plastic wheel with five vibrant colored bubbles, through which he can poke his fingers. Mother watches with interest and delight as he does this and comments on his selection of which bubble to poke. After some time, the baby loses interest and releases the toy from his hands not looking where it lands. He waits, for a while, appearing not to focus on anything. Mother waits as well, saying nothing. Taking his time, the baby lingers in this creative void not knowing what will follow, how next this void will be filled. Moments pass, and the baby looks down at his toys and reaches-for the soft rocking horse, which he grasps-onto and pulls-toward. The subsequent figure of his interest and curiosity has emerged, and he spontaneously and creatively moves on.*

> *Imagine a seven-month-old baby seated on the floor next to his mother, who is talking on her cell phone. Spread out in front of and around him are a plethora of toys. Mother fidgets with a few toys, absent-mindedly picking them up and placing them down while chatting on the phone. The baby looks at his mother and then down at the various toys. He reaches for a soft rabbit, grasping-onto and pulling-toward it. He pushes-against the rabbit, gently rubbing its fur onto his face. Losing interest in the toy, the baby releases it and watches it drop onto the floor. Looking up again, he appears peacefully to gaze in front of him in an unfocused way. Mother, still chatting on the phone, abruptly reaches-for another toy and hands it to him, and he mechanically grasps-onto it. The potentially creative void of not knowing what will come next is too soon filled.*

Each appearing pattern becomes prior ground for the next. Yielding-with-pushing-against is fore-contacting for reaching-for; reaching-for is fore-contacting for grasping-onto, and so forth. The six fundamental movements collapse, like two ends of a spiral coming together, and form the density of the experienced ground from which the next sequence emerges. Once accomplished, yielding-with again moves foreground. Each pattern is like the overlapping waves of the ocean, as one wave crests onto the beach and pulls sand back into the sea which, once sedimented, becomes the ground for the next breaking wave.

The yielding-with at the beginning of the contacting sequence, however, is different from the quality of yielding-with upon its completion. During the sequence, the here-and-now activation of pushing-against-reaching for-grasping-onto-pulling-toward-releasing-from—invited out by the stimulating responsive other, is integrated and assimilated to become the sedimented ground for the next yielding-with phase. The potentialities of these movements in concert and their retaining of the lived past, whether recent or historic, are accessible and can serve as resources. This makes the quality of the next patterns to arise denser, richer, and more intricate.

Fundamental Movements: Summary

The fundamental movements of contacting are expressed through the material body and experienced through the phenomenal body as reverberating feeling tones within the relational field. For example, as person A reaches-for person B through his subtle or overt vocal, gestural, and postural expressions, the qualities of A's reach (soft or hard, abrupt or gradual, hi-intensity or low-intensity, like silk or cement, and so on) are experienced by person B, who moves and feels herself move in response. B's moving-feeling response enables her to know something of her experience, something of how she experiences person A, and something of how they creatively adjust within this co-created situation. The qualities or feeling tones that arise are expressions of ongoing movements of the field experienced and experienceable as one moves and is moved by the other; touches and is touched by the other. From the ground of such myriad meetings and their inherent psychological aspects evolving within the situation, some action completes itself and a multiplicity of meanings can be found and made (Perls et al. 1990, 227).

Through these progressions, we move out to learn ourselves only through the other. Acting in the world, we simultaneously receive the world. The native impulse that initiates this sequence and moves us through the world, is the inspiration to feel oneself as more than previously known. In the doing, we become greater than we were before and always strive toward becoming who we will be.

Relational Moves within the Family Session: A Clinical Example

In the following case vignette, the fundamental movements that inaugurate the sequences of contacting—yielding-with-pushing-against—are more thoroughly explored to illustrate the building of experience and offer a phenomenological relational diagnosis. To be relational *is* to yield-with-push-against in every moment. It is not possible to separate from without the inclusion of the *already there other* from which to separate. Nor is it possible to merge unless there is the *already differentiated other* to include in the merging experience. Both yielding-with-pushing-against are required for every figure of interest, curiosity, or desire, and the concomitant excitement to spring forth. Both are essential for contacting.

In this clinical example, we shall demonstrate how these primordial descriptors of the body situated in experience will sharpen the therapist's skills of observing and feeling. Placing her focus on relational moving patterns, the therapist attends to her tactile-kinetic-kinesthetic awareness and sharpens her eye to the patient's experience. The therapist's interpretation of the situation is set aside as she completely involves herself in the emerging co-created happenings. She knows what to look for, when to look, how to look, and where to look. As she uncovers the meaning of movement in the unfolding relationship, she is privy to the continually forming narrative that springs forward when we stay with the meaning that is lived in the subverbal (Robine 2013).

Case Vignette: Bobby and His Family

A colleague of mine had been seeing twelve-year-old Bobby for individual therapy for several months. Bobby was very anxious and becoming disruptive both in school and at home. Whatever his parents asked of him, whether to stop playing computer games and go to sleep, or to get organized for school, or to walk his dog, he would constantly argue until both parents and son became enraged. Although this behavior was somewhat tempered at school, he now was late with his homework and began to do poorly on examinations. Not doing well in school was a new behavior for Bobby and unacceptable for his highly achieving and anxious parents. After meeting with them as part of Bobby's ongoing individual therapy, my colleague suggested that they see a family therapist and recommended me. After several family sessions together, where I felt more like a referee than a therapist, I suggested I see Bobby with his mother and then with his father. I was hoping that the level of anxiety and overwhelm generated when all four of us were together would be mitigated by this different configuration. In this vignette, I focus on the session with Bobby and his mother.

As we begin, Mom describes what a problem Bobby has become at bedtime. Instead of turning off his computer, as she has asked him to do, he routinely argues from his bedroom, across from and down the long hallway from the parents' bedroom. Bobby presents the rationale for why he needs more time on his computer, why it's unfair to have to turn his game off when he is not finished, and why his parents are always too strict with him. When these arguments wear thin, Bobby comes into his parents' bedroom supposedly to say goodnight or that he is hungry and can he get a cookie from the kitchen, or that he is thirsty and can he get a glass of water. This ritual is repeated on most school nights and escalates until both parents and Bobby start screaming at one another.

As Mom paints this dismal picture of his behavior, Bobby looks toward the floor: his chest hollowed, his shoulders narrowed, and spine shortened. I, too, feel my chest slightly sink, and the weight of my body feels heavier on the chair. Suddenly, in the middle of Mom's reporting, Bobby lifts his head, widens and bulges his chest outward and begins to interrupt her and state his own position: "Well, you said I could…" or, "It's only because…"

Bobby and Mom are now in a battle as to who is wrong and who is right, who will win and who will lose. As they go back and forth, their movements become more abrupt, higher in intensity, and more bound, as do their voices, pushing-against and pushing back with a rapidly increasing excitement that does not seem likely to diminish. As I watch their impassioned exchange, I notice my body lifting up and away from the support of the chair. I feel my neck tighten as I hold my breath. Once I have found my support—feet on floor, pelvis, thighs on chair seat and my back touching the chair's back—I interrupt their engagement and say, "What you are doing is something well-practiced by both of you. Maybe you would be interested in trying something else?"

First, I explain what they will do to see if they have any interest in doing it. Once they give me the okay, I ask them to stand in front of one another. I introduce a 50-centimeter, bright red gymnastic ball, place it between them, and ask each to support the ball by placing their hands against it, fingers upright, in a pushing position. Once the ball is firmly in place, I ask each to see if they can feel the other through the ball. To do this, Bobby and Mom begin to make subtle pushing movements against the ball. This allows them to sense and feel the other through the palms of their hands as well as the whole of their bodies. They meet here at the crossing threshold of experience. The air-filled ball enables each to feel more easily the rebound of the other's pushing hands. In pushing-against the ball, they find the other is already there.

After a few soft and gradual movements, push comes to shove and both Mom and Bobby are forcefully pushing the ball into the other's space and with a lot of excitement. They appear to be enjoying this battle, laughing and smiling. This is the first time in session that I have seen this kind of playful interaction between them, and I am feeling excited and alive as I watch their animated dialogue. After a while, I say, "Here you are again. This seems familiar to both of you," although I am quite sure they are well aware of it, and they agree.

"Yup, this is just what we do," says Mom. "You do it first," Bobby cries out, "And I have to push you back." "No, you're the one who starts this," says Mom laughingly, as she gives the ball another hi-intensity shove and Bobby stumbles backward. The ball drops.

I ask if they would be interested in doing something different from the customary shoving of each other, and I propose another task. This time, I have them face one another, arms-length apart, and with no ball between. I ask Mom to imagine slowly extending her hand to Bobby, palm facing upward. Giving her time to envision the act, I tell her that *when* she feels ready and *if* she feels ready to execute it slowly. Without a pause, Mom rather abruptly reaches her hand outward, palm up and in the direction of her son.

I then ask Bobby to imagine placing his hand on top of Mom's with palm down, and then to do this *when* and *if* he feels ready. Bobby takes his time imagining the move and then, slowly and with a low intensity, places his palm onto Mom's hand. They remain in this position for some moments. Their breathing slows and deepens, as does mine. I feel myself almost swaying, a light and subtle move, as I watch them. Next, I ask Bobby if he can give Mom the full weight of his hand—whatever that means to him. Bobby takes a deeper breath, and his shoulders soften. To Mom I say: "Notice how Bobby's hand feels in yours. How much can you allow him to rest on the palm of your hand?"

Both remain in this position about fifteen seconds, which is longer than I had expected. Although Bobby looks directly at the joining of their hands, Mom looks down, away from Bobby and toward the wall. Now Bobby gazes up at Mom, pausing for a bit. "I like that you are holding my hand," he says, and his eyes begin to water. Mom pauses, as if trying to collect herself. She abruptly looks up at Bobby and says, "Yup! But you never know what will happen." Bobby immediately pulls his hand away.

"Well, I see you found your push," I say. Mom looks toward me and then at Bobby, who now holds his grasped hands onto this chest. He looks down and says nothing. I feel a pervasive emptiness in my chest and a distinct sadness for all of us. The session draws to a close.

Psychodynamics

At the beginning of the session, it was clear how both Bobby and his mother shared a common movement signature or individual pattern of moving. That is, they both had hi-intensity, held, and abrupt qualities of pushing-against with a diminished and less available capacity for gently yielding-with the other. Pushing-against fuels the aggressing, the moving out, in the sequence of contacting, and reveals the effort involved in moving toward or away from the other. The yielding-with is the felt sense of having done so. These two movements are analogous to the process of contacting-withdrawing-contacting, as one moves out to *find* and *make* contact and feels almost simultaneously the experience of *being* in contact (see L. Perls 1993; Bloom 2005). These patterns, working in tandem, influence the qualities of the received pushing back from the other. In other words, one resonates or yields-with the feeling of the other's pushing back, which then influences the next pushing-against and the implied reaching-for. We re-create the other that we are created by.

Without the fluid capacity to yield-with the other, neither Bobby nor his mother could kinesthetically feel themselves resonating within the developing situation. The seemingly unavailable qualities of a lower intensity, freer, and more gradual yielding capacity, left them without the requisite support to notice or reflect upon themselves in relation to the other, and to know the profound impact that each created. Continually pushing-against the other with the demand to be met, both appeared alone and without a necessary home base to return to in their interpersonal exchanges. Neither could gracefully withdraw, influencing their capacity to contact; nor could they contact fluidly, influencing their capacity to withdraw.

Tactile-kinetic-kinesthetic dynamics are experienced within a social frame. There is no *me* without *you*. If an infant or young child experiences ongoing threats to a solid, flexible, and reliable *you*, he loses faith in his most intimate and significant relationship. A coherent experience of himself with another is threatened. In this situation and to preserve himself, he pushes *away* from the other, holding taught his muscles and his breath. This is an endeavor to create a kind of bodily certitude, an attempt to know what comes next. It is the necessary and preferred creative adjusting in a routinely precarious situation. Even though he may appear to look as if he is reaching-for the other, he is ambivalent at best, believing that the other is not easily or at all available. He holds onto himself, neither giving to nor taking from the relationship, and making it difficult to evaluate exactly what is real and true. Over time, the child loses the capacity to feel the other feeling him. That retreat from feeling *me* with *you* is the fundamental source of neurotic behavior (Michael Vincent Miller, personal communication, September 25, 2019). It is a breach in the flow of contacting.

Bobby and his mother needed to be firmly met, but their repetitive and familiar relational moves alienated each from the other. The less each felt met, the more he/she abruptly, intensely, and desperately pushed-against the other. Their individual and similar characteristic movement repertoire, repeatedly stimulated to the foreground in situations of uncertainty, limited their capacity to respond kinesthetically. The weaker the kinesthetic response, the more limited the movement repertoire. By keeping the pushing-against in foreground and with a diminished experience of yielding-with, neither Mom nor Bobby could feel themselves and know what might have been available to them. In a sense, each lost the confidence that he/she could flexibly adjust to whatever was or would be.

The first experiment involving the large red gymnastic ball allowed the pair better to understand the kinetics of how they generally responded to each other. This offered a first step in feeling their movements as their own; a sense of differentiation and position of responsibility. *This is my body moving with yours.* They had a certain comfort in their exploring, and it energized them. They knew that they were with each other, what they could do with each other, and seemed to take a kind of pride in their attempt to dominate the other. Finding humor in their joint task, they both could see the absurdity in shoving each other around.

In the second experiment, Bobby discovered a sense of wonder in his mother's supportive touch. Through touch, he allowed himself to be open and curious, seemingly without preconceived notions of what would happen. He discovered a rare responsiveness to Mom momentarily. "I like that you are holding my hand," he offered. Mom, too, was able to tolerate some moments of ambiguity to the situation, at least until she could not. At that point, routine anxiety displaced curiosity, and she pushed back at Bobby with her attempted joke, "Yup! But you never know what will happen." Given my sense of Mom's history, I considered that a radiant and potentially useful embarrassment about to form was abruptly shut down: one that would have left Mom more vulnerable and receptive than she had the resources to maintain. What could have been was lost.

Bobby could only abruptly push-against himself with what I imagined was the shame of having exposed his desire for closeness. Disappointed and alone, he grasped onto his own hand, and a burgeoning feeling of belonging with Mom had vanished. Mom, too, appeared ashamed. Perhaps it was the shame of so noticeably having failed her son and probably herself as well. While such revelations can feel like a brutal wrenching apart, it is often only through these kinds of wounding experiences that we are called upon to listen closely to the dynamics of our relationship.

Frequently, we lose the profundity of experience in an attempt to make explicit the implicit. For the three of us to have discussed what just had transpired would have taken us away from a deeper kinesthetic knowing—a pre-reflective understanding that requires nothing more than to be lived. It is a holistic apprehension of the unfolding dynamics of relationship from which empathy is born. A different narrative, an alternative way of being and doing with each other momentarily felt by mother and son, exists on the horizon, and once touched upon can be rediscovered.

In this case vignette, Mom and Bobby were invited to explore their movements together. It is an example of how working with movements between and among people can be used to facilitate kinesthetic awareness, encourage relational support, and clarify intentions. It is, however, not necessary to extend an invitation to the patient(s) to move, especially if they are not interested due to various reasons, and if the therapist is not inclined to explore in this way. Yet, even by observing these movements and the feelings they produce during the session, the therapist can diagnose the process of contacting and intervene verbally rather than through movement. Knowing the psychological function of these six movements opens a world of unfolding relational dynamics. The situational conditions that allow movements between one and another to flow unimpeded, or the conditions that disallow the flow of movement, are readily discovered as the underlying themes come to light.

Concluding Remarks

Returning to the core of contact-making once more—yielding-with-pushing-against—we revisit the primary patterns that set the rhythm of every act. These movements organize space as they move us through time and continue their pulsating support throughout the progression of experience. And although we are born into this rhythm, it continually changes. Whether the pulse of contacting is impeded and habitual, or flows unimpeded, is dependent upon the dynamic qualities of yielding-with-pushing-against. For the sequence of experience to stream easily in time, all patterns need to move through foreground-background formation smoothly and efficiently. Figures of interest, curiosity, and desire organize and disorganize in a spontaneous and creative manner with the continual undergirding of these fundamental patterns. The person gives to and takes in from the other: this is the experience of growth. When the qualities of yielding-with-pushing-against-pushing back are not in balance enough of the time, the current of contacting is disrupted; stasis and neurotic function ensue. Nothing novel is gained, no growth achieved.

The sequence of six fundamental movements expresses the moving-feeling-perceiving history retained in the existing now as one moves toward the anticipated future. As these patterns emerge within therapy, they articulate the patient's world formed and forming in relation to the progressing therapy situation. Working in this way discloses the authenticity of experience as it appears, making movement essential in the phenomenological diagnosis of contacting.

"Theory without practice is empty, and practice without theory is blind" (Dan Bloom, personal communication, December 4, 2018). Once the theory of six fundamental movements as the undercarriage to contacting is understood, it becomes background and serves the therapist's intuitions as the ongoing tactile-kinetic-kinesthetic aspects of the situation proceed pre-cognitively or pre-reflectively. Six Fundamental Movements make more tangible and palatable the emerging of experience.

Chapter 4

Moving into Memory

The Interface of Moving and Feeling

The Six Fundamental Movements, discussed in Chapter 3, are described through their dynamic psychophysical features, each moving-feeling pattern working in synergetic coordination with the others and in relation to the environment to form a whole experience or gestalt. The animated and energic body, the body we live, touches and is touched by the world as we move through it. The integrating of these six movements, the verbs and their accompanying prepositions—*yielding-with-pushing-against-reaching-for-grasping-onto-pulling-toward-releasing-from*, form one's gestural repertoire and provide the means by which one feels oneself while adjusting to and engaging with the world.

Intertwining movement and affect, Henri Bergson (2010), noted French philosopher of the early 1900s, asserted that affects "interpose themselves between the excitations that I receive from without and the movements which I am about to execute, as though they had some undefined influence on the final issue" (86). In other words, in the doing of the gesture, we feel ourselves in the process of its execution: some act is completed along with its kinesthetic evaluations and some meaning is found and made. When gestures are routinized, the accompanying kinesthesia is restricted. The individual no longer can clearly appraise the situation, and the possibility of varied, unconstrained creative responses are limited. On the other hand, when moving-feeling gestural patterns form without inhibition, the individual can more readily perceive and assess the situation and adjusts with inspiration and originality.

Bodily Agency

Carrie Noland (2009) places movement and the feelings/affects/qualities that attend movement at the center of agentic experience. Generally, the sense of agency is the human capacity to influence one's own actions, and the course or consequences of those actions, within a given situation. This is primarily and fundamentally recognized through gestural patterns that continually

DOI: 10.4324/9781003266341-4

inform us *that* we are, *where* we are and *how* we are (Frank 2016, 373), so crucial to the orienting within and manipulating of the environment. Noland affirms that first and foremost, the sense of agency is bodily and that humans are "embodied within and impress themselves on their worlds" (2) as the world impresses upon them simultaneously. Continuing the argument, Noland advances the concept that bodily interactions and the affects they produce are core to a developing theory of agency (3), and that any use of the body providing kinesthetic feedback is an organ of "distributed agency," either aware or unaware (16). That is, the sense of agency is not localized to one part of the body only but includes the entirety.

The six fundamental movements and their accompanying qualities of moving and psychological functions co-organize any gesture in relation to the situation in which it arises. They move us out into the world and gather essential information. The six movements may be seen, therefore, as exemplifying the distribution of bodily agency. Even in the act of making one's bed there is the shaking of the sheets with both hands, which can move softly and gradually and with low-intensity or in an abrupt and firm manner with hi-intensity. In both cases, the kinesthetic feedback informs one in regard to the aesthetics of the situation. Gestures of communication also gather information; the gradual reaching for the cheek of another and softly stroking it in demonstration of one's appreciation or, the abrupt and firm push of an index finger to poke directly towards another to clarify one's point of view. The individual must rely on kinetic-kinesthetic experience, the feeling of doing as it is done, in order to function within the everyday world.

A gesture, with its ongoing loop of kinesthetic feedback, shapes itself while shaping space, and can alter during any act. In their capacity to assemble information, felt gestures offer the opportunity to change course as one experiments with a different moving-feeling pattern that is less routinized and could result in more satisfying contact. "Human bodily agency is defined by action and could not exist without the input of kinesthetic experience" (Noland 2009, 65). The sense of bodily agency relies upon the very feel of our moving to adjust as it opens the varied possibilities of responding: "An enhanced sense of agency is obviously related to enhanced kinesthetic awareness" (Sheets-Johnstone 2016, 16).

Kinesthetic awareness "can also lead to fine-grained understandings of the social synergies of meaningful movements that abound in everyday life" (Sheets-Johnstone 2016, 16). The individual's understanding or knowing of oneself within the situation co-organizes meaning, whether pre-reflectively or reflectively. As kinesthetically experienced gestures change, meanings shift and as meanings shift, gestures have the possibility of changing. *How* movement happens is fundamental to the creating of meaning.

The six fundamental movements, at the heart of every gesture, and the affects or the qualities of movement therein, express what one *does*, what one *has done* and, therefore, what one *can do* within a particular circumstance. This process is well described by Husserl (1989) in his observations of "I move," "I do," "I can." It is a temporal happening with its significant placement of "I move," preceding "I do," and "I do" preceding ",," from which then emerges I will. The "I cans" are "both a declaration and validation of agency" (Sheets-Johnstone, 2017, 12). This sequence distinctly can be seen with infants, who experientially learn about their bodies and their world, always in relation to the other. Their desires to move, inaugurated by what attracts them as well as what they attract, underlie their explorations: for example, pushing-against the floor to rise on forearms and receive the parent's warm greeting and smile; reaching-for and grasping-onto an enticing biscuit and pulling it toward an open mouth to satisfy hunger and for comfort. They arrive in the world already integrating information from "all their senses, including their movement senses (and) then there is new meaning to infant's everyday experience, even the seemingly purposeless movements of the very young baby" (Thelen 1995, 90). The "I move" of the subjectively experienced tactile-kinesthetically resonant body of the infant, one reverberating within the environment, "constitutes its most fundamental onto-logical reality, a reality that is its entrée into agency and indeed the sine qua non of there being agency at all" (Sheets-Johnstone 2017, 7). Bodily agency, there-fore, is first and foremost a developmental progression whose origin is there from the very start.

Postural Dynamic Expression

All gestures emerge from a postural dynamic, or the varying positions of the body in its attempt to find balance in relation to the universal forces of field: gravity, earth, and space. The body passes through a variety of shapes to find that point of postural equilibrium—one bodily segment in relation to the other and to the environment—which is in a process of constant change. In ongoing exchanges with the environment, one can both lose and find equilibrium. Moving from stability to flexibility to stability to flexibility, and so on is inherent in the human experience.

Dynamic balance functions in relation to gravity, earth, and space, and is colored by how one experiences these elemental forces of nature in relation to the other; a what or a who. Postural dynamics form an interwoven ta-pestry of moving-feeling experiences. That is, the organizing of muscular synergies position bones in a variety of ways such that they influence the experience of feelings, which contribute to the building of emotions and psychological states of mind. This arrangement configures an overall psy-chophysical shape and expresses our readiness to respond; to do something in relation to the situation in which we live.

Let us look now to the personal other, the one whom we always already answer to as that other answers to us and co-creates myriad opportunities for our moving through the world. Finding equilibrium, in that case, is through that personal other who structures our possibilities as we structure theirs. The actuality of the other is the *point of support* for one's body (Merleau-Ponty 2012). One experiences oneself only through that other; exists only in relation to that other; and is embedded within that other. The forming of posture, then, is an attempt to find a sense of equilibrium in a world of others. In whatever ways one might find oneself in relation to the other, it is always necessary to find stability, a kind of certainty within the uncertainty of relationship, however, ephemeral. The verity of this fact enables one to risk the more stable structure of living to adapt flexibly to a novel event and, thereby, grow and change; a new point of stability follows. Achieving balance, in this sense, is experienced both physically and phenomenologically through one's subjective reality.

Postural Dynamics and the Universal Forces of Field

To begin a more detailed explication of the social dynamics of postural balancing, and to exemplify its process, it is necessary to look through a developmental somatic lens. In observing and analyzing the processes of infant relational somatic development in the first year of life, it becomes obvious how kinetic and kinesthetic processes are central to contacting. The forming of contacting or experience is always through interaction.

Esther Thelen (1995), motor developmental psychologist and theorist, was among the first researchers to demonstrate that infant movements arise always in response to the universal forces of field—gravity, earth, and space—as well as to the infant's physiology and biomechanical potential invited out by the tasks the infant is exploring. Her ground-breaking theorizing was based on the work of Russian physiologist and biomechanical researcher, Nikolai Bernstein, whose 1960s classic studies on the structure and function of movement came to light during the period of *glasnost* in the 1980s. Before that time, the west had no idea of his brilliant contributions to the field. Bernstein demonstrated that it was not possible for the brain to be responsible for every movement executed, and that its structure and function had much to do with the continually adjusting of tensile or spring-like properties within tendons, ligaments, muscles, etcetera, in response to the universal forces of field. The brain does not do all the thinking: the body also does its share.

Bernstein's contributions were in opposition to research and theorizing led in the 1940s by Americans Arnold Gesell and Myrtle McGraw, who conceptualized infants as passive and their moving patterns as the result of a genetically determined developmental plan. As the brain develops, they surmised, movement emerges, a simple paradigm of cause-and-effect. Priority was assigned to the nervous system and only a secondary role to the infant's experience. So effective were Gesell and McGraw in demonstrating that motor skills were reflected in the regularities of brain development, a process common to all infants, that no further studies in that field were thought necessary. Researchers now assumed they had sufficient information from the field of motor development, as this genetically de-termined theory seemed to provide the ground for the more appealing psychological research into cognition, language, and social behaviors. The field of motor studies was abandoned.

In her own studies, and stimulated by Bernstein's work, Thelen too be-came intrigued with the structure and function of coordinated movement. In particular, she noticed the stepping patterns of young infants. When held on their feet, newborns could step in rather sophisticated, rhythmic patterns, but within the first two months the stepping response stopped and did not return until almost the end of the first year and before walking patterns emerged. It had been thought that the early stepping pattern was reflexive and originating from the low brain. As the infant developed, higher brain progression was considered responsible for diminishing the stepping reflex.

Questioning these prescriptive theories of development, Thelen (Thelen and Smith 1994) carefully studied the "life of the limbs" as she attended to the specific movement patterns infants spontaneously made during experi-mental periods of observation. In one of her many elegant experiments, she immersed infants chest-high in water at an age when their stepping response had disappeared on dry land. The water reduced the effect of gravity and the infant's stepping patterns emerged once more. Thelen concluded that the ratio of fat-to-muscle in these older infants made it impossible to execute stepping patterns on dry land. Underwater, the dynamics of gravity had changed so that the movement was easily performed. Toward the end of their first year, infants gain enough muscular strength so that stepping on dry land is now possible and a prelude to walking. Through ongoing ex-periments such as these and many more including infants on treadmills, in harnesses, crawling, and walking across see-through platforms, Thelen concluded that movements were not prescribed before their elaboration. Every act of movement was emergent rather than a product of context and history. No component, therefore, had causal priority.

Understanding that movements self-organize always in relation to environ-mental conditions, Thelen (1995) further elucidated that developmental change could be seen in dynamic terms of a series of stable and unstable states and that "change is heralded by the loss of stability" (84). Something must be disrupted for transformation to occur, and such disruptions might be due to "growth or biomechanical factors... in early infancy, whereas experience, practice or en-vironmental conditions may become dominant later on" (84). Developing pat-terns of moving take place in relation to real-time events in which the infant plays an active and necessary part. The infant's *experience* of universal forces of field in particular contexts affording a variety of relationships is of primary importance in development. Looking at movement as precisely and descriptively as possible and from a phenomenological perspective, the field of movement theory "may again provide theoretical leadership for understanding human development in general" (Thelen 80).

Complementary to Thelen's thinking, my first book develops the idea that young infants experience universal field forces primarily through the bodies of their significant others as they are picked up, placed down, rocked, hugged, played with, comforted, nourished (Frank 2001). The native sensitivity of the infant to the other's facial, gestural, postural, vocal patterns has been well-documented (see, e.g., Trevarthen, Stern, Tronick, Meltzoff, Moore, Bruner) and relies on a developing sense of one's own body, which facilitates the distinction between *me* and *not me*. This internal receptivity enables infants to respond delicately to the moving patterns of their significant others. Infants watch parents walk toward or away from them; observe their parents' gestures; listen to their vocal tones; and feel themselves carried from place to place. From the parent's body, the child interacts with the world (Welsh 2013). The parent responds in kind, and an ongoing moving and vocalizing dialogue develops; one that is kinesthetically experienced. Patterns of posture, gesture, gait, vocal tone, and breathing always surface in relation to the other and against a background of universal forces of the field.

The Process of Movement Coordination

Gravity presses downward and through the body, while the earth thrusts upward and, in this way, the interaction of pushing-against-pushing back appears. (All patterns are present in the forming of any experience, and this is no different. Pushing-against is lifted out of the sequence of the six fundamental movements here for teaching purposes). Every move we make as we shape space requires something or someone for us to push-against. For example: as I sit on my chair, I feel both pelvic bones push-against the seat to keep me upright. In order to rock from side-to-side, I push the right pelvic bone more firmly against the chair, which shifts the weight of my body to the left. To rock back, I push the left pelvic bone against the chair and feel its pushing back, and my weight shifts to the right. As I move back and forth, shifting my weight from side to side, I realize that the only way I *can* move is through this pushing-against-pushing back interaction. Similarly, to rise, I push both pelvic bones against the seat of the chair and my feet against the floor and with concomitant push back from both chair and floor sequentially, I can stand. Without the pushing-against-pushing back, we cannot move and without moving, we cannot feel. Even in the simple structure of an inhalation and exhalation, these fundamental movements are found in the pushing of the lung walls against the area of the ribcage, which offers a subtle push back during inhalation. The ribcage, then, pushes-against the area of the lungs as they deflate in exhalation.

So too the social ground is always already offering the containing push back against which we push. How infants feel themselves as they move and are being moved in relation to the other forms a *ground* of social relations. It is upon the veritable ground of the other, *the point of my support*, that I exist and that ground co-organizes how I exist. I propose that the myriad ways in which the infant kinesthetically resonates with their significant other, whether in satisfying moments of being with that other or those less satisfactory, are similar to how that child experiences the literal ground underfoot. This is also true for parents in ongoing exchanges with their child. The moving-feeling experience is not limited to one part of the body alone; rather the whole of oneself attunes to a particular invitation from the environment, and one responds. It is as if the others move through our body as we move through theirs; a pushing-against-pushing back response. The postural dynamic, one's attempt to find a momentary stability that one can move away from and return to, whether infant or adult, expresses the sense of equilibrium of both social and literal ground.

When the attempt to find and make stability becomes habitual, one loses the spontaneous capacity necessary for risk-taking and diminishes the resultant novelty of experience that engenders growth and change. This attempt to stabilize can appear in a rigidified posture or one too malleable. In either posture, the literal experience of ground underfoot may not feel reliable, predictable, or dependable enough. This also reflects in the social ground as one's clear difference from the other, so necessary for fluid, lively contacting, is not well-felt, and so the meeting between one and the other is not well-perceived. In such cases, kinetic-kinesthetic awareness of *how* one pushes-against, and *how* one experiences the other's push back, is not clarified: thus, an essential differentiation of *me* with *you* diminishes.

Infant-Parent Case Vignette

The following case vignette of infant and parent illustrates the process of stability and flexibility in their social relations and its reflection in ongoing expressions of posture and gesture.

Leon, a single father, brought his eight-month-old baby Topher to see me. Leon had wanted a child all his life and now the child he had dreamed about was here. He wanted to make sure he was the "best father possible" for the baby. A rather anxious man in general, Leon now was worried because he did not think Topher focused on him but was always looking past him. He seemed convinced that Topher suffered from autism, and he genuinely wanted to do whatever was possible to help him.

As I observed Topher, I saw that he, in fact, did prefer to focus on objects in the distance rather than close-up. He appeared especially fascinated by the fan circling overhead and could stay for quite a while absorbed by its movements. I asked Leon how Topher liked to be embraced and learned that he preferred to be held loosely rather than snuggle up to his father's body and favored extending out rather than flexing in to fold himself up, whether in father's arms or on his bed. He also was inclined to stand, with father's help, whenever and wherever possible. His son's inclination or movement signature was interpreted by Leon as a lack of interest in father and a desire to "get away" from him.

As we were seated on the floor, I noticed that Topher was well-balanced in his seated positions, in that his spine was long and sufficiently supported around the area of his collarbones, which were wide. The verticality of his upright posture was maintained by its width in the horizontal. Wherever Topher moved, he would return to this balanced seated posture. I hypothesized that the support offered by the ground beneath him was enough for Topher to form a fundamental and necessary ontological security.

Leon, appearing to reduce himself, sat with his different set of postural dynamics: shortened spine, narrowed in the collarbones, concaved chest and head pushed downward and reaching forward. This was the preferred posture that Leon frequently returned to and how he found balance within the relational field.

With no objections from Topher, Leon picked him up and placed him on his lap as he and I were talking. His hands around Topher's waist allowed the child to grasp onto his father's fingers. I noticed that when Topher began to look around at various objects in the room that captured his fancy, Leon would gently bend his head so that Topher primarily saw his father's face rather than the object that initially had grabbed his interest. While emersed in our conversation, Leon continued placing his face in front of his son's face and seemed unaware of his own actions. This was a similar behavior when we three had moved to the floor to let Topher explore. As the child crawled over to investigate a large red ball, Leon crawled alongside of him and placed himself close to the ball, appearing to redirect the child toward himself. These tactics did not work well at all as Topher, with desires of his own, began to object. He promptly sat himself down and looked away from his father and began to fuss. Leon then moved closer, as if to comfort Topher, which seemed to encourage the child to fuss more and make low, growling sounds. Now Topher's seated posture took a different shape as the area along his collarbones narrowed, his upper chest shortened, and his shoulder bones lifted towards his ears as his head slightly fell back. His now fisted hands grasped onto his T-shirt. The literal and relational ground had, for the moment, shifted for Topher. Leon's posture, too, had changed. His head pushed further forward and downward and, as he reached his upper torso toward Topher, his chest folded inward, shortening, narrowing, and hollowing.

In the subsequent session, and when he and Topher were seated on the floor, I invited Leon to follow his son's gaze rather than occlude it, and to get curious about what Topher was looking at. I then asked whether Leon might want to tell his son what he was noticing when he followed Topher's gaze. Speaking softly to the child and pointing toward the objects that Topher was looking toward, Leon said: "Oh, I see you're looking at those big blue blocks in the corner. How many blue blocks? Four? Bigger than the ones we have at home. And there are a lot of little ones as well." As Leon continued talking and vigorously animated the dialogue with his arms and hands, Topher looked at his father and pumped his hands up and down as if excited. He then crawled over to the blocks to explore while a now smiling Leon remained seated and continued to talk to his son. "I know that blue is your favorite color. Like the blue trucks we have at home."

Once Leon showed interest in his son's explorations, Topher could follow what attracted him and without interruption. With this new freedom and with father's support, he could look back at Leon while he played with the blocks that were now the topic of conversation between them. Father and son spontaneously included the other in their experience. When Leon noticed how his son was now attending to him, he remarked that he felt more settled. I saw that Leon's head lifted and his spine lengthened, to some degree, as the area of his collarbones widened. He now could more easily adjust to the unfolding situation. The formerly routine pattern of *chase and dodge* that had developed between them destabilized for the time being, and a different pattern emerged: one with the greater flexibility required for change and growth.

Once we had resolved, to some extent, that Topher was not autistic, Leon and I agreed that he continue in individual therapy with me and bring his son along on some occasions. At our next meeting, Leon told me how he and Topher were apparently progressing "somewhat" better. He reported that he could "catch himself" more often when he "intruded" upon the baby but "not enough of the time." I inquired: "How is it for you when Topher looks away?" "Bad," he said: Not really knowing his experience, I asked: "What does bad feel like in your chest or abdominal area?" At first Leon did not know how to respond, as he had not much experience looking inside himself. I waited, and instead asked: "What does it mean if Topher does not look at you? What does it mean about you?"

Leon sat with himself for a while and then responded, "It means I'm not important to him." The concavity of Leon's chest exaggerated, and he grasped onto the fingers of one hand with the other while he simultaneously pushed his head downward. I waited for some time as we sat with his profound statement. Then I asked: "And if you're not important to him?" Immediately Leon said: "I won't be loved." I again paused and then repeated, "So if you're not important to Topher, you won't be loved." Leon remarked: "Yes." Then he took his hand and made swirling movements in front of his chest and said: "I feel kind of hollow here, or maybe empty just after you said that. Like I'm not important to Topher if he doesn't look at me. He doesn't love me." As he made that statement, Leon abruptly lifted his ankles and toes up and off the floor. I asked him if he noticed that movement. "Yeah. My feet are clenched." I wondered aloud: "Do you feel the couch under you or behind you?" Leon paused then answered: "I really don't know." Taking more time, he responded again: "I'm kind of lifted off the couch, too." All the while, Leon continued to glance down at his hands. With a deep sigh he said: "It's sad." I asked, "You're sad?" Tears began to form in his eyes, and Leon appeared to stay with his experience. As I sat with him I, too, felt an empty sadness descending in my chest.

Leon slowly placed both feet on the floor, his body appeared softer, he slightly opened his chest, lengthened his spine a bit, lifted his head, and gazed directly at me. I paused for some moments meeting his gaze, and asked: "I wonder how you see me?" Taking a few deeper breaths, Leon said: "You look supportive, like you're here." I responded: "I do feel here and with you." I paused again and then said: "I see your feet are now flat on the floor. How is that for you?" Leon shuffled his feet around as if in exploration. "Now I feel the floor. I feel the floor."

Psychodynamics

Caring for his son rekindled Leon's earlier kinetic-kinesthetic "enduring relational theme" (Jacobs 2017). Slowly and over time, Leon began to understand the root of his dilemma, as it clearly emerged in these kinds of situations with Topher and in other relationships with friends, family members, and colleagues at work. In time, he was able better to perceive the actual child and all that Topher could bring to the relationship, rather than the wished-for child; the one who would rid him of this feeling of being unimportant so that he finally could feel loved.

As Thelen (1995) portrays in her work with infant movement patterns, "Some changing components of the system must disrupt the current stable pattern so that the system is free to explore and select new coordinative moves" (84). This actuality can be applied to behavioral patterns within the relational field. Applying this theory to the real-time explorations with Leon and Topher, the destabilizing of the former relational patterns allowed a novel psychophysical pattern to emerge. Although the existential issue that arose in therapy, with attendant patterns of posture, gesture, gait, and breathing, did not disappear for Leon, he could better attend to his moving-feeling body and alter the course of his interactions. Thus, a more developed and enhanced sense of bodily agency began to emerge. Leon's expanding awareness of his routine kinetic-kinesthetic perceptual patterns, and the long-held beliefs about himself anxiously held within, along with the therapist's essential interventions, were the disruptive elements needed to facilitate change. Equally important were Topher's different responses in relation to his father's newly forming spontaneous responses. They were central to their building a fresh and fluid experience together. In this way, Topher learned that his nonverbal language could influence his father and thereby co-create more satisfactory experiences between them. That is, the actual responsivity of both partners, with as much developmental awareness as possible, opened the possibility of choice.

Every appearing gesture, posture as well as patterns of breathing and gait that were primary creative adjustments in an earlier field, now anticipate and co-design the next moment. The more anxiety in the moment, the more solidified the routinized pattern becomes. Such habitual moving stories are a remnant of the past reconstituted within present engagements. As advantageous, creative adjustments that functioned early on, their use will be preferred in any unstable situation as an attempt to make secure what is impossible to secure—the future.

Time Consciousness and the Process of Remembering

The rhythm asserting the temporal nature of the process of contacting can be further understood in Edmund Husserl's (1964) illuminating exposition of time consciousness and explored through the passage of the six fundamental movements. Husserl's radical theory explores how time appears to us as temporal; how we experience the flow of time. He finds phenomenological confirmation for the just-passed experience, which he refers to as "retention" and the anticipation of that which is just about to occur, or "protention." These are what Husserl designates as the structural features of consciousness. It is a consciousness of what has passed and what will be, that accompanies every moment of perception. In other words, in the existing now, or primal impression as Husserl refers to it, there is a retaining of the previous phase that has just passed. What has just passed also includes or retains its prior phase and that phase includes its prior past and so on. The protentional phase, the future horizon, lends itself to the intention that there is something more to happen, and that happening is anticipated. In the existing now, there is the retaining of what was and also the anticipation of what will be: "Attending to one's experience, one finds always both an anticipatory sense of what is about to happen, however, indeterminate, and a continuing sense of experience that one has just lived through" (Gallagher

2020, 27). That anticipated something more gives the sequence its direction as intentionality moves toward its intention. The beliefs or certainties that are anchored in the lived past stream through the existing now with the faith that there is a next, as yet unspecified. This is a continual series of figures emerging from ground, which become ground for the next figures of interest to spring forward. It can be exemplified by the simple task of walking, which is like a kind of falling forward. As the left leg pushes-against the floor underfoot, the right leg slightly lifts and reaches forward toward time-future, while the left fades into the background to become time-past. As that right leg momentarily remains in the air, the individual briefly loses a more secure balance until it lands upon the floor, which counteracts the direction of the fall and finds stability. The individual must have some degree of faith in the anticipation that the floor, once again, will be underfoot; the inevitable something that comes next. The quality of that something to be, however, remains unknown.

Husserl chooses a melody to illustrate temporality as it is "something that is not confined to the punctual now" (Russell 2006, 131). When hearing a melody, we are not hearing the bar of music that went just before or the bars yet to come, rather we listen to the melody in its entirety instead of singular notes. Similarly, we do not see the dancer's separate movements as she pirouettes across the stage. We experience the flow of choreography in its entirety and not in discrete steps. In this now-phase, we see and feel the just past as it moves into the anticipated future. Internally aware of our experiencing, we are aware of a continuum (Taipale 2014). When the dancer executes a *grand jete*, or leap, she pushes against the floor with one leg, feeling the solid enough push back of the floor, while reaching high into space with the other. The pushing against-pushing back experience is retained in the just now impression of her grand leap, as is the anticipated landing of the reaching leg, which will complete the form; complete the gestalt. How this dancer may land, with poise or ineptness, is so far unknown. The existing now, illustrated by the dancer-in-mid-air, appears like a threshold from past to future.

As Aristotle recognized, "only when we have perceived before and after in motion that we say that time has elapsed" (*Physics*, 219a 23–25). The primordial six fundamental movements are implicated in every interaction, every contacting. The earlier figure formations, supported by a background of coordinated movement potentialities, serve as the ground for the possibility of later anticipated figures and their accompanying background supports to emerge. Similar to consciousness, movement has a flow, a structure, and an intentional direction: "Without movement, there would be no *befores* and *afters*, or in terms of internal time consciousness, no protentions and retentions" (Sheets-Johnstone 2014, 254, emphasis mine).

Recalling the example of the dancer's *grand jete*, I reach-for my glass of lemon water. The reaching movement is against a background support, that of my pelvis pushing-against the chair beneath me and finding the push back of its seat. This reciprocal movement allows my spine, to lengthen which enables and secures the forward trajectory of my arm. Contained within the existing now of my reaching movement and the attending kinesthesia, there is also the implied and anticipated grasp of my fingers onto the glass and the eventual pulling-toward my mouth in completion of a hoped-for satisfying experience. If the lemon water has grown sour, my anticipation ends in disappointment. My expectation of what would be was not fulfilled; the expectation not coming to fruition (Gallagher 2020, 28).

The rhythmic processes of contacting are interactive by nature and, as such, the six fundamental movements are indispensable to the temporal structuring of consciousness; a kinetic-kinesthetic-perceiving consciousness that awakens us to the environment in which we are always already situated: "Movement is integral to time and time is integral to movement" (Sheets-Johnstone 2014, 254).

> *Imagine a five-month-old infant playing on her belly with a series of interlocking chains. Supported by her elbows and forearms pushing-against the floor to keep her torso upright, she stretches the chain between her grasped hands. Gazing at the varied colored links, she chooses the yellow one in the middle, releases the chain from her right hand, and shifts her weight to the left elbow and forearm. Now she has enough bodily support to grasp-onto the yellow link with the finger and thumb of her right hand. Soon after, she reaches her head downward toward the link with open mouth, while simultaneously pulling that hand directly toward her mouth. As she continues her investigation, each link is scrutinized and chosen until almost all the links have been grasped by both her mouth and free hand. This series of arising creative adjustments progresses spiral-like as the interactions that bring the infant in sharp relation to the various links appear to collapse in on themselves and provide the perceptual foundation for the next emerging act.*

What is retained from the passing present can occur moments ago, as in the above scenario, or can be preserved from one's earliest history. In the latter situation, what is retained can be in relation to those significant others who have made lasting impressions on the individual at consequential times in development. The historic kinetic-kinesthetic past *collapses* in on itself and forms and is informed by the existing now experience. What is lived past is shaped and being shaped within the existing now of *what is* and anticipated in the future horizon of *what will be*. In other words, what is retained generally is predicted. Sometimes this is a necessity, as in completing the lyrics of a well-known song or the established warm greeting toward a familiar friend. Here, what came before concludes a now fluid and satisfying gestalt. Other times, however, the process of retaining the past can be challenging.

For example, what has been retained along with its beliefs and certainties can be a historic mistrust of both the familiar and unfamiliar other and this mistrust can be anticipated. To predict the other, one who is not yet there, as untrustworthy keenly exemplifies the neurotic moment as routinized behaviors leave no place for novelty to be found and made; no growth garnered. The continual anticipation of *what was* is essential to neurotic formation as the customary habitual figure of the anticipated next becomes the ground for what then will be retained.

Kinetic-Kinesthetic Remembering

The processes of time consciousness can be useful in understanding how remembrances of the past move through us, form, and reform in this passing present, and participate in the anticipation of the future next. Here, Husserl has remade temporality in terms of continuity to demonstrate how past, present, and future interweave. Close attention to descriptions of lived bodily experience will enhance our apprehension of *how we experience time,* exploring the temporal flow of contacting.

A phenomenological study of remembering is a subject that many contemporary theorists have undertaken, and all have placed bodily competence as the centerpiece of the processes of remembering: "Body memory alludes to memory that is intrinsic to the body, to its own ways of remembering; how we remember by and through the body" (Casey 2000, 147). (See also, for example, Fuchs, Sheets-Johnstone, Gendlin, Behnke, Gallagher). Throughout the first year of infant development, the process of remembering occurs through moving-feeling happenings always already in interaction with significant others in the infant's life: "In the structures of the lived body, the others are always implied: They are meant in expression and intended in desire" (Fuchs 2012, 15). Accordingly, the body's dynamic capacities, expressed through the six fundamental movements and their various attendant qualities within a variety of contexts, serve as the ways by which the processes of remembering can appear. The discussion here will be limited to the kinetic-kinesthetic processes that underlie, form, and reform the experience of remembering. This is not a cause-and-effect position as if a remembrance formulated then/there is reenacted in the here/now. Rather, I offer an emergent perspective; an exploration as to how remembering constitutes and is constituted as it folds and unfolds within the continuity of retained past/passing present/anticipated future. In terms of the root practice of therapy, it is not as if the patient is enacting something in session formed in an earlier relationship with significant others and over time, a one-person therapy model. Instead, the evolving therapy situation invites such experiences and their expressions on the part of both patient and therapist, a two-person model.

To further clarify the processes of remembering, another of Husserl's formidable concepts will be invoked: that of the developmental relationship he abbreviates as a progressing from "I move," to "I do," to "I can." Sheets-Johnstone (1999) expands upon Husserl's concept—"movement forms the I that moves before the I that moves forms movement" (138)—in the context of how babies spontaneously move, and how such movements form the foundation of the ongoing developing of bodily agency, that is, the power to influence the other while being influenced by that other. It is, in fact, only through moving that the once vaporous *I* becomes solidified, an actuality, once the mover perceives the move. Although moving-feeling-perceiving interweave, it is the process of perceiving, not the kinesthetic experience alone, that is necessary to accomplish the forming of subjectivity and the building of the experiencing *I*. The kinesthetic qualities are always there as we move; however, they are experienced to different degrees as they motivate us to move and are motivated by our moving. For example, I hardly notice my felt experience as I abruptly get up from my desk in search of my cell phone, which hides somewhere in my office. Rushing from place to place in my desperate search, my felt body moves background. I barely notice feelings emanating from my feet as they push-against the floor, nor do I kinesthetically attune to my arms and hands as they overturn cushions and inspect behind stacks of books. The lived body, a directly felt experience, has been subsumed for those moments by the object body as it supervises the course of its movements. This is the perceiving and perceivable body. In other moments, kinesthetic experience moves foreground, as when I sit with a sad friend and tentatively place my arm around his back while not knowing if he will be open to me. In response to my touch, my friend deeply sighs, and I feel a softening quality under my arm and a heaviness lift from my chest. With greater clarity, I draw him closer to me. Here I attend to my lived body, a body living in the fine-tuned dynamics of movement.

The six fundamental movements—*yielding-with, pushing-against-reaching-for-grasping-onto-pulling-toward-releasing-from*—figure in the operation of "I move," which precedes "I do" and "I can" in the making of memory. Sheets-Johnstone (2017) puts it well: "A repertoire of 'I cans' is inscribed in kinesthetic memory in the course of normal development, which is to say that habitual ways of moving can, and commonly do flow forth effortlessly, but only because their qualitative dynamics are familiar kinesthetic themes—themes with possible variations according to circumstance" (12).

The two movements supporting and initiating experience or contacting, yielding-with-pushing-against and the epiphenomenon of pushing back, create an ongoing loop; a curve that crosses over and passes through itself. (Once again, the first two of the six fundamental movements are made figure for the sole purpose of teaching, although all are implicated in the making of experience). I refer to this phenomenon as moving I-feeling Me. Thus begins the passage of moving I, which traverses the other and, in turn, the concomitant counter thrust of the other's push back that enables the feel of the move, the feeling Me. Simply put, an ongoing kinetic response organizes the

I, the maker of the act, while the kinesthetic response organizes the Me, the recipient of that act. The moving I motivates the feel of Me, which in turn and almost simultaneously motivates the moving I.

It is not as if young babies develop the concept of "I" or "Me" as they learn themselves and the world through their moving-feeling-perceiving bodies. These identifications come in time and with the developing of verbal language and cognition: "It is not until reflection that the subject of consciousness is named 'I' and that reflection is therefore necessarily operative when we use expressions such as I 'perceive'" (Taipale 2014, 73). Moving I-feeling Me, then, is a pre-personal, pre-reflective experience until the capacity for reflecting moves foreground. Its usage is to clarify the bi-directional passage of contacting by examining its cardinal elements as precisely as possible.

Yielding-with-pushing-against-pushing back is primary to the experience of subjectivity. It is the continual response, or the pushing back of the other, that gives form to the moving I as subjectivity emerges. Both are the necessary elements for a primordial and developing core sense of self, one that is highly relational. With effort and growing ability, moving I extends into the environment and brings back that which forms Me. This is how we grow and change. It is a given that there will always be this counter force to meet, a fact of the universal forces of field—gravity, earth, space. This is the only way one comes in touch with the other in various degrees of attending and perceiving. Yielding-with-pushing-against is in dialectic relation to pushing back, as touching is to being touched. One experiences oneself in the world already always through the repeating and unifying processes of responsivity and response.

This concept can be exemplified by a simple kinetic-kinesthetic experiment. As you stand, press your two hands together, palm to palm, hands flat against each other. Now move your hands so that the base of your thumbs are placed in front of the base of the sternum, fingers pointing at approximately at 45% angle upward and elbows widened and pointing downward. Notice your shoulder bones and allow them to release and come to rest. Once you have found this position, place your attention on your right hand and notice how the palm of that hand pushes-against the left hand. You need not use more effort to do this as it is already happening. Give yourself enough time to attend from the perspective of the active right hand as it meets the left. Then switch your perspective and notice that same right hand in the position of receiving the touch of the left. After a while, you might also switch your perspective again, and notice the palm of the left hand pushing-against the right and then receiving the touch of the right.

In this example, the pushing-against of the right hand *makes* the move, which is simultaneously accompanied by the receptivity of that same hand yielding-with, which *finds* the feeling. This is the elemental level of touch-touching-touch: the double sensation that is part of all contacting experiences. If you were to keep your hands in that particular position for a period of time and with none of the subtle movements necessary for the adjusting of one hand to the other, you would not experience this double sensation. In this state of confluence, there would be no felt difference between one hand and the other. Without difference, contacting is muted. *Touch requires movement and movement requires touch.*

This ongoing passage of moving-feeling is an expression of kinesthetic resonance, that is, ongoing reverberating feeling tones generated from one to the other. *The world moves through me, and I move through the world*: a field phenomenon. It is as true between or among persons as it is between persons and non-human elements of the field. For example, when I walk through a grassy knoll on a cool and windy day, I am yielding-with-pushing-against the surrounding elements of nature and feel their push back. How I move influences how I experience the air around me and the grass underfoot; how I feel these elements influences how I move. This is like seeing the much longed-for first crocuses in spring on the other side of a waist-high fence. The sight of the flowers generates feelings of lightness throughout my body, which dissipate as I perceptually attune to the possibilities of how to cross over the fence. My kinesthetic experience, lived body, moves background to the body that negotiates the fence, object body. Once the crossing is made, kinesthesia moves foreground, and the sense of lightness, once more, returns. Affect, movement, and perception form a unified whole of experience.

Merleau-Ponty (1968) describes the "double-sided nature" of touch-touching-touch as an intertwining or chiasm. This subtle interlayering of responsivity to response is analogous to the *middle-in-mode* of Greek grammar: though in the active voice the subject causes the action, and in the passive voice the subject receives the consequences of the action, in the middle voice, on the other hand, the subject is part of the action as both act and actor, agent and experiencer. Rather than a bifurcation of experiencing, there is feeling in the moving and moving in the feeling; one often cannot be distinguished from the other. The lived body is that crossing threshold, the loop of reflexivity, where moving I, the touching, and feeling Me, the touched, meet. Taipale (2014), for his part, expresses it this way: "Through double sensation, we experience the peculiar articulation of internal and external and understand that the field of sensing and the pre-objective lived body are one and the same" (51).

Moving I-feeling Me is an attribute of the physical body and constitutes one's psychic reality. These elemental movements underlie and contribute to forming the intersubjective dimension from which subjectivity emerges. Looking at the continuity of this dialectic, it is now possible to consider how the passage of moving I-feeling Me explicates the contiguous interweaving of past/passing present/anticipated future. This is all in relation to the developing progression of "I move," "I do," "I can" in experiences of both healthy and neurotic functioning, and through the language of movement.

Every retained past, passing through the present, and anticipating a future-next is part of the clinical ground of therapy. The aesthetic diagnosis of the relational field is one of form-forming-form. This is so for moments of healthy, spontaneous, and creative functioning as well as for moments of neurotic or habitual functioning. In the former, contacting arises relatively unimpeded; figures appear and smoothly fade into the background; desires are clarified and expressed; and satisfaction is gained. Each of the six fundamental movements and their attendant qualities of feeling act as support for this temporal passage; they are well-integrated with the others to form a completed act, a fluidly animated gestalt. The person chooses to approach and welcome what the other offers or avoids and rejects what is offered, and in that case reaches for the next presenting and attractive possibility. In that instance, moving I (pushing-against the other) bears only as much effort as necessary to meet the creative challenge the situation invites. This invitation is experienced through the qualities of the other's push back. What has been retained passes through the now of the primordial present and into the anticipated future. This process of remembering is: "always directed toward action, based in the past and looking only at the future" (Bergson 1896, cited in Fuchs 2013, 10). There is faith that there will be a next, but *how* and *what* that next might be remains unknown. Will there be novelty and surprise, or familiarity and a certain inevitability?

Here is an example: person A enters a room to greet a relative stranger, person B. As she reaches toward this other, A's movements appear gradual, firm, light, and free. Perceiving herself and the other, A opens to discover what can be made and found between them. Here A's sedimented past is stimulated in the arising situation and serves as background support for her unfurling interests. There is wonder and curiosity, such that the other's push back, that is A's *experience* of B, is neither anticipated as intrusive nor neglectful. Risk-taking appears on both sides of this crossing threshold as each partner moves with and through the other. With faith that ground will be found, the inevitable distance between the two can be cleared such that they can meet. *I* and *You* become *We*. From here, the anticipated future, now retained, sketches the coming now, and so on, and so on.

The form of the neurotic situation does not proceed fluidly and appears blocked in its forming and stale in its form. For example, imagine in this different scenario that there is a constricting in the yielding-with-pushing-against, such that person A approaches the environment with considerable timidity and restraint. His gestural patterns, a low-intensity effort—loose, gradual, and indirect—contour his perceptions and influence how he anticipates and receives the responding push back of the other. The moving I with its retained and sedimented past experiences, stimulating and stimulated within the current situation, foreshadows and co-creates the anticipated next, which now seems to require considerable caution. That is, as person A reaches for person B, the retained significant and earlier experiences of how he reached and how his reach was returned are kinetically-kinesthetically remembered in this now moment: "The dynamics of movement are felt as they unfold. They are felt kinesthetically" (Sheets-Johnstone 2012, 45). In his perceiving himself and the other, person A imagines and predicts that something in this situation probably will be disappointing or even despairing. The constriction of his moving, which brings with it a diminishment of feeling *You* with *Me,* provides a protection for the inevitable crash of hope into dread. *Having kinesthetically experienced the earlier others moving through me, I prepare for a similar experience with you.* This is not to say that person B does not bear a significant role as she, too, is influencing and influenced by what presently unfolds. The influencing others do not necessarily need to be in the actual moment. What is imagined, fantasized, and thought about also brings with it the experience of pushing-against-pushing back.

In both healthy and neurotic functioning, what each person can and invariably will do in the emerging situation is made known through the kinesthetic temporal progression of the unfolding kinetic patterns. They are the foundation of responsivity to ongoing response. These gestural postural patterns are familiar as they have been practiced in some form since the beginning of life (including the womb) and then are specifically shaped and adapted to fit certain situations throughout life: "The dynamics are not only behaviorally observable; they are experienced by the self-moving body creating them and thereby potentially the basis of kinesthetic memory" (Sheets-Johnstone 2012, p. 51). Thus, an ever-developing kinetic-kinesthetic repertoire unfurls centered on "I move," "I do," "I can" and inevitably I will—and with you.

Case Vignette

The following case vignette exemplifies how patterns of posture, gesture, breathing, and gait carry our kinetic-kinesthetic histories, or moving stories, as they are retained from the past, constitute, and are constituted in the primordial present, and anticipated in the future-next. They are the "memory cores" that most closely and profoundly connect us with our biographical past (Fuchs 2013). A past not necessarily recalled but lived.

This vignette was recorded during an international training program held virtually on an internet network and then transcribed for purposes here. Similar to any therapy illustration performed during workshops and trainings, these illustrations support the progression of theory into practice as we move from knowing through cognition to knowing through the lived body.

Internet technology enables participants to be placed into small groupings or "break-out rooms" to have privacy as they work among themselves. In our trainings, we often form dyads so that students can silently explore certain movement patterns with each other, and then verbally process their explorations together. Therapy illustrations generally follow such group experiments.

As with all our moving investigations, before performing the actual task, students are encouraged to notice themselves in advance of the experiment. They are invited to attend to their feet and notice how much or how little they find themselves pushing-against the earth, how much or how little they experience the earth's thrust pushing back, and how that experience lives "within" them. Rather than looking at their partner on the screen, the student gazes downward, while the head remains upright. This requires that the upper palate remain parallel with the earth and not descend downward along with the gaze. Once students make note of their situation, they slowly bring their gaze to eye level to find their partner on the screen. Students now are asked to notice if their kinesthetic experience has changed in this different context and, if so, how the difference is subjectively experienced.

In this encounter, the group was given a *reaching-for, grasping-onto-pulling-toward* experiment. Person A was asked to slowly bring both hands together just above the pubic bone and gradually raise his/her/their arms and hands upward, through the midline of the body, and stop at the level of the heart. From there, A was invited incrementally to reach-for Person B. Moving as slowly as possible, A could decide how far he/she/they wanted to extend their arms and hands toward B. If A began to feel anxiety in advancing toward B, A could retreat and bring the arms and hands closer to the chest once more. If there was enough excitement in reaching-for the partner, A could reach-for and grasp-onto the on-screen image of the other and, if that felt comfortable pull that other toward him/her/themselves. A could monitor when and how a felt experience of reaching-for-grasping-onto and pulling-toward B flowed smoothly or when and how these supports for contacting became blocked. A was encouraged to feel the possible building of anxiety as these movements were executed in relation to B, and to retreat until anxiety lessened, and then possibly to try again. This back-and-forth movement would allow A to take subtle risks moving forward, expressing a YES and then retiring, expressing a NO. B also was invited to notice arising kinetic-kinesthetic experiences in relation to A as B was reached-for. Once A finished the moving exploration, B began his/her/their movement journey toward A. Once completed, A and B processed their experience.

Theory is always explored through these kinds of moving-feeling-perceiving dynamics, as it is the single best way to understand the principles underlying the developing of contacting, of experience. From this simple experiment, as is true when making any one of the six fundamental movements figural, awareness is heightened and meanings emerge, whether interacting person-to-person or online.

Overall, the experiment foretells how each partner experiences a sense of belonging with the other, and to what degree. There is never a right or wrong way to execute the pattern; rather the goal is to discover one's potentiality through and with the possible other.

When I asked for a volunteer for the therapy illustration, I saw a hand immediately rise with all five fingers stretched outward which then slowly curled inward at the tips. I was surprised and delighted to see Ben volunteer as he had been rather quiet in the larger group during this module, and in other modules taught earlier in the program. For all therapy illustrations held online, participants are told to mute their microphones and shut off their videos, so as not to be a distraction to me or the volunteer. Both Ben and I pin the other, such that I only see his image on my computer screen, and he only sees my image on his.

Different from in-person training groups, where participants are seated in various configurations around and at some distance from the instructor/trainer and volunteer, internet technology allows participants a more intimate view of the therapy experience as they can see and feel the unfolding session from a more proximate perspective. This illustrative session is recalled in present tense, which allows readers to feel themselves more sharply with both therapist and patient.

Ben is a young man in his late twenties, rather small with a slight frame and compact build. His face has a tapered look, his jaw appears held, and his eyes narrowed, as if overly focused on someone or something. As we begin, I notice that his spine is lengthened in the vertical dimension, and his chest holds a slight convexity or bulge as if there is a hand between his shoulder blades, subtly pushing him forward. The lengthening of his spine appears to originate at the level of the diaphragm giving the impression that he lifts himself up from that horizontal circumference. There also is an almost contradictory slight hollow at the edge of each collarbone such that the tops of his shoulders roll inward.

As the session begins, I tell Ben that I need a moment to transition from working with the group to sitting with him. With both legs folded, yoga-like to rest on my chair, I place my head down on my hands and become attentive to my breathing. Once I discover my breathing pattern, I lift my head and, before looking directly toward the screen, I find my experience of yielding-with-pushing-against the chair under my pelvis and legs and behind my back. The push back of the chair provides the necessary ground for me to attend to Ben and experience both of us as clearly as possible.

Turning to Ben, I see that he reaches his head upward and to his left, toward a large window. Maintaining this position, he begins slowly to look up and around, as if inspecting the ceiling before turning back to the window. He inhales more fully, seemingly in an attempt to pull air into his body and then looks toward me. Feeling an open softness in my chest and abdomen, I say: "Take a moment, and notice what it is like to look up and away, and then to look toward me. No one place is better to look than another. Take your time and see if there is a difference between looking at me directly or looking at the ceiling or toward the window." As Ben still faces me, I notice a marked shift in his postural dynamic as the verticality of his spine reduces, and the bulge of his upper chest modifies to take on a slightly hollow shape. In a low, soft voice Ben says: "I find it easier when I don't look at you and I look outside and see the tree." I propose: "You're more than welcome to stay with the tree and notice what might make it easier for you to look at it rather than at me."

Ben takes me up on my suggestion and looks out the window once more. He sighs deeply and further deflates his upper chest. "I can believe the tree is just there." After a pause, Ben looks directly toward me again and I hold my breath: "You just came back to look at me. Did you want to come back to me?" Ben places both hands on his chest: "Yes, I did. And I feel unsure." He makes circular motions with one of his hands, while the other drops to his lap. The hand motion continues for a few beats until it again comes to rest, palm down, on his chest. I remark: "Can you say more about what's happening between us that makes you unsure?" Ben seems to hold his breath, as he replies: "I'm not sure I'm welcome. And as I say this, my heart starts racing." Ben's hand remains on his chest. Still facing me, his eyes move upward toward the ceiling and then directly back to face me. He makes another audible sigh, which deflates his chest once more, and then he forcibly attempts to pull in more air. With a softer voice, I suggest: "The tree gives you something that I don't or might not give you." I, too, spontaneously, and lightly place my hand on my chest and gradually shift my torso towards his image on the screen. Ben's hand remains on his chest and continuing to look at me, he says: "Yea." Ben tightly closes his lips and the corners of his mouth turn down.

With a firm voice I say: "You might want to go back to looking at your tree and see what it gives you that I don't, or maybe can't give you." Ben makes another audible sigh, lengthens his spine upward, and moves slightly forward in his chair reaching-for the window. He divulges: "It's the tree I see, but I also see the person I was with in this last movement experiment." Now Ben is looking directly toward me and returns his hand, once more, to his chest: "I feel that person still with me." His fingers spread wider on his chest and his eyes begin to tear as he utters yet another audible sigh. Choking he says: "That gives me some comfort." I feel a soft descending movement in my chest and my eyes moisten: "Yes, take your time with that feeling." I also take my time to find the chair under and behind me and attend to my breathing as I extend my exhale.

I feel deeply touched. Ben tilts his head farther upward to look at his tree. I now imagine what he is seeing: a tree that is solid and majestic as it reaches toward the sky. I wonder aloud: "You have told me that the image of the tree, and that remembering your partner in the earlier movement experiment, give you comfort. How might I give you discomfort?" Ben looks back at me, shortens his spine and his shoulders roll farther inward. Whereas in his upright posture, I imagined a hand between his shoulder blades lightly pushing him forward, I now imagine a hand lightly but firmly pushing-against his chest. He says: "I don't even think it's you that makes me uncomfortable." I affirm: "Well, I am here with you now." Realizing we are not alone, I add, "And with the group members." I extend my arms to make a circular movement, indicating the now invisible nevertheless surrounding group members, whose videos have been turned off and microphones muted. "It's funny," I say, "at first, when I referred to you and me, I had forgotten about the group. And then I quickly realized that, of course, there is a group here with us."

Stretching his arms to either side of him and with flexed wrists, Ben pushes-against the imagined group: "Yes, I think so. I see thirty people behind you." Ben immediately pronounces, "I'm happy to be with you. There is such excitement." He now shakes his head. "But... but I'm not sure why... I don't know... something happens. I don't know what keeps me so far from you," he says measuring the distance between us, fingers touching his chest and then reaching for me. He suddenly drops his head to his chest, lifts it up again, and blows out a stream of air from his pursed lips. He and I pause for several beats. "Just to clarify," I submit, "You are telling me the group looms large for you." "Yes," Ben affirms and pauses to inhale more fully and then exhale rather quickly; a now-familiar deflating of himself accompanies his sigh. I ask: "How did the group become so large now?" Ben reveals: "I think that I'm taking something away from them."

Ben blinks rapidly, looks out the window, and starts to tear. This time the tears are more fully formed and roll down his cheeks. "That brings up a lot of feeling." I state. Ben bows his head into his hands and covers his eyes as if to hold back tears that seem impossible to restrain. "Yes," he agrees, and reaches-for some tissues to wipe his cheeks. "And I am taking away from them what is not really mine," he adds. Repeating this I say, "What you are taking is not..." Before I finish the sentence, Ben asserts with a higher intensity, "*Mine*. What I'm taking from them is not *mine*." Ben looks at me and attempts to pull in air by forcing his inhale. I hesitate for a moment and then state: "You believe that you are taking away from the others in the group because you are here with me?" Ben nods his head and affirms, "Yes, I'm taking time away from them. It's not my time." Ben looks up and toward the tree outside his window and reiterates: "That's what is not mine. The tree will not complain about those things. People will." Looking back toward me, Ben smiles, blinks rather rapidly, and appears to hold his breath on the inhalation, which prevents him from exhaling completely. He touches his chest with the fingertips of one hand, and his back pushes-against the sofa behind him. Ben struggles to take the next inhalation, which must ride on an incomplete and unsupportive exhalation.

I declare: "Well, you're right. Some people do complain about that sort of thing and some people don't. And about you... what are your complaints, Ben?" He smiles and lengthens his spine, vaguely bulging the area around his heart forward. Looking directly at me and with a higher intensity push to his vocal quality, he announces: "Oh, I have a lot of complaints." Feeling the strength of his voice, I feel a rising excitement in my chest. "I'd like to hear them," I say. Ben laughs and looks up and outside the window toward his tree. He pauses, "Uhm. I complain a lot. And I'm not sure you really want to hear them." Looking back at me, Ben now maintains his smile and there is no blinking. I question, "Are you sure *you* really want to say them?" Ben leaves me and returns to his tree. "Well," he repeats, "I'm not sure you want to hear them." His fingertips return to his chest, "Hmm, maybe I... maybe I can make a few complaints." Ben now looks at me and I feel a slight holding of my breath, as if he is waiting for me as I wait for him. I ask: "What would you need *from* me to help you complain *to* me?" Immediately Ben replies: "I need a number. Like how many complaints I can make. That would be helpful." I spontaneously exclaim: "Five!" Ben smiles and exclaims, "Wow, that sounds like a lot." I am touched by his lack of sureness; I experience a kind of innocence with him and feel a warmth spreading throughout my chest. "Well, you might start with three and see how you feel. I want to know what feels satisfying enough for *you*." With my hand touching my chest I say: "I'm interested in your experience of complaining to me, to us."

Ben gazes toward his lap and appears to be organizing his thoughts. He then raises his eyes to look directly at me and shares in a soft voice: "I would love that. I want to complain about... the immigration system as it dominates my thoughts." His vocal tone soon shifts, and there is a higher intensity and firmness as he continues, "I have a meeting tomorrow morning and I am so angry at how much it affects me. I feel hated." I feel Ben's push has a greater solidity and he is more animated than usual. Somewhat surprised and confused by his statement, I question with equal firmness, "You feel hated?" Ben asserts: "Yes. It's as if I'm asking too much from them to get this paper; this paper I need." Ben's eyes shut, his jaw is steadfastly held, and his upper and lower lips push-against each other. Tears stream down his cheeks and, although Ben attempts to wipe them away, they appear undeterred. He continues: "It's as if I have to prove I'm worthy." I add, "It's as if you have to prove you are worthy of taking what should be yours." Saying this, my hands reach-for his image on the screen as I grasp-onto some imagined object and pull it toward me and repeat, "Taking what should be yours." Ben slumps onto the couch with hollowed chest and abdomen such that his collarbones descend and shoulders round. "This is so painful," he says. I enquire: "And familiar in some way?" Ben cries more deeply: "It makes me angry and so sad." I interject: "You are showing me your grief. This is *your* anger, *your* sadness." I lengthen my spine, widen my chest, and hear a sturdiness in my voice and feel greater solidity throughout my body. Ben responds with a surprised look as his eyebrows rise, his jaw softens, and his mouth slightly opens. He repeats now with a gentle vocal tone: "*My* sadness and *my* anger. My feelings. I wish I didn't need this piece of paper to be free. I wish I wasn't so affected by this whole process. But that's where I am, and that's sad." I respond: "I don't know how you could be elsewhere." Ben agrees: "I don't know how I could be elsewhere either."

I feel a softening in both my face and abdomen and continue: "I don't think that this kind of grieving is only on an individual level. I think there is a whole world of people you are grieving with and for." Ben lengthens his spine and advances toward my image on the screen. "I'm not without support," he says as if realizing this now. "When I saw Kamala Harris on stage yesterday, accepting her Vice Presidential nomination, I mean, she is the daughter of an immigrant. Black and Asian. She did not have to say a single word to help me feel free. To help me feel welcome. Hearing her was so powerful." Tears streak down Ben's face and he allows them free reign to fall wherever they will. I pause to feel my own moist eyes, linger in the closeness I feel with Ben, and then suggest: "Maybe we could do a little exporting/importing. Maybe you could imagine Kamala here with us, along with the comfort tree and your partner from this morning's movement experiment." With excitement in his voice, Ben says, "Yes. Yes." I go on: "You took in her words, and they became yours." I repeat the fundamental patterns of reaching-for-grasping-onto-pulling-toward the screen as I say this. The movement echoes the earlier experiment and is pertinent to what Ben describes he felt during Kamala's acceptance speech. Ben remarks: "Yes, I could grasp-onto that and take it in."

We both pause for some moments as I notice Ben's breathing becoming deeper. He is no longer pulling in air, but more smoothly exhaling to allow an easier inhale. "And where are you and I in this moment?" I ask. He replies: "I think you are here." I wonder, "Is it thinking, rather than knowing?" Ben's surprised look returns, and one of his hands springs up, lightly smacks his forehead and remains there as he states: "I imagine you as a tree. I don't know the name of this tree in English, but there is a tree in my country that I like a lot and I just saw *you* as that tree."

We both smile and I take a slow deep inhalation and a longer exhalation. I pause and then declare: "Trees have very deep roots." As I say this, I take my hands and arms chest-high and hold them in the center of my body, the midline, and gradually move them down and then out spreading to either side. "If we were two trees, my roots would go deep down into the earth and spread out to touch yours." I repeat the spreading movement several times. Ben slowly replicates the movement and smiles: "Yes, I somehow felt that. I felt that through my arms and my legs." He sighs deeply but this time does not deflate himself.

After pausing for a while, he says: "I could actually picture some of the group, the individuals, as a forest behind you." Ben places both hands on his cheeks, lifts his eyebrows and opens his mouth, appearing astonished at this thought. I say: "Yes, and all with very deep roots." Ben adds: "All touching." His tears return as he discloses: "I want to be part of that forest." I quickly and softly comment: "What makes you imagine you're not?" With a softer voice Ben says: "It's very familiar for me to imagine I'm not part of..." Not waiting for him to complete his sentence, I say: "Yes, somewhat of a habit. A habit you well know." Ben calmly retorts: "It's my trauma and I have lots of stories to support that." I settle back in my chair: "Have you ever seen trees with knots in them? They're called burls, and some scientists who study trees think they are reactions to stress. The burls are a covering for their injured areas, a covering for their wounds. All the trees in our forest, the forest behind me and in front of you, are in various stages of healing their wound." Ben has a wide smile, and his eyes smile with him. I continue: "I have one more fact about the life of trees. When one tree is in trouble, maybe with Elm disease or something like that, that tree will signal to others to share its distress. An essence comes out of the leaves and travels to other family members. The other trees learn of the distress and, perhaps, they also know what could spread to them as well." Ben responds, "That's good to know. I hoped that they communicated with each other. I thought it might be like that." I continue and spread my arms wide, "We all are in this forest. Sometimes you will imagine this forest, this family of trees, is welcoming you, and sometimes you will go back to your old habit of not being able to imagine that you are part of that forest, a part of us." Ben says: "Thank you. I feel that family with our roots touching." I suggest: "Take some time and let yourself feel that." We both breathe more deeply and stay focused on one another and remain like this for some time.

Ben says, "I have to miss our training session tomorrow morning because of my appointment. That's lousy!" I add, "Oh, you snuck in another complaint." Ben responds: "Oh, I only needed two, huh?" "Well," I say, "You only needed two for today." We both laugh. Sitting upright and seeming wider in his chest and broader in his face, he says: "I'm going to imagine this beautiful forest with me tomorrow. I feel better about it already. Thank you." I feel very full as Ben and I finish for the moment and say: "Let's invite our forest family to turn their cameras back on, unmute, and come join us." The session ends.

Psychodynamics

The above therapy session exemplifies the process of remembering as a lived body experience expressed through kinetic-kinesthetic shifts. In the simultaneously fluid-forming sequences of moving I-feeling Me, a clarity of subjectivity allows the individual to orient within his/her/their world. *I feel myself here with you and know that you are there with me.* Moving I-feeling Me intertwine, such that the coordinating of pattern ensures that movements, feelings, and perceptions are unified wholes, synergies of experience. When the reflexivity of yielding-with-pushing-against-pushing back lacks flexibility and flow, a necessary separating from while including the other in experience is lacking. Without sharp differentiation between one and the other, contacting is impaired and the subsequent forming relationship, the epiphenomenon of contacting, is not well supported.

In the opening moments of our meeting, it became obvious that something was arousing Ben's palatable discomfort. As we progressed, it was revealed as to how I and, in particular the group who could see him, but whom he could not see, were part of his tenuousness. Without having to tell the story of Ben's past, a rupture in the flow of temporality of contacting was palatable. What was retained from earlier and injurious situations with significant others echoed in this passing present and was now anxiously endured and anticipated with certainty. It was not as if Ben had a memory of a represented past; rather, Ben was *living* the experience as it emerged in the moment-to-moment of our unfolding therapy relationship. It seemed as if Ben steadfastly knew in advance what he could do and, thereby, what he could not do with me and the group, and what we could do with him. In these moments, Ben was attached to his fixed depiction of prior experiences and could neither discover nor generate the possible novelty within this newly arising situation. Without novelty, there is no growth and so Ben, in those moments, lived as if stuck in time.

As I closely monitored Ben's glances from the tree just outside his window, back to me and back to the tree again, I felt how he pushed-against himself with such hi-intensity that the effort necessary to push-against me and the unseen group was diminished and ambiguous. Ben believed that he was taking something away from the group by having the solo time with me. He imagined their complaints and, by doing so, experienced an unwelcoming push back from them. With the debilitated experience of *moving I*, and therefore the collateral damage of *feeling Me*, the smooth operation of giving to and receiving from the other, the essence of contacting, was inhibited. The experience of a potentially lucid subjectivity lessened.

My intention was to be alongside Ben as we uncovered the situation we were living together, with its possible frustrations and dangers. In the words of Laura Perls, oft repeated during my ongoing studies with her, I offered Ben "as much support as necessary, as little as possible." That is, by discovering the shifts of my flow of movement, I could appraise the developing situation and adjust myself in creative and spontaneous ways, co-constituting an environment from which Ben could gradually take support. Accompanying him and listening to his words and, importantly, listening to my own bodily happenings, refashioned Ben's experience. What had been retained was now made figural, and Ben noticed his well-practiced habit of not taking what was deservedly his. Taking responsibility for this behavior, Ben now could take the risk and choose a less familiar course of action. He was able to stay with his feelings of grief and with me. Working together, Ben was able to see/feel his situation in a new light to inaugurate new possibilities of moving, which shifted feeling and perceiving.

Ben surprised himself by imagining me as a tree, one that he liked and that grew in his country of origin. I trusted that the image supported a furtherance of our growing intimacy. Embellishing the evolving tree image by depicting its deep roots spreading and touching the roots of other trees, the background of our developing sense of belonging was made figural. My spontaneous and more personal responses to Ben were not solely about my own feeling; rather they were an expression of the situation we together were creating. My lack of restraint encouraged Ben's burgeoning liveliness, and he was able to move from a constrained self-consciousness to a heightened sense of the actuality of our collaborative situation. From here, with our sharing of the forest metaphor, Ben's anticipation of the unwelcoming others shifted, and his desire to allude to the past and anticipate its repetition became less interesting. Communicated in my own way of being with Ben was the prospect of a larger containing, a larger forest of belonging.

Concluding Remarks

It is human nature to make the unfamiliar familiar enough to be lived through. The mother's breast milk has a similar smell to that of the amniotic fluid, and so the neonate moves toward the nipple with enough necessary familiarity to accept the newness of experience. The fetus also has practiced grasping the cord as well as grasping its thumb during its time in the womb. When the nipple of bottle or breast is presented to the baby, the movement of grasping-onto has been familiar enough to make this novel task doable. From fetal experience and throughout the lifespan, sequences of "I cans" are kinetically-kinesthetically retained and anticipated in relation to the situation that invites them out. That is, in every kinesthetically resonating situation, there is the familiar and remembered past that is part of and performed within the present of the newly arising situation and anticipated in the future. When the anticipation of the unknown is believed to contain too much novelty, the child, adolescent, or adult firmly grasps-onto what was familiar, though uncomfortable and often unbearably anxiety making. This is an attempt to make oneself safe through what is known rather than chance what is not.

As the therapist attends to her/his/their own progressions of moving I-feeling Me encounters, a different order of push back for the patient is created; one that reflects a novelty that the patient had not before experienced or experienced enough. The openings between therapist and patient must happen incrementally, and with the therapist always attending to the kinetic-kinesthetic experience of the patient's push back. This lets the therapist know how the patient is integrating and assimilating what has been offered. How does the patient reach-for-grasp-onto-pull-toward the therapist to incorporate the other into the experience? In other words, the therapist attentively monitors the patient's developing sequence of "I move," "I do," "I can," and with you. The giving to and receiving from the other gradually lays a familiar foundation from which the novel situation springs.

Chapter 5

Diagnosing through Movement

A Two Person Therapy

Psychopathology is generally thought to provide health care professionals with elementary and critical information regarding the phenomena that affect and influence the spontaneous creativity of human experience and its expression. It is an endeavor to describe patients' experiences in relation to their world, an investigation into subjectivity. Psychopathological diagnoses, however, sometimes can be misunderstood as a perspective solely oriented toward illness, looking at patients' complaints as symptoms (Stanghellini and Broome 2014, 169). All too often, the treatment of these various symptoms can be an attempt to rid patients of them. This is a *one-person therapy* perspective in which patients are the primary focus of attention, as if the symptom is something they suffer *internally*. This approach minimizes the simple fact that the symptoms brought to therapy are the best way individuals can adjust to the ongoing difficulties developing in their varied environments (Spagnuolo-Lobb 2013b, 90). They are a person's most efficient, practical endeavors to meet and be met by the other, to find and make contact. Symptoms, or routine behaviors lacking spontaneity, are *attempts to cohere*; to achieve some sense of completeness within the arduous and often incomprehensible situations in which patients repeatedly find themselves. "All contacting is creative and dynamic" (Perls et al. 1990, 230) and, therefore, must be regarded and appreciated as such.

A *two-person therapy* perspective concerns "subjects as they interact with the environment, or more precisely, the *interaction* of subjects within the environment" (Francesetti et al. 2007, 60). Rather than the suffering existing within the individual, an *internal* experience, what suffers "is the relationship between the subject and the world" (61). In other words, although perceived and expressed by the subject, suffering becomes animate at the *crossing threshold* of experience as *I move through the world, and the world moves through me.* Without available and sufficient support from the other, the symptom has a crucial function: to assist the patient when and where possibilities to garner support from the environment are few and far between.

DOI: 10.4324/9781003266341-5

A phenomenological approach to psychopathology, therefore, must explore the symptomatic distress and the interpersonal processes in the co-organizing of such distress. Whether patients live under an emerging cloud of depression, debilitating anxieties, obsessive thoughts, compulsive behaviors, and so on, symptoms are patients' endeavors to cope within their world in the most fitting ways possible. They are creative adaptations, achievements in contacting.

As said previously, observing the earliest developing relational fields betters our comprehension of *how* we eventually become who we are in the immediate present. Here we explore the continuum from healthy to neurotic functioning through clinical phenomenological procedures that detail the arising of lived body experience. Clinical phenomenology, as a process for examining the structures of subjective experience, "may also be considered the foundational science for psychopathology" (Fuchs 2010, 546). It is imperative to know that rather than giving attention to assumptions made from any causal accounts—one's behavior now due to some past happening—the focus remains on the descriptive analysis of emerging experience, granting insight into the fundamentals of its structure. The methodology is based on aesthetic criteria as we attend to that which we see, feel, hear, touch, taste, smell, and the varied meanings made of such experience. Experiencing is something given within the phenomenal field of every person—a field of myriad possibilities. Though experience can be *known*, it is primarily *felt* (Gendlin 1997, 242) through a continuous stream of *moving* along with its kinesthetically experienced qualitative dynamics. Beginning at the beginning, with first-person or subjective accounts of the lived situation, the co-constitutive procedures in the forming of implicitly felt movements, perceptions, and their meanings are made known. Present phenomenological psychopathology addresses emerging symptomology from its roots in such pre-reflective experiences. Exploring lived body, moving-feeling experience, "allows for the detection of the critical points where the constitution of self and world is vulnerable and open to deviations or derailments" (Fuchs 2010, 548). The building of our sensuous environment is conjoint to our bodily self-constitution in that "we can be conscious of the environment only insofar as we are bodily self-aware, and our bodily self-awareness correlates with, and thus also *outlines,* our awareness of the environment" (Taipale 2014, 33). Knowing how contacting develops in fluidity and agility forms the basis for understanding *how, when,* and *where* the flow of contacting is modified, such that inhibitions and hindrances are cultivated. A phenomenological diagnosis, then, analyzes the emerging rhythms of continuously lived experience, subjective experience, through a dynamic temporal flow manifest within the here-and-now of therapy. What are the conditions by which rhythms form melodic flow, and what are the conditions by which they lose their cadence and continuity? While in the former, there is novelty and growth, in the latter there is redundancy and the all too familiar.

The Phenomenological Study of Evolving Subjectivity: Fetus/Mother Hybrid

From the mid-1970s, researchers in the field of infant development began sophisticated in-depth studies into the role of subjective experience in the life of the developing child. Through the decades since, there has been a plethora of information from varied researchers (Brazelton, Bruner, Campos, Fogel, Meltzoff, Moore, Stern, Thelen, Trevarthen, Aikin, Tronick, Rochat, and more) gleaned from an array of illuminating experiments with infants as they investigate varied objects, explore familiar, significant others, and interact with the unfamiliar stranger. Their observational and theoretical findings have proved supportive ground for phenomenological descriptions of the unfolding relationship between the parent-baby dyad in the first year of life, and its functional similarities to the therapist-patient dyad in the moment-to-moment of therapy (Frank 2001; Frank 2005; Frank and La Barre 2011; Frank, 2013; Frank, 2016; Frank 2021). A diagnosis through movement directly focuses on bodies as they interact to form contacting through a longer timeline of that first year and its application to the forming of contacting in the real time of child, family, couple, individual therapy treatment. Now, it is possible to incorporate studies of development from an even earlier phase of life, that of the evolving fetus/mother hybrid. This opens new pathways not only to gain further information regarding the forming of experience but also to realize and appreciate the crucial acquisition of self-movement and its accompanying felt qualitative dynamic.

Though studies in fetal life date back to as early as 1929, researchers and theorists in the fields of psychology, medicine, neurobiology, developmental motor studies, and philosophy now firmly place the spotlight on the fetus/mother hybrid. Recent 4D ultrasonography offers computerized images that reconstruct the fetus in motion and illustrates its astonishing capacities. In the future, and with the development of even more state-of-the-art instrumentation, the knowledge gained from fetal studies will be as revolutionary as the past forty years of ground-breaking research in the field of infant development. Phenomenologist Jonna Bornemark (2016) refers to this unique period of fetal life as anonymous experience or *asubjectivity*. The study of the fetus is not "pure transcendental phenomenology," she states, as fetal experiences lie outside the realm of our first-person experience. However, and importantly so, "these specific experiences tell us something about the genesis of all experiencing and subjectivity" (252). Such investigation has always been a central task of philosophy (251).

While an in-depth discussion regarding the topic is beyond the scope of this chapter, it remains vital to consider that "development of the fetus in gestation is shown to be one of the most consequential periods of life" (Smith 2016, 19). In sketching several of the occurrences within the nine months of fetal life, we discover a lens through which we can learn something about the organizing of *pre-contacting* and its furtherance in the developing of contacting postnatally and throughout life. Within these pages, there is a blending of recent fetal research, movement theory, and the critical concepts of phenomenologist Edmund Husserl. The interweaving of approaches will emphasize the verity of tactile-kinetic-kinesthetic processes arising from their inauguration and their crucial role in clinical phenomenological diagnoses. Awakening to the ever-changing qualitative dynamics of moving bodies in relation, we awaken to the basic elements of our human condition. Generated from our most primitive phase of life, we move to learn ourselves and our world. We learn in order to grow and grow in order to learn.

Psychology and Fetal Studies

The field of psychology often begins its descriptions of human experience with the neonate rather than the fetus. Information regarding prenatal history with its multitude of phenomena either is ignored or not sufficiently known. At the same time, there have been certain schools of psychology that have made interpretations from adult memories of fetal and birth experiences and/or stories told about such events. From this unsound information, generalized and fragile conclusions have been drawn. These are "adultomorphic speculations of what happened in the womb or at birth" (Piontelli 1992, 7). Distinctly different from this method, a phenomenological account of prenatal life describes, with as much clarity as possible, what appears to us. In observing motility, fetal perceptions can be investigated directly (26).

Let us underscore once again that the focus of phenomenological exploration is upon emergence and not cause-and-effect. Whatever occurs in the moment-to-moment of our aliveness is a matter to be explored. It is the substance, the essential nature, from which meaning is made. Though it is true that a relational foundation is laid during early experience, a phenomenological approach looks at how what has been retained from such experience is stimulated and brought forward within the presently lived situation and anticipated in the future—the next step. That perspective is different from imagining that one's present feelings and behaviors are a reenactment of or a result of something that happened at a far earlier time in our developing. There are, of course, individual preferences that spring from a simultaneous melding of the use of space, time, and qualities of moving that form dynamic patterns. These are accompanied by familiar enduring relational themes acquired over time and that always arise in relation to the lived situation (Jacobs 2017). They are *developing* in the moment and do not come already *developed* from a preceding time. It would be an error to imagine that what is happening at the moment of meeting—whether another person, object, idea, fantasy, rumination—is the direct result of something that occurred in our primeval history.

The Fetal Environment

The life of the fetus is substantially different from that of the neonate, though even within its warm, dark, relatively silent fetal surrounds there is also continual change. Formerly, the world of the womb was thought to be a homogenous, steady environment in which the fetus is protected from intrusions by stimuli. Contrarily, and through varied empirical studies, the fetal-mother hybrid has its many challenges, which enable the pathway to transformation. A persistently changing environment invites the organism to move from phases of stability to instability and back to stability again. This back and forth is an essential characteristic of the human organism (Sparling 1993, 9; Thelen 1995, 84). In relation to the fetal environment, these phases influence the qualitative dynamics of its movement. For the fetus, this entails the shift in levels of amniotic fluid, which increases in the first two trimesters, levels off, and then rapidly decreases (Sparling 1993, 9). As in all environmental shifts, this substantial adjustment presents a challenge for the fetus, and the temporary instability fosters the development and expression of further competencies (10). The amniotic fluid is smelled and tasted though not related to hunger. In later fetal stages, the fluid is swallowed and excreted. In the dark environment, the fetus' eyelids are sealed until approximately twenty-seven weeks. At this time, the eyes can open and will blink in relation to light shined upon the womb and, by thirty-four weeks, the fetus can track its movements. Moving and hearing are not separated in the earliest trimesters as the sound of mother's voice, intestinal rumblings, mother's beating heart, and breathing are felt through the vibrations of the amniotic fluid that create a pulsating of soft fetal bones. There is no distance between the sound and the experience of hearing/feeling. What is heard is what is felt, and what is felt is what is heard. The umbilical cord, sides of the womb, and the fetal body (hands, face, mouth, tongue, fingers, limbs) touch and are touched. At the same time, "there are no objects in the sense of autonomous and thematized 'things' that are identified in the stream of perceptions" (Bornemark 2016, 255). One perception knits together with others, such that there is no distinction between *Me here* and *You there*. In other words, there are perceptions in the womb, but not an *it* who perceives. In uterine life, all is one.

The Six Fundamental Movements in Fetal and Infant Life

The Six Fundamental Movements and their varied qualities are the means by which contacting takes form. Their dynamic emergence—qualitative flow, use of space, continuity through time—comprise individual and unique characteristics of one's movement signature. These are the particular and preferred characteristics that underlie and shape our experiences and expressions and denote *that*, *how*, and *where* we discover and build our connection to the world. From infant to adult, foundational movements appear as: yielding-with (or being-with)-pushing-against-reaching-for-grasping-onto-pulling-toward-releasing-from. All movements conjoin to support the forming of experience or contact. They are the means by which we dynamically animate ourselves and accomplish myriad tasks of everyday life through the support of these six intertwining movements. Every movement is followed by its preposition as all movement sequences are always already in relation to the other that is different from us. That is, one either is drawn toward or repelled by that other, whether person or object, to fulfill an intention.

The varied rhythms and shapes of these sensorimotor supports for contacting begin to form in the very earliest weeks of fetal life, a *pre-contacting phase of developing*. They outline the foundations of a repertoire of movement that will be available for use throughout the lifespan: "No neonatal patterns can be considered to originate at birth, as the fetus has already the full repertoire of movements which will be found in the neonate" (Piontelli 1992, 30). The patterns also evolve with preferences or dispositions; certain ways the fetus enacts these six movements while lying, sucking, stretching, crouching, and so on (Wynn 2002, 10). As the fetal body develops in relation to the changing environment of the mother's womb, these six movements will transform to shape a coordinated whole of experience postnatally. What the fetus learns in the womb is readily transferable ex-utero (Rochat 2011, 61). There is yielding-pushing-reaching-grasping-pulling-releasing in the womb. Perceptions, however, are not recognized as belonging to objects (Bornemark 2016, 255), and so the prepositions *with-against-for-onto-toward-from* that express a difference between one and the other are not applicable to fetal life. Without objectivity, there is no subjectivity. There is no *other* in the fetus/mother hybrid, only the totality of experience. The process of differentiation begins in the neonate and, in time, *other* comes to be.

Sketching Yielding and Pushing Movements in the Womb

The most potent stimuli capable of generating changes in fetal motility are the vibrations carried along the amniotic fluid (Piontelli 1992, 34). Vibrations move through the fetal body and create pulsations or rhythms. These moving rhythms are relatively experienceable qualities: otherwise, the fetus could not adjust itself to the environment. There is as much background awareness as developmentally possible in the fetus, but a lack of focused attention. The latter would require a sense of *alterity* or a greater knowing of the difference between what is itself, and what is other than itself. The capacity to abstract, to take away some idea from what is happening, is simply not there. All six fundamental movements are the potentiality of the organism waiting to be invited out by the possibilities of the environment. The first movements appearing in the womb between seven and a half to eight weeks of fetal development were first described by neurologist Heinz Prechtl (1984, 1989). These are referred to as holokinetic movements, whole movements. They vary in combination and continually adapt to changes of the fetus and within the external conditions of the environment. That is, with its growing capacities, the fetus influences its surroundings as these surroundings influence the fetus. Each co-contributes to the ever-changing fetus-mother hybrid.

Though the whole body moves during this phase of development, there are neither distinctive patterns nor repetitive sequences of parts. No matter how variable these movements, they "appear always graceful in character" (de Vries et al. 1984, 46–64). Before ten weeks, early coiling and uncoiling motions are seen although "barely perceptible and have an oscillatory swimming-like quality" (Piontelli 2010, 8). At this phase of fetal development, the fundamental movements of *yielding-pushing* in relation to the plentiful fluids of the womb come into play. The fetus appears to be carried or held by the fluids surrounding and containing it and, at the same time, also pushes the fluid with head, spine, and buttocks. A dynamic kinetic-kinesthetic experience emerges right from the start. The organism is responsive and responds. The flow of pattern is primarily a whole-body interaction although the limbs hardly enter into the execution of these general moves. By weeks ten to thirteen, however, the limb of the head now can push the uterine wall and, by this means, occasionally can *pin* itself such that the whole body will rotate around it. With this first more effortful push of a limb, a primordial happening of pre-differentiation continues as a foundation for the later process of differentiation prepares itself. The fetal body rapidly grows and changes in proportion; the length of the muscles increase, bones ossify, there are shifts in spatial freedoms and constrictions, and so forth, enabling different patterns to awaken for use in the process of adapting. These evolving patterns are the fetus' way of interacting or adjusting to the challenges of the changing environment. Soon after the push of the head arrives, the participation of legs and feet are seen to enhance the whole-body motions and become essential driving forces. They extend to and push the uterine wall and, in doing so, create a thrust that moves through the fetal body (Piontelli 2010, 8). The legs can work together or alternate as if slowly bicycling. Although the arms and hands join the movement, they appear independent and not synchronized with the push from the legs. With the newly acquiring force of the legs, the fetus can crouch with bended knees and push the uterus with greater strength. Here the hands are placed on the knees and appear to push down, perhaps in an attempt to lock the movement. With the thrust of the legs, the fetus now jumps around the womb. In later weeks, the arms and hands seem to reach out to stabilize the pushing movements.

At twenty weeks, and with greater spatial constriction, the head vigorously pushes the uterine wall as the flexible tissues of the uterus respond with a push back. Kicking movements from the legs, especially when the fetus is on its back, grow more forceful. In this position, there is responsivity of the fetus to the responding push back of the amniotic fluid. The pushes of legs and feet along the wall, different from the pushes in relation to the viscous environment, are registered as relatively minimal but still qualitatively different. This is especially true with the smaller motions of touching the uterine wall, fluids, cord, or touching parts of its own body. In other words, although the fetus experiences varied kinesthetic qualities, there is no meeting of an identified one with an identified other: "The kinesthetic feeling of movement is not yet connected to movement in a world, and there are no bodies experienced as entities that would be held together, neither of the self nor of others" (Bornemark 2016, 255). That would require the fetus to be able to distinguish more clearly a *this* from a *that*. Variations in pushing movements—stepping, kicking, cycling, hopping—are all seen by twenty-four or twenty-five weeks of development. In the final month of gestation, the earlier and well-practiced yielding-pushing movements serve as the foundation for denser yielding-pushing movements of head and feet in relation to the push back of the mother's womb. Through the climactic duet of responsivity-response within the mother-fetus hybrid, a baby is born.

Primal Animation and Primal Sensibility

Husserl often employed the phrase *animate organism* throughout his works. Using this term he highlights, in a most primary sense, the crucial significance of movement to the maintenance of all "creaturely" life (see Sheets-Johnstone 1999, 134). To move, an organism must feel a particular urge or impulse, always co-constituted within the environment; that feeling shapes the flow, direction, and effort of the movement: "Animate organisms are moved to move and kinesthetically experience in felt bodily ways the particular qualitative dynamics of their movement (...)" (Sheets-Johnstone 2014, 248). *As the organism flows through the world, it feels the world flowing through it.* Animation and the feel of its flow is of utmost significance to the developing organism. After birth, these dynamic, relational, situational exchanges lend the movement its rhythm and shape, its mode of contacting. Yielding-with-pushing-against the world, the animate organism touches and is in touch with a world that touches back in return. The impulse to move and the feel of it exist from the very initiation of life. Being animate is simply being alive.

Husserl also and importantly refers to *primal sensibility*, asserting that "sensation, etc. does not arise out of immanent grounds, out of psychic tendencies; it is simply there; it emerges" (cited in Sheets-Johnstone 2014, 248). Primal sensibility is the way in which we approach the world with and through the aliveness of our animate bodies. It is implicitly the quintessentially human ability to receive (Zhao 2020, 25). Primal sensibility is integral and rudimentary to the realm of primal animation. Co-equal and co-emergent, they are always already there and are the essence of our living as temporal and spatial beings. The realm of moving (primal animation) and the accompanying realm of receptivity (primal sensibility) form the sub-stratum of experience. They can be demonstrated by persistent transfor-mations observed within the fetus/mother hybrid that continue throughout life. From the earliest forms of human development, we experience the in-imitable fact that our receptivity and responsivity are the conditions through which we are alive.

"I Move" "I Do" "I Can"

The incipient fetal movements of yielding-pushing become the essential sup-ports for contacting postnatally as they now continue to organize always in relation to the environment. For example, when the baby lies in the parent's embracing arms, there is a functional similarity to that of the fetus embraced by the amniotic fluid. The baby yields-with-pushes-against the parent's arms and, in the giving over, a complimentary pushing back is experienced. As develop-ment proceeds, slowly defined differences between the infant and the other, person or object, are clarified. Movements that support contacting, a reaching-for-grasping-onto-pulling-toward-releasing-from, always in cooperation with the experiences of yielding-with-pushing-against, describe an evolving in-tentionality. Intentionality is composed from something prior that shades the novelty of the moment with something familiar. Both the familiar and the novel support the capacity to co-inaugurate the next to come. In the fetus, the six fundamentals, dynamic patterns of movement attended by their varied quali-ties, indicate the antecedents of an infant's developmental progression. Clearly stated by Husserl, "the child in the womb already has kinaesthesia and ki-naesthetically moves... it already has its acquisition of experience from its ex-istence in the mother's womb (...)" (see Smith 2016, 35). From the beginning, kinetic-kinesthetic experiences are seamlessly interwoven, and one does not happen without the other. These attributes, exceptionally early human faculties to develop, are of great importance for survival. They are different sides of the same coin and reciprocal in nature.

As an example, when you walk down the street and toward your office, you may pay attention to the feel of your gently swinging arms and/or vigorously striding legs in their coordinated pace. In this case, you experi-ence the body that you are, a moving-feeling happening. Perhaps, however, you are preoccupied, even obsessed with myriad challenges that await you once you arrive at work. This is your well-practiced and familiar way of being. Instead of being in touch with the qualitative dynamic flow of ex-perience, you unknowingly desensitize your body and cannot evaluate clearly the situation you live. In those repeated moments, where anxiety has replaced excitement, you lose the capacity to flow through the world and receive the world as it flows through you. Deprived of your subjective experience, your body becomes an object, a thing in the world, disconnected from what you truly desire.

The tangible kinesthetic response, the primal sensibility that contributes to the animated feeling of aliveness, can be repressed or diminished, as in the latter example, but can *never be eliminated* (Jeannerod 2006, 56). It is always already there if we are willing to notice ourselves, either when excited and lively, or anxious and dulled. When we become aware *that* we desensitize ourselves, we can attend to *how* and *where* we numb, fix, shut down, or cut ourselves off. Only after taking response-ability for *how* we live the situation we now live is it possible to act in a different manner. There exists a continuum from anxiety to excitement at the prospect of increased competence in being and behaving in novel ways. This process requires patience, perseverance, and ongoing practice.

Following an evolutionary path from womb to postnatal experience, Husserl vividly describes a developmental progression beginning with "I move," preceding "I do," and "I do" preceding "I can." Behavioral scientists Kelso and Fuchs (2016) have explored, in a reconceptualization of a classic experiment, the importance of body and consciousness gained from an understanding of this developmental sequence. The earlier experiment, Mobile Conjugate Reinforcement by Rovee-Collier and associates, was administered in a research laboratory and part of a study of the patterns of learning and retention. Three and four-month-old babies lay on their backs in a crib. Their legs were lightly tethered by ribbons to an overhead mobile, which moved and made noise as the baby kicked. It was discovered that babies were able to find and make very specific hip and knee movements that differed in both duration and direction, provided they were accompanied by the sounds and movements of the mobile. According to researchers, those responses that were more vigorous produced a "reward," and the greater the experience of "reward," the more vigorous the kicking (Rovee and Rovee 1969, 35).

Inspired by the work of Sheets-Johnstone (2019), who understands the kicking of babies as a vital source of energy, Kelso and Fuchs (2016) reformulated the mobile experiment. In further investigating, they looked at the transition from merely spontaneous movements to purposefully coordinated movements. The latter movements were referred to as "the eureka moment," in which the infant realizes it *can* make things happen. A switching or kind of "eureka effect" occurs between the essentially spontaneous and intentional movements (Sheets-Johnstone 2019, 144). This transition rests on "an infant's dual kinesthetic-kinetic awareness: an awareness of its movement and of how its movement can make things happen" (143). Being able to move and feel oneself move is the foundation for any specific bodily "I do," and the potential "I can." According to Husserl, the ultimate task of philosophy is to clarify how the world comes to exist for us, and how it comes to be taken for granted. His elegant, experiential sequence, explored in Kelso and Fuchs's reformulated experiment, distinctly delineates how we learn to learn from infancy to adulthood. Evolving through this progression, we make meaning of the world in which we live. All experiences "share the common feature that they *reveal* themselves to the subject that lives through them.... These are not processes to which the subject has an external relation, but something that the subject immediately undergoes" (Taipale 2014, 21). Subjectivity is composed of aware moving-feeling experience. As we advance from "I move" to "I do," to "I can," we tune to the dynamic kinetic-kinesthetic body: a body of awareness.

The reformulated baby-mobile experiment reveals how spontaneous movements, "I move," I do," form the ground for an emerging "I can." Using the descriptive vocabulary of the six fundamental movements, the baby's pushing-against the mobile (the "I move") receives the immediate feedback from the mobile pushing back through the sound it makes. The capacity to yield-with (or be-with) allows the mover to *feel* itself move and *hear/feel* the accompanying sound elicited from the mobile. In other words, the "I do" happens through the almost spontaneous felt experience of I have done. With rehearsal, the spontaneous evolves into spontaneous *and* creative as infants (also children and adults) adjust to the situation they live and learn *what I can do with the other* and *what that other can do with me.* The streaming of the six fundamental movements, and their qualitative kinesthetic dynamic, supports "I do" which, with practice, becomes the "eureka" of "I can." In this discerning progression, Husserl gives assiduous analyses of animate organisms that "document their foundational unity with psyche in the fact of 'feelings,' feelings especially in the form of kinesthesia that precisely distinguish an animate organism from any material thing" (Husserl cited in Sheets-Johnstone 2019, 146). The movement alone does not complete the act; rather, the feel of the movement, or kinesthesia, is of utmost significance in its satisfactory completion.

Though the extent and range of "I can," in terms of learning new skills and in relation to personal interactions continues to enrich through time, it can be temporarily or permanently eroded through illness, injury, and through aging. A diminishing of "I can" also occurs within environments that are constricting and, all too often, demoralizing. Such environments present acute and chronic ongoing frustrations and dangers in myriad ways: early environments of chronic alcoholism, sexual mistreatment, illness of a loved one, dying or death of close relations, severe neglect, psychological abuse, criticism and bullying, routine inadequate attunement. This concerns any situation where babies, children, adults had to cope with what was intolerably beyond their capacity to move through, and where there was no significant, reliable, consistent enough other to offer support, counsel, and compassion. In such situations, these individuals learned very well what they could not safely express nor even feel fully experience. Repressing moving-feeling capacities can serve as necessities for one's capacity to survive. Over time, however, what was an attempt to preserve and protect the individual *then* has become stale, repetitive, and inadequate in terms of its usefulness *now*. Rather than risk the anticipated and all too painful dangers and frustrations that present challenges beyond one's ken, the individual seems far safer desensitizing the body and shutting out the environment. A world of imagination, uncomfortable but familiar, is preferrable to hazarding the unknown. Desires are muddled and contacting modified, such that intentionality cannot fluidly or satisfactorily move toward intention. The diminishing of kinetic-kinesthetic experience can sometimes be so powerful that the possibility of its restoration can seem almost irretrievable.

Diagnosis through the Six Fundamental Movements

The word diagnosis, from the Ancient Greek, means knowing-through or *coming to know*. Using this somatic and developmental approach as diagnosis, we come to know by attending to moving and the accompanying feeling of the move as an assemblage of faculties—a series of "I can" that we live in relation to the world. These faculties engender a sense of agency, the capacity to influence others. They underlie the forming of form and delineate the structure of experience. How and what patients believe they can and cannot do with therapists, and what patients imagine therapists can or cannot do with them is observable in the moment-to-moment of therapy. Each of the six fundamental movement patterns has a succinct psychological function that operates together with the other patterns. Not only can we observe the physical movements in our patients and ourselves, but more importantly we experience them in the phenomenal field. In other words, when I see my patient move, I too respond with either subtle or overt movements in relation to what I see. There can be changes in my breathing, the tilt of my head, focus of my eyes, or my postural shifts. These movements always are influenced by the other and are attended by the varied dynamic qualities of moving or kinesthesia. For example: as my spine shortens and collarbones narrow, I might experience a sense of emptiness in my chest, heaviness in my abdomen, tightness in my throat. Conversely, as I slowly extend my spine and widen my collarbones, a lightness and fullness may emerge from my lower abdomen and rise upward through my chest and throat. This is how I experience myself, how I experience my patient, and how I experience the situation we both co-create. As we engage, we are involved almost continually in understanding the immediate world and thereby each other. From this crossing threshold of experience, a *trans-corporeal* meeting, meanings are co-created: "Meanings are formed and made through an interaction" (Gendlin 1997, 1). Meanings have their roots in lived experience, the animate, and the sensible.

The living body is a medium of the subject's relation to the world (Fuchs 2005, 1). As contacting develops, the kinetic-kinesthetic body must inaugurate and build a relationship between subject and world. It must establish a difference between itself and the other, a who or a what, or else there would be a melding of one into the other and a loss difference, of uniqueness. At the same time, to experience the difference, there must be a merging with that other that provides the who or what to be different from. To feel oneself with the other, one also must find and make a separation creating a difference from while including that other. This sets the fundamental rhythm of contacting or "any movement of the field" (Robine 2015, 48). The body is not an object in the world; rather, it is the person's potentiality in relation to a worldly field of possibilities. The fundamental movements of yielding-with (being-with)-pushing-against, and their psychological functions, are important for a phenomenological investigation where the focus is the body as directly experienced by the experiencer. The necessity to be with, and almost simultaneously separate from while including the other, begins the sequence of contacting, of experiencing. When these moving patterns show distortion, the additional and essential supports—reaching-for-grasping-onto-pulling-toward-releasing-from—are modified in varied degrees. The greater the distortion, the more impaired the sequence of contacting becomes. The distinction between perceiver and perceived is muted. Either there is too much attention given to bodily efforts and a minimizing of the other, or too much attention to the other who looms all too large, and minimal attention to bodily experience. As the individual loses bodily potentiality, the possible affordances of the environment are misperceived.

Case Vignette

The following case vignette takes place in person. Anne and Richard were referred by their friends, a couple whom I had seen for therapy some years prior. Anne and Richard have been partners for five years and have a three-year-old daughter. In our first session, they reported that they had been in couple therapy before, and each wished to return to therapy as they continued to feel "stuck." It can be useful to understand what the felt experience of particular and important words can mean. In this situation, however, rather than explore the significance of the word "stuck," I thought its structure would be revealed to all of us as we got to know each other. The following is a description of our second meeting. It has been reconstructed from my notes taken directly after the session.

Anne and Richard sit at each end of my deep, seven-foot couch with their bodies slightly angled toward each other. Their heads sometimes look in the direction of their partner, but mostly toward me. Anne is of medium height and weight with bright red hair and round freckled face. She primarily sits with her shoulder bones subtly rolled inward; her upper chest hollowed. In this position, she appears to have reduced herself. Occasionally, however, she punctuates what she is saying with a lengthening of her spine, concomitant widening of collarbones, and a push of her head forward. In the former postural dynamic, Anne appears to blend into the back of the couch, while in the latter, her forward pushing torso holds her away from it. Rather than the pushing-against of her pelvis on the seat of the couch to support her more upright posture, Anne instead rises by the lift emanating from her ribcage. It looks as if she exerts some extra effort to maintain the hi-intensity and gripped qualities of this vertical posture. The switch from Anne's shrinking pattern to that of greater expansion is accompanied by her hi-intensity vocal expressions. At such times, I feel a holding in my chest and a slight lift of my shoulders and wonder, to myself, if Anne is feeling desperate in her attempt to "right" herself. Anne's hands are most often lifted off her lap and grasping-onto each other. All the while, her thumbs take turns massaging themselves. Anne seems to notice the moments when she is not breathing fully and then sharply inhales. Even so, her exhalations remain truncated. Her breathing, therefore, does not maintain the even flow necessary to support an excited aliveness and the spontaneity of creative expression.

Richard is rather tall, of solid build, and with a generous amount of wheat-colored hair surrounding his pale complexion. Most generally, Richard maintains the verticality of his spine and wide chest, firmly held in place and bulging slightly. The palm of each of his hands remains placed on his thighs, with fingers closely gathered. Richard's postural dynamic and gestures do not fluctuate often. In moments of agitation, he solidly and abruptly pushes-against the back of his chair and slides his hands, still placed on his thighs, closer to his hips, as his chest slightly rises. Usually, Richard's vocal tone is even, of low-intensity, and his words emerge in measured phrases. Appearing to take in the merest spoonsful of air, his breathing patterns remain shallow. Like Anne, his inhibited breathing patterns transform the possibility of excitement into the surety of anxiety.

After we settle onto our respective couch and chair, I take some time noticing my own experience. We are new to each other, and I have some anxiety at this second meeting. I am not so anxious about what will transpire among us, as much as I am anxious as I sit with the unfamiliarity of our meeting. I am a stranger to them, and they are strangers to me. First, I support myself by finding my back pushing-against the back of the chair, with my pelvis and crossed legs pushing-against its seat, as I feel the concomitant push back from both. I take some breaths to be with myself, then look more directly toward Anne and Richard to enquire as to how each is feeling. This *starting situation* forms the background for what next will emerge for the three of us. Like our first meeting, Anne says she feels anxious as she does not know what will happen. She is unsure what Richard will say or do, and she feels "unsafe." Richard reports that the first session went "well enough," so he is feeling "just fine." He says he is "already prepared" for Anne to say something that: "I won't like. This is usual for me." I do not ask Richard what he is feeling as he shares this with us. I know from our first session, and again from this "just fine" response, that Richard has his own vocabulary to identify his experience. If I persist and ask him for a more in-depth response, it would be as if I had an agenda for him. In asking him what he yet cannot do, Richard could easily imagine he is not doing what I want him to do, or not being how I wish him to be. There is some good reason that Richard has truncated his moving-feeling experience, and I want to respect and appreciate that. What I do register, as Richard speaks, is my own kinesthetic experience. I notice I hold my breath and feel an elusive, vacant feeling throughout my torso. This experience is of the phenomenal field, meaning that it is not my experience alone; rather it emerges from the situation we each contribute to. Just now, there is something of a vacant feeling among us, as if we cannot connect with each other but float in our own separate orbits. I catalogue this and will wait to see if, when, and how this feeling may shift.

Hearing what Richard said, Anne begins to cry: "He is like that. He's just waiting for me to do or say something he doesn't like." Each go back and forth accusing the other of having done something wrong. Anne psychologizes Richard and points out: "You don't make yourself vulnerable. You don't listen to me." Richard, sharpening his tone of voice, tells Anne that she is constantly criticizing him: "There are always things from the past that you bring into every argument. Why should I listen to that?" From here their "stuck" experience is made known. The hurt of not finding an intimate path toward each other enough of the time is concealed by the familiar repetition of their impassioned accusations. The power of their indictments circle around each other in unrelenting spirals of experience. On the one hand, each accusation seemingly points toward, but apparently lands nowhere near, the other. They hear the other's words, yet do not register their own feelings or imagine those of their partner. Their firm push-against the other lacks the yielding-with so necessary for this kind of reflection. Without these fundamental supports in place, they can neither decipher whether their partner could be available to reach-for, nor can they take the risk that such reaching-for would require. Holding on to her dynamic posture of lengthening up from her ribcage and away from the couch, Anne grasps-onto her hands with greater intensity. Richard pushes-against the back of the couch, hands closer to his hipline. The more they maintain the *rightness* of their positions, the further they drive the other away.

After listening to the content of their monologues that build with increasing effort on both their parts, I interrupt and simply state: "It seems like you both accuse the other, and that seems rather familiar. It's something you have learned to do and can do easily. Perhaps this is how you get stuck." Saying this, I have divided the responsibility so that Anne and Richard can each be each *one-hundred percent* accountable for co-generating these exchanges. They pause for a while, look toward me, each other, and back to me. I question: "How is it for each of you that I accuse you of accusing the other?" Anne slightly smiles. Her head drops down to her chest, and she exhales more fully. Richard laughs and his hands slide forward and back on his thighs. I wonder if Anne's smile and Richard's laugh are due to an embarrassment. Perhaps they have been caught in some behavior they were not aware of prior to this moment. In realizing what they have done, they realize what they can do and will continue to do. I took a risk in sharing my observation with them, and now I feel some relief. My breathing deepens.

We pause for a while and register what has just happened. Anne slowly lifts her head, looks up at Richard, and says: "I am sorry if I accuse you." Immediately responding, Richard again sharpens his tone and retorts: "You think you know better what I should do and say to you. It is always the same thing." Once more, he firmly pushes-against the back of the couch, lifts his chest, places his hands to his hipline, and appears to have hardened. As he continues to devalue Anne, I again intervene: "It seems you have returned to accusation mode. I wonder if that helps you?" Richard looks at me, looks down, and then up and toward the ceiling. Anne now has become more sorrowful and reaches for tissues to wipe away tears that stubbornly will not stop. Looking toward Richard, I feel a vague and distant sadness. It is as if sadness is there, but just beyond my reach.

I ask Richard if he will look at Anne and only describe what he sees. I tell him: "There is no right or wrong in your perception. Notice how Anne appears to you right now." Richard takes some time and then responds: "I see she is upset and crying. I see she needs a lot of tissues." Anne, who has been looking down, lifts her head to see Richard. She smiles. Richard reveals to me: "She looks so sad. I don't like to make her sad." I say: "Maybe you could tell that to Anne." Turning to her, Richard softly says, "I'm sorry to make you sad. You know that." Not having gestured much during the session, Richard extends one hand in Anne's direction and then deftly and quickly drops it to his lap. I ask Richard if he noticed that he reached-for

Anne with his hand. "Yes. I noticed that. I think I'm sad." I reply: "Well, it is a sad situation." I pause for a while and then ask Richard if he would be willing to slowly repeat this gesture. He looks down at his hand and agrees to try and see what will happen. Looking directly toward her, Richard gradually extends his hand, holds it there, and gently returns it to his lap.

Through her tears, Anne says: "This is what I want from you. I want you to be vulnerable. But you're not really there." I ask Anne if she recognizes she is accusing Richard of not being vulnerable at the moment of his vulnerability. She abruptly looks at me, as if realizing what she so easily can do with Richard. She again apologizes and says: "I'm sorry," as she places her hand over her heart and leaves it there, fingers splayed. I ask: "What does the palm of your hand say to your heart?" Anne waits and then reveals: "My hand says I'm here." I again question: "And what does your heart say in response?" Anne's crying continues more fully, and she says: "Thank you. My heart says thank you." I suddenly realize that my hand also rests over my heart. I look to Richard, and he seems visibly moved. His body has softened, as has his face. I ask him if he would be willing to place his hand over his heart. He instantly agrees: "Yes." We three remain in this experience until Richard states: "I am sad. I am sad too." This time he is unequivocal in his response. He no longer "thinks" he is sad; the whole of him is sad. In touching Anne's sadness, Richard touches his own.

As the session is ending, I tell them that they have found a heart connection to themselves and to each other. I suggest: "The sadness that you both feel now is a grief that you avoid when you fight each other. There is a lot of hurt, a lot of wounding, a lot of grief that you both bear alone. Now there is the possibility that you can bear this together." They linger with hands on hearts, slowly release them, rise from the couch, pack up their belongings, and move toward the door. Richard has his hand on Anne's back as they leave. When I close the door, I need some time to stay with my own feelings. I am touched for the intimacy they have remembered and for the love and caring that remains, and sad for how difficult it has been for them to find each other. They have made a start. It is enough for now.

Psychodynamics

Anne and Richard's chosen form to achieve their intention, the desire to be seen, heard, and felt, was through an admonishment of the other. Clearly, this behavior was well practiced in their relationship and, most likely, learned earlier in life. If we see Anne and Richard's behaviors as pathological, we will be referring to normative ways of being that are "external to the experience of the person, set by someone who is not immersed in the situation" (Spagnuolo-Lobb 2013a, 34). Sitting with them, I could sense their strong and similar desire to be understood by the other; to be well-held, carried, or sustained in the best of ways. I also could strongly feel the held-back grief of a litany of hopes crushed and longings dashed. This informed me as to where next to go. The limited capacity for Anne and Richard to yield-with or be-with the experience of themselves, and with the other, was obvious from the start. This came across as I listened to their choice of words and their rhythm and intensity, seeing/feeling their postural dynamics and gestures, and almost simultaneously attuning to myself with trust that my feelings revealed something important about the situation.

Anne and Richard had set their minds as to what their partner should or should not do for them. The passion of their fighting, though seemingly futile, is what they could do, and its fervency fastened them together. The less one could impact the other, the more ardent their desire to do so. At the same time, this mode of contacting also arrested their growth and impaired the possibility for intimacy. As they expressed their longing guised in a familiar and routine form, their list of angry accusations, the original intent was obscured to themselves and to each other. Anger is a fine and necessary form of differentiation, but when one loses the bodily supports for anger, it can become suffused with rage so that the other is turned into an object. Monologue replaces dialogue and there is no satisfaction gained.

After some back and forth between incriminations and accountabilities, Anne repeated her apology and appeared to stay with the truth of her words. I encouraged Richard simply to notice Anne, and he did so without evaluation. Seeing her upset and realizing his part in it, he opened once more and risked becoming vulnerable. His reaching gesture said even more than his words and was not his alone. It had been invited out by a softness developing between them. Noticing Anne's hand resting over her heart and guiding her to reveal its meaning—"Thank you. My heart says thank you."—I supported the intentionality of contact, the desire to meet and be met by the other. Asking Richard to place his hand in a similar position, the creativity of intentionality moved to creation. Although this session ended in the reciprocity of contacting, that was not necessarily my purpose. My goal was to heighten awareness of *what* they were doing with each other, and to notice *how* they were doing it. In other words, to experience the "I move," which sketches the flow of intentionality and precedes "I do" and "I can," which demonstrate its intention. From a kinetic-kinesthetic heightening of immediate experience, Anne and Richard were able to restructure the familiar "I can" of their behaviors and practice the novelty of a different "I move," and "I do."

As our couple therapy continued, both Anne and Richard came to realize that each wanted different things from their relationship that were not to be had. Nevertheless, their desire to maintain the family was crucial. To remain together, they needed to learn to live with their considerable differences and the accompanying disappointments. Initially, disappointment sank into an ongoing and familiar despair for each of them. But in time, they learned to support themselves and each other through moments of appreciation and shared disappointment. They remained a family and together made a life.

Case Vignette

At the time of this in-person session, Gina and I had worked together weekly, and for four years. The case vignette has been reconstructed from notes taken directly after our meeting.

Leaving her shoes at the door, as is our custom, Gina walks into the room and carefully places her coat and purse on a chair. Routinely, she takes a moment to fluff her shoulder length hair, secures it behind each ear, and walks toward the couch. She arranges pillows behind her back so that she can more easily touch her feet to the floor. With supports now in place, she grasps-onto her hands and places them on her lap, where they will remain. Gina is strikingly tall, big-boned, and solidly built. Her face is narrow, and her large eyes most often are opened wide, as if she does not want to miss a thing. She maintains a long spine, which appears to be lifted from the area of her naval. Her upper torso is wide, though each shoulder bone appears to be pounded into its respective socket. Her held verticality and gripped shoulder bones give Gina the appearance of being in a kind of vice. Her postural dynamics are unchanging, and so are her gestures. This unchanging quality is echoed in Gina's vocal pattern, steady without much variation.

Gina and I take a moment to withdraw and find ourselves. Learning to do this has been helpful for Gina as she can discover what is happening now, rather than script the session in advance. Keeping her eyes fixed on her hands, Gina tells me that she was very critical toward her husband the night before. Slowly she reaches-for me with direct and open eyes, though I am not sure that she is receiving my looking back. I feel somewhat wooden and notice a kind of awkward, uneasy feeling forming between us. Gina pauses and then tells me: "I had a bad day yesterday. I was angry with myself for not completing everything on my list at work." Gina further reveals that when she arrived home, she found that her husband had ordered dinner but not *exactly* what she had requested, and she began to berate him. Though this is a familiar behavior for Gina—blaming herself and then placing blame on her husband—she tells me: "If he only listened to me, we would not be having these kinds of fights.

He doesn't pay attention." Inevitably, this becomes their usual struggle. She criticizes him, he stands up for himself but to no avail. Now it seems as if *she* does not listen. As Gina describes this encounter, her hands, still placed on her lap, grasp-onto each other with hi-intensity. Her breathing is almost imperceptible. I, too, feel my breathing diminish and take some time to extend my exhalation, which spontaneously enhances my next inhalation.

I ask Gina: "Are you interested in describing what you now feel in your chest or your abdomen after telling me this?" After four years together, Gina is familiar with these kinds of questions. Attending to the kinetic-kinesthetics of our building situation, we simply move from content to process, from form to forming. Immediately, Gina responds: "I feel a steel rod up-and-down from my neck to my gut. I felt this last night with Tony [her husband]." The experience of the steel rod is familiar to Gina, and we have learned that this feeling lends support and binds her together at times when she feels lost, powerless, and does not know what to do. Along with this bodily manifestation come the brutal self-criticisms for not being "perfect at work or at home." Gina attempts to find relief from self-recrimination by blaming Tony. This behavior has been well-practiced in their fifteen years of marriage and often feels impossible to alter. Gina's *steel-rod* provides the internal force needed, a push-against herself, as she valiantly tries to hold together. Similarly, she pushes-against Tony with abrupt, hi-intensity efforts. Her pushing endeavors invite Tony to meet her with his own repertoire of hi-intensity moves. These exchanges usually create a chilly ambiance that permeates their home for hours. Though this pattern has become less frequent since she and I began meeting, it has not lost its potency. When the fighting subsides, Gina faces another round of regrets and self-criticisms; she further punishes herself for punishing Tony, yet does not apologize to him.

I question Gina: "What do you imagine your steel rod is saying now, and to me?" While this is a question I have posed before, Gina's response is often somewhat different each time. Its meaning changes and depends on our evolving therapy situation. I am interested in how the feeling of the steel rod functions in the immediacy of this moment. How might Gina now feel lost and powerless with me? What is precarious about our being together? Her eyes look down, and with a stifled voice, she states: "I can't be open to you." I tell Gina that I appreciate her revealing herself, and wonder if she would change the *I can't* to an *I won't* and say it directly to me. For the first time, Gina abruptly lets go of the grasp of her hands, lifts them, and firmly drops them onto her lap. Just as they land, she looks directly toward me and says: "Ruella, I *won't* open to you." Impressed by her energetic response, and feeling my own growing excitement, I ask: "What now happens to the steel rod as you say this?" Gina continues looking toward me and states: "It gets more firm, more solid." I tell her: "I see how important it is not to open to me, and keeping that rod in place helps you do this. What do you imagine would happen between us if you were to open?" Her eyes lowering to her lap, Gina pauses and discloses: "I would disappear. I would be nothing." Her eyes grow wet, and she reaches for a tissue on the low table in front of her. Rather than explore what it may mean for her to disappear and lose herself, I propose a moving exploration. After explaining it, I ask Gina to stand, and I take my place to the side, rather than in front of her. I want Gina to feel herself as distinctly as possible, and without too much of my influence. I ask: "Does the rod remain solid and firm as you stand?" Gina responds: "Yes, nothing has changed." I ascertain whether Gina would prefer to do the exploration proposed alone or with me. She asks me to join her.

Gina and I lie on our backs upon the wood floor. We take time to feel ourselves yielding-with-pushing-against it and experience its push back. We also attend to our breathing, not to change it but only to observe its flow. Gina and I make subtle snake-like movements in place and imagine we are gliding through a pool of calm, freshwater. Doing this, we discover whatever space we can find and make within the joints of our bodies: the spaces between the bones of our spinal column, within our elbow joints, wrists, knees, ankles, and so on. Slowly and gracefully, we begin sinuously to snake our way along the floor. Using as much effort as necessary and as little as possible, we gradually lift our limbs lightly off the floor and shape the space around us. When we feel finished, and continuing our snake-like moves, we bring ourselves to stand. Once on our feet, I ask Gina to now hold still and notice what she experiences, if anything. With some excitement she tells me: "I'm still moving. I'm moving inside. It's strong." I share that I feel something similar; a moving all through me, an aliveness. I now stand directly in front of Gina and notice that her eyes softly reach-for me. I feel as though a gentle wave moves between us. I ask Gina what she notices as she looks toward me, and she says: "I feel open." I respond: "Open with *me*?" Gina laughs: "Yes, open with *you*." The session ends.

Psychodynamics

At the beginning of our therapy, to notice Gina at all would raise discomfort. To observe her was perceived as being *critical of* her rather than *interested in* her. It took the necessary time for us to build enough support in our relationship for Gina slowly to come to trust me. Taking relational support, and becoming kinetically-kinesthetically aware, was a simultaneous procedure. As she began to believe in the genuineness of my interest, curiosity, and concern for her, she began to foster those traits within herself. Her pervasive anxiety, that of having to be perfect or to disappear into nothingness, was not easily replaced by curiosity. Gina was, nevertheless, up to the challenge. In time, moving-feeling explorations became part of our working together. We first explored her kinesthetic experiences; then we investigated her gestures as to when they emphasized what she said, or when they said something different; next we moved to standing and walking around the room. In these latter explorations, Gina and I considered our different relational, emotional, perceptual configurations. Building a supportive therapy relationship takes perseverance, and we found ourselves at odds with each other more than once. Each time I miss-attuned to Gina's exquisite sensitivity, she clearly and directly told me so, and I listened as best I could. Working through these mismatching moments we found our way back to each other, and our relationship strengthened.

When Gina revealed the fight with Tony, I noticed that her eyes were not so much reaching-for me as pushing-against me. When there is a modification in contacting, one or two fundamental movements remain held in foreground, while others remain less available. Gina's strong and routine push-against herself was also a push-against me; yielding-with or being-with me, and the vulnerability that movement pattern could supply, remained background. This diminished a possible liveliness between us, which was diagnosed through the awkward, wooden feeling I experienced: a co-created happening. When Gina firmly stated, with gesture and vocal tone, "I won't open to you," I felt the authenticity of her more animated bodily experience and an excitement building between us. Rather than exploring in-depth *what* she was saying, I chose to work with *how* she was saying it. Placing the exploration of form at the nexus of our work, Gina's experience of her steel pipe restructured. In its place, a more adaptable form emerged; one that was more adequate to the situation.

I had no agenda for our moving exploration on the floor. Perhaps Gina could have experienced a sense of *primal animation/primal sensibility*: the always already existing competencies of human experience, and the underlying structures of contact-making. If this occurred, she could have learned a different way of supporting herself rather than relying only on the feeling of her familiar and routine steel pipe. Or perhaps she could have noticed her unyielding constrictions as she moved along the floor and became more familiar with how these constraints lived within her. In this case, we would admire the tenacity of Gina's holding pattern, in that such constraints were a creative adjusting that protected her from an unrelentingly, difficult early environment. Keeping the uncompromising steel pipe in place seemed the best way she could advocate for the child she had been. In the end, Gina courageously took a risk. Receiving the necessary support the floor offered, and with my support by her side, a new bodily narrative was created; a new meaning made.

Concluding Remarks

Bodies are dynamic patterns of movement. In spontaneity and creativity, these patterns play out in the immediacy of the moment. Exploring through movement, patients and therapists understand *when*, *where*, and *how* they excitedly open to the other, and *when*, *where*, and *how* they anxiously close. Each learns to register and appreciate aesthetic influence in the co-creating of the situation they live. Phenomenological diagnosis is based upon the aesthetic and reliant upon our capacities of responsivity and response; one does not feel without doing or do without feeling. The more sensitive we become to ourselves and to those we treat, the more we understand how we make meaning of experiences we build together: "personal experience always emerges, maintains itself, and transforms within relational contexts" (Orange 2009, 237). Human subjectivity, therefore, is embedded within a world of relationship, and our bodily capacities, the six fundamental movements, act as its mediator. Therapists need to understand the psychological function of each movement pattern, and how each works in concert with the others, to diagnose the *forming of contact* in real-time. As Henri Bergson (1992) expressed it: "Every form has its roots in a movement that traces it: a form is nothing but recorded movement" (279). By employing the six fundamental movements and their attendant qualities, we investigate the forming of form.

It is not always possible and certainly not necessary to introduce movement explorations into the therapy session. To do so, like with any intervention within session, therapists must first attend to the kinetic-kinesthetic experiences, which delineate the movements of the field. In touch with kinetic-kinesthetic happenings, therapists take measure of the phenomenal situation made perceptible by the unity of all senses. Sensitized to this unfolding therapy situation, they come to know what they can and cannot do with their patients, and to imagine what patients can and cannot do with them. Moving-feeling experience is a sensuous aesthetic diagnosis of the immediate situation, a diagnosis of contacting. Even if movement experiments are not introduced immediately or at all, one can continually diagnose contacting through a diligent analysis of the structure and function of its moving-feeling supports. After any intervention is made, the same attention to lived bodily experience enables the therapist to evaluate how that intervention has touched the patient.

To use the six fundamental movements as diagnosis and treatment within therapy is not to *fix* the patient, that is, not to coach them to move or feel in more spontaneous, creative ways. Rather, the six fundamental movements provide a prism through which therapists and patients can register and respect attempts to preserve a sense of cohering within the relational situation. What *is* can be valued and understood, instead of what *could be*. Once the newly realized, reliable but inadequate form is appreciated, an exploration of its qualities and meanings can follow. The next step is not so much analyzed as found. It is a rhythm already forming within what is occurring and can be listened to. In the aesthetic diagnosis of form, therapists move beyond familiar modes of analyzing their patients' symptoms and delve into the unknown of the present moment to explore in novel ways.

Chapter 6

The Bodily Origins of Developmental Trauma

Traumatic Attaching

According to the traditional perspective on the development of trauma, in the first years of a baby's life, the parent initiates what is thought to become a habitual traumatic reaction in the child. Consequently, the baby reacts to the parent in ways that are rigid or overly malleable and generally repetitive. This understanding of developmental trauma, however, does not take into consideration the relational and contextual dynamics that are part of any organizing experience. Emergent experience, which is where we clinical phenomenologists focus our therapy practice, belongs neither to the organism alone nor to the environment: "When the deliberate dichotomy between 'external world' and 'body' is not made, what you then experience is the organism/environment field—the differentiated unity which comprises you-in-your-world" (Perls et al. 1990, 94) Emergent experience, then, arises at a *"crossing threshold"* as the experience of each person, informing and informed by the other, takes shape (Michael Vincent Miller, personal communication, May 2016).

Observing baby and parent interactions from a relational, contextual, dynamic perspective, and through micro-movements, it can be seen how the baby's behaviors can powerfully impact the parent. When the parent experiences the baby's influence as negative in nature, it can generate the threat of re-traumatization for the parent. Parents, in an attempt to avoid the pain of this re-traumatizing experience, avoid feeling themselves with their child, and inadvertently traumatize the child with a lack of attuning. It is imperative that the young child attaches to the caregiver for survival both emotionally and physically (Bowlby 1982, 39). There is also an ongoing emotional survival that is part of a parent's experience of attaching. That is, the developing of self-esteem by the primary caregiver can be threatened in chronic experiences of re-traumatization in relation to the child. Healthy attaching is the result of predictable, reliable, and consistent enough ways one joins with another, offering stability and flexibility in relationships. Creative and spontaneous adjusting to the novel situation eventuates in

DOI: 10.4324/9781003266341-6

relational growth and change. Traumatic attaching, however, refers to how one joins the other in such a way so as to create an implacable relational stability with diminished flexibility. Creative and spontaneous adjusting is replaced by all too familiar repetitive patterns. The lack of unique interaction impairs the creating of novelty and therefore lessens the possibility of relational maturation.

This chapter will explore the developing of traumatic attaching from its roots in the infant-caregiver dyad, as well as the inevitable re-traumatizing experiences that are part of the ongoing psychotherapy relationship for both patient and therapist. A developmental perspective on the emergence of trauma is crucial to our continued investigation of how we become and continue to maintain who we are. We need to look at our infancy, which provides the ground of our current experience; the earliest history forming the legs upon which this present moment stands. Rather than the word trauma remaining as an abstract notion, the experience of trauma will be analyzed through a somatic and developmental lens, emphasizing the most fundamental moving experiences that comprise traumatic reaction. This phenomenological approach invites us to look at the emergence of traumatic reactions occurring in everyday life and especially in psychotherapy. The developmental trauma, originating in the there-and-then of an earlier relationship, must be addressed as it emerges in the here-and-now.

In the first year, the foundation for attaching appears and is seen and felt most clearly through movement. Here we see how traumatic attaching and intergenerational traumas develop. These psychophysical heirlooms are often delivered through unaware and often subtle bodily postures, gestures, and gait along with their attendant feelings. These stories form from a foundation of tactile-kinetic-kinesthetic expressions and experiences passed on through a certain kind of affective sensitivity, such that this next generation moves through the world in some ways similar to the earlier world of parent, grandparent, great grandparent, and so on. The stories are sometimes verbal but primarily subverbal and expressed through movement: how the child is picked up, put down, carried, reached-for, touched, spoken to. The parent's story lives through the moving-feeling body and expresses an unspoken legend whose meaning and message, although unconscious, holds utmost significance.

Cause-and-Effect

Many psychotherapists now look to varying psychotherapy modalities grounded in neuroscience to work with and to understand the passage of trauma. Simply put, neuroscience studies the function of the nervous system and brain. It can be used to characterize a person's neural-mental state from an objective, third-person perspective. A clinical phenomenological description, however, looks at how persons live the situation they live, a first-person subjective perspective. Neuroscience, though extremely valuable to our scientific learning, can greatly reduce the complexity of body/mind/environment when brought into psychology or the practice of psychotherapy. Incorporating neuroscience into psychotherapy is a determined effort to make higher-order processes into more predictable causal accounts. These scientific approaches to experience are concepts that attempt to make sense of the human condition. They are not truths. People are mysteries that we wish to unfold and not solve through intellectual analysis resulting in the formulation of certitudes. With this kind of reductionistic thinking comes a host of techniques which, in creating a kind of certainty, leads to categorizations. For example, it could be determined that a patient's unique experience indicates either a hyperactive or hypoactive reaction to a re-traumatizing experience. In those cases, particular techniques are used to work with one reaction or the other. Human experience, however, is much more than a fragmentation of the experienced world of neurons. We cannot look at a particular adult behavior in the present—the effect—and attribute it to something that happened in our infancy, childhood, or adolescence—the cause. In contrast, as clinical phenomenologists, we pay close attention to how we make something together—a bi-direction event—and do not impose theories of cause-and-effect. In attending to direct experience, we look at and describe what appears between one and the other without naming what is normal or abnormal, or what we surmise to be true or not true. We look, instead, to *my* subjective experience and *your* subjective experience as it emerges now. And although I have mine and you have yours, we continually influence each other to create a *trans-subjective* experience. In other words, we together form our experience, the process of contacting.

Everyday Traumas

The traumatic experience is part of day-to-day reality. We experience all kinds of losses including the loss of income, position; we lose loved ones through death, lose a sense of ourselves through divorce, physical and emotional abuse, devastating illness, war, natural disasters, pandemics, political upheavals, racial and religious persecution. It is impossible to find anyone who has not lived through some kind of traumatic experience inherent in the course of living. And though some have more enduring experiences than others, trauma remains a shared thread and is "built into the basic constitution of human existence" (Stolorow 2007, xi). No one escapes the necessary existential experience of having been traumatized at one time or another, and to some degree. The word trauma can be attractive to clinicians wishing to help their patients who suffer from deep, chronic wounds to their psyche, and who become easily re-wounded in session. The word trauma, however, is used to describe so many different situations and experiences that it has become an abstract notion, a label. Psychotherapists dealing with their patient's traumas may develop a particular attitude they bring into the therapy session. Patients are identified, categorized, and diagnosed before or during the session if and when they exhibit certain symptoms that fit the label *traumatized*. When separating out the patient from the unfolding therapy situation, the patient is objectified rather than personified.

Developmental Traumas

Developmental traumas, the background for other later kinds of traumatic experiences, occur when the caregiver is not able to respond to the child in such a way that the child feels well-met enough of the time; satisfactorily recognized, heard, and seen. This is especially so when overwhelming, intolerable experiences arise and feel unbearable for the child, and there is no one to offer substantial help. An absence of steady attuned responsiveness to the child's affect states leads to "significant derailments of optimal affect integration and to a propensity to dissociate or disavow affective reaction" (Socraides and Stolorow 1984/1985, 106). Not finding the necessary protection from these massively overpowering feelings, children learn to abate them. They anticipate there will only be gross miss-attunement from the caregiver if their feelings of vulnerability and great distress surface and are expressed. To subside their feelings, children bind their muscles, which restricts breathing; conversely, restricting breathing binds muscles. The processes of contacting, of experience, are greatly modified. The intense feelings may appear to stop, but they never truly finish.

This does not happen for the child alone. With these kinds of chronic miss-attunements, the parent also suffers since their early kinesthetic, relational themes are stimulated and move foreground. Often parents have not had adequate caregiving attunement in their childhood and cannot bear to relive the feelings they too had to avoid in order to survive. No one was there for these parents and so they did not learn how to be there for their child. In avoiding their own pain as a means of protection, parents avoid the loss of a full-lived bodily experience and its meaning. They are no longer consistently enough in touch with themselves and the world.

In the process of development, both parent and child alter their reactions to the anticipated actions of their partner. These patterns emerge as unique forms of communication within dyads that transcend the discrete behaviors of each individual, that is, mother or infant (Stone et al. 2012). Through these patterns, each partner develops a sense of certainty: *I know what I can do with you, and what you can do with me.* This reduces some amount of relational anxiety. Knowing how to predict and respond to the other is a crucial aspect in any relationship, and it begins very early in our development. These regulatory patterns of adjusting offer a kind of stability and familiarity. It is how we order our world; the more uncertain we are in the moment, the more we utilize our most familiar patterns to sustain ourselves under adverse circumstances. It is how we endure. The child does not respond only to the *trans-corporeal* data received from the situation. There appears a moving-feeling logic that forms itself; a kind of primitive symbolizing rather than a set of innate fixed responses. Caregivers respond to their children in similar ways through individual moving-feeling patterns that hold meaning, whether these patterns are made explicitly aware or not.

Mother and Samuel

The following story is a description of the ground from which traumatic attaching emerges.

> *Five-and-a-half-month-old Samuel sits in his hi-chair facing his mother. His movement qualities are low-intensity, soft, gradual, and free. Excitement emerges slowly for him and dissipates quickly. When Samuel reaches-for mother, he extends his hands and legs under the tabletop, advancing them halfway in her direction and soon moves them back. Mother, on the other hand, has a hi-intensity, sudden way of moving. Her shoulders are often raised as she presses her head forward, reaching-for her son with constricted muscles that appear to burst out of her skin. Mother's excitement rises quickly and does not dissipate easily. She often quickly advances toward Samuel, who then abruptly drops his head downward, his chin to his chest; or he turns his head to his right at a 45-degree angle away from her. When mother's abrupt advancing builds in intensity and frequency, Samuel angles his head to his side this time at a 90-degree angle, his eyes staring upward but appearing not to see. A circular pattern emerges between them: mother lunges into Samuel's space and he averts his eyes and head, raises his shoulders, and hollows his chest in response. Seeing him turn his head away from her, mother places her hand on Samuel's chin and moves it in her direction. He now tries to turn his head to the left and simultaneously puts his thumb into his mouth. "No, don't suck your thumb," mother tells him, as she pulls his thumb away from his face. Her voice has an even, firm, and moderately intense quality. Samuel, shoulders raised upward once more and eyes now squinting, attempts to reach-for his mouth and now with both hands and fingers. Again, mother grasps-onto them: "No sucking your fingers now. This is our play time," she says with the same even and firm tone.*
>
> *This chase and dodge continues for some minutes more before mother sighs and gradually sits back in her chair, unknowingly offering space between them. After a brief pause, Samuel looks directly at her. Seeing her son meet her, she says, "Samuel!" as if surprised and in a softer tone, "Saaa-muel, Saaaaa-muel." With every repetition of his name, mother's*

voice becomes more gentle and more flowing. Samuel smiles and softly reaches his fingers toward her. "There you are. I see you," she says. Still gazing at mother, Samuel's legs and feet reach out, and he smiles and babbles. Mother continues: "You're smiling!" Showing some excitement, Samuel abruptly kicks his feet against the tabletop with a higher intensity. He makes several banging noises, while opening and closing his fingers as he reaches-for mother. Still smiling, he lengthens his body upward and suddenly shortens it dropping chin to chest, as if to take a necessary break from his building excitement. Immediately, mother responds to Samuel's postural shift and abruptly lunges forward and, with a firm, hi-intensity slap of her hand on the high-chair tabletop, says: "Samuel," but this time with a sharp vocal pattern that matches her slap. A startled Samuel flinches, simultaneously raises his shoulders upward, his head descending into his hollowed chest.

Through the dialogical dynamics of nonverbal communication, both child and parent form patterns of traumatic attaching, distinctly shaping their way of contacting. Perhaps mother never felt loved consistently enough throughout her infancy, childhood, and adolescence. She comes into this relationship hoping to receive the kind of attention she sought when she was young, yet routinely could not find. As the traumatic attaching experience continues, it becomes a way the relationship stabilizes, albeit losing flexibility. This oft-repeated pattern leaves both mother and child unsatisfied and perhaps confused as to what to do to be seen, recognized, and accepted by the other. Rather than interactions created through mutual and co-ordinated participation by both individuals, Samuel and mother participate in disruptive and unengaged unilateral exchanges that diminish the developing of a fluid co-regulating dialogue (Stone et al. 2012). In such unfavorable circumstances of ongoing dynamic, situational, and relational uncertainty, holding in, back, and down with an accompanying restriction of breathing, circumscribe the child's movement potentialities, reducing kinesthetic experience—*the feel of our moving.* When the liveliness of kinesthetic experience is diminished, the capacity to adjust creatively and spontaneously to possibilities of the field are hindered, sometimes greatly. The child loses an aspect of core intelligence: a bodily knowing how to orient clearly and to maneuver freely through the world. It is a loss of bodily agency; the power to do. The parent experiences a similar fate. The habitual and rigidified repetition of a psychophysical and fixed *ordering pattern* in relation to her child emerges with its accompanying theme: *Something is wrong with us. I cannot find you and you cannot find me.* The belief, often unaware, is nevertheless background as it is confirmed from the past, organizes in the present, and projects toward anticipated future horizons, expressing the mother's isolated state. To find order, certainty, and stability within this relational field, mother and child form these kinds of habitual patterns. And although sometimes they do meet, there are enough moments of missing each other such that patterns of traumatic attaching easily surface. Each partner has grown sensitive to and anticipates such discordant experiences and adjusts, as best they can, to their circumstances.

Paradoxically, mother's desire to avoid the pain of her re-wounding experience in relation to her son leads to its recreation. Stimulated by her hopes to find the *wished-for child* rather than the *child that is,* she inadvertently passes her earlier and enduring re-traumatizing experiences on to her son with each fixed move she makes and held breath she takes. Mother feels threatened by the uncertainty of the moment, Samuel's seemingly indifferent responses to her. Feeling desperate in her quest for a more desirable response, she tries again and again to get the kind of attention she longs for in her attempt to feel loved. But Samuel is unable to meet his mother the way she wishes him to and, likewise, mother is unable to meet Samuel. The desired intentionality on both of their parts does not culminate in a fluid, clarified, and ultimately satisfying intention. The certainty of belonging—Y*ou are mine and I am* yours—does not emerge often enough, and when it does, it dissipates all too quickly. Longed for hope is replaced by dread. Although uncomfortable, there is a consistency and predictability formed by these ongoing scenarios, which saves mother from a deeper existential uncertainty: that all is in flux, and nothing can be continually certain or secure.

The process of attaching is the relational function of a forming self that is part of development; otherwise, we would not survive: "The relational function orients us towards the human other" (Bloom 2016, 77), and we do whatever it takes to establish and re-establish these kinds of connections. For the growing child, it is necessary to find the other as someone who can be there reliably enough, and when not, predictably will return. When this meeting is threatened, the ongoing uncertainty of the presence of an available other becomes entrenched in lasting, sedimented, and kinesthetic experiences that leave traces throughout the lifetime.

Evolution and the Experience of Safety

In the world of evolution, the infant gorilla held in the mother's arms often gazes into mother's eyes as she gazes back. There appears communion, and we can imagine a sense of safety or containment for the infant. But when the mother looks away, the infant follows her eyes and traces where the mother is now looking to identify a possibly perceived threat (Anni Bergman, personal communication, September 2009). With this kind of learning through movement, the infant gorilla distinguishes between the experience of safety, enfolded in the soft quality of the mother's gaze, and its loss as the mother abruptly looks away in search of a possible threat. The infant gorilla learns that I am safe here with you, and what is unsafe for the moment is out there.

For human infants, what is safe and unsafe is not as clear as for the baby gorilla. For humans, primary caregivers hold both safe and unsafe positions. The threat itself is not from the outside world of predators but from within the individual's own social world. At times, the parent provides a safe enough environment from which the child takes as much support as necessary to continue to develop well enough. At other times, the caregiver becomes the uncertain, unpredictable other and the child, who relies on this other for survival, grows perturbed.

Particularly for the infant, but also throughout our lifetime, we are called upon to respond to and even rely on those we do not know completely; those who are strangers (Waldenfels 2011). We have *our* experience of the other, but it is not *their* experience. We can see, hear, touch, and sense them, but we cannot be them. We have the commonality of our shared cultural, social, historic environment, and the fundamental patterns of moving-feeling through this environment. The unique qualities, dimensions, and lived spatiality created by these patterns, however, can be dissimilar enough so that we do not always understand that other. We are completely dependent on the other that is not fully known; a different and strange other who is sometimes there, and sometimes not.

Infants come to learn and then know themselves through a developing *trans-subjective* matrix. They learn their bodies through moving, and primarily with the significant others who care for them in the important first year. The developing lived body "conveys the practical knowledge of how to interact with others and how to understand their expressions and actions against the background of the common situation" (Fuchs and Schlimme 2009, 572). Developing from birth, this knowledge is gained through interactions with others. When there is a cohering experience of child and parent; a moving-feeling experience of one part of the body in coordination with another part *and* with the caring other, a coherent and articulate meaning of the situation is made. For these coherent, meaning-making experiences to emerge, there must be a kind of stability within the relational situation, whereby each partner is available enough to the other. It is a world wherein parent and child can discover and build the ground of *Me* with *You*. There is a sense of belonging. This is a flowing harmonious world; one in which the child has sufficient resources to equilibrate the pressures of the field and can meet the developmental challenges of the task at hand. But in periods of traumatic attaching, there is a lack of the coming together of my body and yours (Stolorow 2007). The capacity to make meaning of the situation is fragmented. Perception and movement are disjointed, and parts of the experience are broken apart from the whole and no longer make sense. The child experiences an unrelenting and dread-filled vulnerability in a world in which she/he/they cannot cope. The flow of harmonious experience is interrupted, sometimes rather suddenly and violently. The world of the other can feel as if it is intruding upon the child, leaving no space to feel a developing separate self: anxiety moves into panic. Or the world of the other can seem far away and completely out of reach, which also leads to an anxious and unending longing, eventually crashing into depression. A basic trust that there is order in the world breaks down.

The animated experience that comes with a fully functioning lived body is now replaced by a kind of lifelessness. A troubled tactile-kinetic-kinesthetic involvement with the world results in a "basic sense of detachment that may pass over into a threatening alienation" (Fuchs and Schlimme 2009, 572). A world to be discovered by the child's intrinsic sense of wonder, the sub-structure of curiosity, is now flat.

The Moro Response: The Phenomenological Equivalent of Uncertainty

Despite this common thread of traumatic experience in our early years, the roots of developmental trauma or wounding perhaps have not adequately been attended to from a phenomenological perspective. To further this investigation, it is necessary to look at the earliest expressions and experiences of disruption in the first five months of the neonate's life: the Moro Response. In doing so, we are exploring basic and primal physical processes and their psychic consequences rooted throughout the course of evolution and observed in our earliest moments of life, as well as in fetal development.

Almost everyone is familiar with the Moro Response, formally called and still referred to by some developmental motor theorists as the Moro Reflex. Let us recall the difference between a reflex and response. A simple reflex arc in general is seen as a movement performed automatically and without conscious volition, such as when the tendon of your knee is tapped, it produces a knee jerk. James Dewey (1896), however. denounced the accepted theory of reflex arc as it created a separation between stimulus and response: to this philosopher, a simplistic breaking into cause-and-effect for what was a more complex unity of coordinated action. Almost 100 years after Dewey, Esther Thelen (1995) supported his theory stating that no movement is prearranged before its amplification. Instead, any movement emerges during its performance in relation to the physical environment of the external world and the biologic environment of the internal world. Thelen was referring to the universal forces of field—gravity, earth, and space. Moreover, the universal forces of field are experienced through the caregiver's body as the baby is lifted and placed down, rocked, cuddled, vocalized to, gazed upon, and all with that caregiver (Frank 2001; Frank and La Barre 2011). How the infant's moving patterns emerge both influence and are influenced by this unfolding dynamic, relational situation. A movement-based understanding of the developing of experience, the process of contacting, is always and already evolving through interaction: dynamic, contextual, and relational.

The Moro Response is primarily elicited when the baby is being put down into the crib and the head is dropped, slightly lower that the torso. Sometimes, the Moro is elicited through unexpected, external environmental sounds; or in response to something happening internally; or if someone displaces the baby's weight by suddenly sitting upon or firmly pressing a hand onto the bed the baby lies on. In the first sequence of the Moro, when the balance of head and torso shifts out of alignment, babies appear to be falling. This is observed primarily in the upper body as torso arches and head falls back, while arms, hands, fingers extend to either side, eyes and mouth widen, the area around the eyebrows lifts upward. Because the extending muscles on the baby's back are not yet well developed to recover from this falling movement, the flexing muscles on the front of the body are brought into play. These muscles are more practiced for use at this point in development, and baby immediately flexes head and torso to draw all parts of the body toward the center. Simultaneously, arms and hands move in front of the body while fingers grasp to complete the act. The flexion movements are a spontaneous and natural attempt to restore balance, such that stable ground is once more reclaimed. Though the Moro Response is universal, how it is carried out is particular to each individual human infant in situ.

All moving responses of the infant, practiced over and over, teach something about adjusting to a continually changing world. From a psychophysical perspective, the Moro Response can be seen as the phenomenological equivalent of uncertainty beginning with the abrupt loss of presence of the supporting other, and the inevitable attempt to find that other and, once more, grasp-onto the world. The Moro demonstrates that the process of losing and finding equilibrium is inherent and therefore necessary to a developing understanding of what it is to be human. A radical shift in experience reorganizes the infant-world configuration. From this new and strange moment of loss of balance, infants learn how to restore themselves as they simultaneously restore a more familiar world: a place of belonging, of home.

The Startle Response: The Phenomenological Equivalent of Resisting

Between three and five months, the Moro Response no longer becomes necessary as the extensor muscles of neck and back, which have been strengthened in the practice of moving, now are stronger. Infants find equilibrium in a variety of ways that enable them to eventually sit up and reach-for others while using newly developing muscular support. At this time, the Moro Response generally becomes integrated within the Startle Response, which lasts throughout our lives. The Startle Response has been thought of as a "start" or "jump" in the English language, which describes that there is a movement but does not provide a more detailed description of the specific kind of movement. The German word for startle, *fahren*, is suggestive of *going*. Added to the prefix of *zusammen*, it becomes *zusammenfaren bin* or going together, as the periphery of the body gathers toward the core. Whereas the Moro is the grosser and more noticeable pattern, with its emphasis on extension, it may contain elements of the startle (Landis and Hunt 1968 (original work 1939)), which often can be subtle with its emphasis on flexion.

The startle has a profound purpose evolutionarily and developmentally. In the startling situation, a whole-body experience, the child is hyper-focused on what is occurring in the environment, which could present a danger, and the child is primed and attentive to what is out there. Evolutionarily, the animal would either move toward the danger in fight mode or move away in flight to find safety. The infant or young child does not have such choices. When the rhythmic harmony or fluid coordinating patterns between the child and the surrounding environment is lost, an existential uncertainty arises along with resistance to it. The familiar kinetic-kinesthetic experiences the infant has grown accustomed to now are disturbed. What felt familiar and stable a moment ago is unaccustomed and strange. The Startle Response, lasting one and a half seconds (Landis and Hunt 1968, 127), alerts infants (children, adolescents, adults) to the immediate, precarious situation, and they are better able to appraise it. In situations of apprehension to impending danger, a rapid sequence of movements arises: jaw and forehead contract, eyes squeeze shut, shoulder and neck muscles tense. As shoulders lift toward the ears, the head is brought forward, elbows bend, palms turn inward. The abdominal muscles contract, bringing the torso slightly forward, pulling down the ribcage to inhibit breathing, and the pelvic floor contracts. Finally, knees point toward each other, ankles and feet roll inward (Hanna 1988, 50–51). Though this is considered the classic posture, there are as many variations of this posture as there are individuals, and no one individual necessarily will respond with all these postural adjustments. Most all, however, will feel the grip of shoulders, neck, and abdominal holding as well as a sharp inhibition of breathing.

After this immediate hi-intensity response, there appears a sequence of unique and individual secondary postural arrangements (Landis and Hunt 1968, 29; original work published 1939). Again, rather than being an all or nothing response, the startle differs from person to person and can be dependent on one's expectations. If the startle is elicited with regularity, children are primed to expect the next startling situation. In anticipation, they begin to hold their bodies together as sensible protection, which exacerbates the startle to come. In all the various possible postural configurations, the function of the startle response is to provide protection from a temporarily, yet acutely threatening, world. The startle response, however, is not always about experiences of shock, as one also can be pleasantly surprised. In such cases, the secondary response is soon diminished, and individuals return to their usual postural configurations.

Maxine Sheets-Johnstone (2016) has investigated the startle response in relation to the exploration of schizophrenic disturbance noting: "It is important to emphasize from the beginning that, contrary to traditional phenomenological practice in both methodology and theoretical sense, what is natural is in this instance is being taken as a clue to the pathologic and not the reverse" (93). That is, the substratum of pathology is an augmentation of what is a natural and healthy response to an abrupt and unanticipated alteration in the concordant experience of the world. The startle "allows one to examine the experience of discordancy, what amounts to be a break in the familiar flow of everyday life, and thereby gain insight into the fundamental aspects of the pathology of schizophrenia" (94). In agreement with Sheets-Johnstone's approach, here we continue the exploration of the startle as the ground of neurotic development.

Though the startle can be elicited in many ways and in varied situations, it becomes fixed in time and plays a part in upending the developing of creative and spontaneous adjusting from infant to adult. The startle, a natural expression of disruption in the seamless flow of harmonious experience, intrudes in its habituation upon the flow of contacting and attempts to protect against the all too uncertain future. In uncovering the most elemental movement dimensions of the fixed startle, a substructure of physiological and psychological development, it is possible to understand better the nature of traumatic attaching and its treatment.

Sedimented Isometric Contractions

In the ordinary development of chronic and habitual startle responses, an isometric holding pattern organizes—an inadvertent muscular contraction where one movement is pitted against the other (Hanna 1988, 67–68). This can be exemplified if one places both hands, palms touching, in front of the chest, and pushes them firmly against each other. The hands do not move but muscles of the chest will contract (73). The isometric contractions are never static but are made and remade in an ongoing kinetic-kinesthetic fashion (Behnke 1997, 188). Unlike voluntary movements, they are the unplanned consequences of adjusting within a chronically dangerous and frustrating environment and have become part of the unaware background of aware contacting. These micromovements are simultaneously shaped and halted; the person wishes to move out but holds back and in and down to preserve a hoped-for sense of safety. These repetitively made shapes sediment, and over time organize a synergetic series of muscular patterns that position bones in a variety of ways, influencing movements, feelings, emotions, and their consequential meanings. The assemblage of isometric patterns at one time assisted or literally supported the individual through difficult and demanding situations, and were co-creations within an environment and not of the individual alone. In time, these holding patterns narrow the capacity to experience oneself and consequently limit one's expressions (Perls et al. 1990, 260–261). They become a *secondary physiology* and being unaware, do not lead to the developing of a more flexible and spontaneous adjusting (402).

False Floors: The Attempt to Find Support

Isometric holding generally organizes in circular bands along various horizontal dimensions of the body. One can hold at the level of the eyes, jaw, throat, collarbone, diaphragm, pelvic floor, hips, knees, and ankles, as they move progressively down the body to form the background of a fixed or bound gestalt. The isometric binding is unique to each person and its expression will, therefore, vary as to where the held pattern most often is employed. In other words, at what horizontal bodily dimension are these contractions brought into play? For example, one person may bind at ankles and knees repeatedly, whereas another holds firmly at the level of shoulders and collarbones. All holding patterns express an endeavor to make stable ground from within when the possibility of the other is not available often enough to offer firm ground from which to take support. The isometric bindings, or *false floors,* were and still are thought to be the best solution found and made in a difficult situation: they are accomplishments in contacting. Faced with the loss of an available and desired other, and the dread that this hoped for other may not be found soon, these *false floors* attempt to anchor or ground the infant, child, and adult. They are a pseudo-support that was functionally useful during moments of disquieting and sometimes terrifying uncertainty. As children pass into adulthood and their world shifts and changes, the earlier constructed *false floors* are not as useful as they once were and can delimit the full experience of the new moment. Tactile-kinetic-kinesthetic history overwhelms present reality; what *was* discourages what *could be.*

Developmental Traumas Emerging within Psychotherapy

As stated previously, whatever traumatic situations a person experiences throughout life, there is always the underlying background of developmental trauma based on an earlier lack of sufficient attunement. This lack sets a relational foundation that surfaces in later adult contacting and naturally in the psychotherapy session. It occurs when the presence of therapists is not felt, and patients imagine them to be not *for* but *against* them. The therapist now seems all too similar to the patient's original family, populated by those significant and often mal-attuned figures. The patient does not explicitly remember the earlier situation but now lives it.

This process rides on the experience of kinesthetic remembering; for example, standing and walking toward the other is an outgrowth of one's kinetic-kinesthetic remembering of how we crawled toward our earlier significant others. It is essential to how we learn to learn. It is a lived-bodily remembering and an assemblage of "I Cans" (Sheets-Johnstone 1999, 135–137); the implicit knowing of what I can do and have done with you and what you can do and have done with me. It is a clear demonstration of how present enfolds past and indicates future horizons.

For example, as one reaches-for the other, there is a moving-feeling knowing—a re-membering of how one executed this reach in earlier experiences. There is always already a dynamic relational form to remember. Kinesthetic remembering, then, is etched into the body as specific moving-feeling dynamics. As they are enacted, they adapt to the situation in a play of figure-ground. We initiate the flow of our movements based on our retained kinesthetic past, which also influences what will come next. Again, the retained moving-feeling pattern that emerges influences and is influenced by the present situation. The earlier reaching pattern and accompanied feeling experience is always background to experience. On occasion, however, the present situation can easily re-stimulate the past along with its historic, kinesthetic theme, and dominates here-and-now situations.

The lived body conveys practical knowledge of how to interact (Merleau-Ponty 2012). When those experiences of re-traumatization occur in therapy and lived body is diminished, the patient becomes detached, and there is a loss of natural self-confirmation. It is a loss of orientation; evidence that I clearly am *here*, and you clearly are *there*. In the event of re-traumatizing or re-wounding, the body loses the ability to feel itself move through the world, and it becomes an object. During therapy, this can be seen as an erosion of the patient's relatedness to all that is. As the body is our "general means of having the world," (Merleau-Ponty 2012, 147), any repetitive loss of bodily experience is not only the feeling of a loss of bodily belonging but also a loss of belonging in the world. What the world can offer is neither seen nor felt, and the possibilities of creatively adjusting to the situation are greatly limited. The certainty that the other(s) upon whom one depends upon for consistent, predictable, and reliable exchanges will always be there is now disrupted (Brothers 2008). Banished from a familiar world, the re-traumatized person lives now in a world of outsiders. Without the certainty or essential trust that stable ground is present underfoot, the experience of a clear reality is replaced by guesswork. The patient becomes involved in having to figure out what is happening rather than directly living what happens. Without a fuller sense of themselves, they lack a fuller sense of the other.

The Developing Session

The goal of psychotherapy is to explore the functioning of emerging phenomena; the purpose they serve for the patient rather than the causes from which they arise. The phenomenological field is centered within the tactile-kinetic-kinesthetic body, or lived body, which functions as background to all experience. The phenomena to be explored—what is seen, felt, touched, heard, sometimes even tasted, and smelled—always emerges in relation to what is disclosed within the therapy dyad. The investigation by both therapist and patient explores the manifold ways that such phenomena now emerge. The essence of the work is to heighten awareness of the patient's tactile-kinetic-kinesthetic experiences and to create an environment from which the patient can take relational support. In the same way that the baby's kinesthetic experience is discovered through moving explorations with the parent, the restoration of these animated and authentic experiences is discovered in relation to the therapist. This is crucial to all efforts in psychotherapy, especially so when working with those moments of re-traumatization. Paradoxically, the re-traumatizing experiences arising in session for both therapist and patient are the passage to healing.

Not all children who have experienced some form of developmental trauma carry this with them throughout their lifetime. When children over time attune to their wounded feelings well enough, these wounds do not completely transfer to adulthood. They do impact the adult but without deeply distressing outcomes (Epstein 2014). This does not mean, however, that when these less-traumatized patients come into the therapy re-traumatizing moments do not emerge. No matter how good enough the parenting is there are always enduring feelings of insufficiency that are a natural part of the human condition. Subtle or overtly expressed moments of re-traumatizing on the part of both therapist and patient are important materials for continuing development.

For patients who enter therapy with their history of ongoing and passionate psychological conflict in the world, there comes the idea that something must be deeply wrong with them. The baby's and the child's naturally intense feelings in their early development were experienced and expressed in a position of solitude. No one was there, and so the unattended feelings became unbearable. Without consoling others to help process the intensity of the feelings, they did not integrate into the child's affective development (Stolorow 2007). The symptoms that brought them to seek therapy are seen as shameful aspects of the person, clear evidence of their flawed existence. Patients who feel besieged by shame are occupied by an ongoing critical evaluation of themselves and the world in which they live. In the diverse attempts to shut down their feelings and cut out the shaming environment, kinesthesia is diminished as dissociation eventuates. Coming to therapy, the patient wishes for the therapist to excise these shameful parts that strangle the capacity to respond freely, creatively, and spontaneously, and dreads that the therapist cannot or will not free them. Dread and fear readily emerge whenever there is some mis-attunement within the relationship. The exquisitely sensitive patient immediately is re-traumatized, and there is a threat to a coherent sense of self. The Startle Response at the ready is naturally provoked, and the held muscular synergies that organize varied *fixed floors* and their attendant meanings are brought into play. These are patients' best attempts to protect themselves in an environment that has become both precarious and deeply disturbing.

The Startle Response and Therapist

In any session, and especially working with patients with a history of profound neglect and abuse, many feelings and emotions occur. These are the sense of frustration or anger, the sense of the body lifting off the floor, or the sense of a heavy weighted-ness, the sense of exhaustion, and even boredom on the part of therapists can be attempts to diminish their own feelings of re-traumatizing. Unknowingly apprehensive, therapists may take one of two positions. These positions are employed as an attempt to make an uncertain situation more manageable: *I don't know what to do next and I must do something*. In the first position, subtle elements of startle occur, perhaps held breathing, constricted abdominal muscles, tense shoulders. Unaware of these subtle yet startling moments, therapists hold on to their familiar and habitually rigidified *or* overly malleable configurations, enthusiastically reaching-for or moving tersely away from their patient. There is a change in the qualities of their vocal tone and gestures. Reaching-for the patient in these ways can be an expression of exaggerated empathy and/or over-identification. Therapists may feel pulled in by their patients' expressions of deep emotion that demand therapists to end their suffering. If some relief for patients does not come soon enough, demanded upon therapists can feel they have failed. At those moments, they have difficulty feeling the abundance of available air to breathe, the ground under their feet, the chair beneath their pelvis, and behind their back. These are primary and fundamental supports for our *going on being* or the continuing of an animated and authentic creative self (Epstein 2001, 11). In the process of intensely attending to the other, there is a loss of fluidly withdrawing or checking in with oneself. The idea of having to support the patient is so central that a true support of oneself in the process becomes lost. Mis-attunement eventuates.

The second position therapists may take when startled is to move away from their patients with an unfelt yet heightened pushing-against the back of their chair and, with a matching loss of the feel of the chair beneath and the ground underfoot. Breathing grows shallow, and gestures are restricted. This is the disappearing position as patients' affects and/or disclosures may feel like a threat from which therapists need to hide. At such moments, therapists may feel inadequate as to what to say or do, and to say anything might demonstrate their inadequacies. Or perhaps therapists may have an agenda, and their patients are not cooperating with it. Conceivably, patients can also be certain in their beliefs that nothing their therapist can do will be sufficient or useful. This attitude states the profundity of aloneness and isolation that accompanies patients' experiences of trauma. The depth and expression of patients' suffering, along with therapists' feelings of inadequacy, can cause therapists to freeze: become immobilized and/or go blank. In this disappeared position, therapists are primarily attendant to their bodily restrictions and lose contact with the other. Miss-attunement eventuates.

There is a third position that therapists may take, especially when they are startled into states of re-traumatization. In this position, therapists become precisely attendant to their kinesthetic resonating experiences within the situation: *How do I experience myself now and with* you? The triggered isometric holding patterns, *false floors*, are brought foreground, and therapists can pause to notice how they push-against themselves holding in, down, and back. Awareness of their own *false floors* serves as a clue to the situation; therapists garner information as to what presently is happening within the relational field. To have waited through the aftermath of the startle by exploring their secondary responses or bodily fixations is not for the purpose of relaxing these held positions but of understanding *how* and *when* they emerged in reaction to the patient. Therapists, throughout the course of their praxis, need to become familiar with their characteristic moving-feeling patterns; long-held *isometric contractions/false floors* that are part of the human condition, and that become exaggerated within the re-traumatizing situation to modify contacting.

How therapists move within session *is* a therapeutic intervention. Suddenly reaching-for or pushing away from the patient is an expression of how that patient is being held by the therapist; one holds the other as one holds one's own body. Once therapists have identified the kinesthetically felt qualities of their own *isometric constrictions/false floors*, held along various horizontal bodily dimensions, and pause to experience fully these fixed gestalts, they can open to their meaning. As therapists now bring their attention to the earth underneath, the space surrounding them, and the air they breathe, they discover the possibility of support. These supports assist in forming a basic ontological security, finding the ground of *Me* with *You* and a sense of belonging. They are the "counterpoint to the existential vulnerabilities of being alive and finding oneself in a discordant world" (Sheets-Johnstone 2016, 88), allowing one to wait for the next and trust that there will come a next. There is always already a following breath to take and a next move to make. Finding these supports, the grasp-onto oneself slowly and incrementally lessens as the static muscular synergies and the meanings they produce reorganize. With ground underfoot, literally and metaphorically, therapists allow their patients to impress them without impulsively evaluating, interpreting, or acting upon these impressions. Whatever the startling impulse was that led them apprehensively toward or away from the patient is felt as it is forming. In other words, the impulse is not acted upon but experienced. There is a *being with* the other rather than a *doing to* the other. Recovering their ground, therapists create an environment from which patients can take support. In touch with lived body, a moving-feeling consciousness, therapists do not try to make something happen; more exactly, they allow themselves to move into the unknown without the usual certainties and wait to discover the happening that is already there. In the waiting, the figure has yet to form; all possibilities are open.

The Startle Response and the Patient

The intention of contacting is to find *Me* with *You: I feel you are here with me, and when you leave, I know you will return.* We reach-for the other and feel the other as they reach back to us. In the process, one becomes greater or more than what one was before. This is a cumulative process of how we grow and change, and reliant upon an evolving tactile-kinetic-kinesthetic body. The lived body opens the phenomenal field, a field where others are already included. In situations of re-traumatization, there is no implied other that can be easily found as one is braced within oneself. Figure/ground fragments and the relational field narrows and constricts (Fuchs 2007). The possible affordances of the world are neither noticed nor expected. Trauma appears to stop time, and during startling re-traumatizing experiences patients are thrown into an earlier zone; a time when no predictable, reliable other was available to help the child suffer excruciating affects. A terrible and ongoing aloneness developed and continued, and the patient enters therapy having lost faith in the intimate environment. A lack of a cohering of body/world experience ensues, and dissociation follows.

In an attempt to recover a sense that one must and will continue to exist, to *go on being*, the patient forms a kind of steadfast certitude rather than risking the insufferable experience of its lack. The certitude is enfolded within a story *about* why the patient is correct to hold in, back, and down in the face of the perceived threatening environment. Either the patient imagines the terrible suffering that can happen if one becomes vulnerable in and receptive to the world, or the patient cannot begin to imagine what will happen, a different kind of horror. There is no working through of the re-traumatizing experience when the patient identifies with the story surrounding the trauma. It is not that recovering a primal memory or a therapeutic interpretation is the healing (Epstein 2014). To find the available other is to give up the story that binds the trauma together; the kinesthetically persistent relational theme that attempts to create confidence where there was and is none. Patients hold onto their certainty: *No one was there for me, so why should I think that you will be there? I can take care of myself, as you will only fail me.* Desire, curiosity, interest must be grounded in a sustainable uncertainty, an uncertainty that can be metabolized. Patients' attempts at grasping-onto an inflexible certitude paradoxically creates its lack.

Patients often report feeling not much or nothing at all, an inevitable product of having survived traumatizing experiences by shutting out the perceived dangerous world and cutting themselves off from their overwhelming feelings of frustration and/or emptiness (Perls et al. 1990, 263–265). The experience of nothingness and the *false floors* that contribute to its making are crucial to maintain. Without someone to hold onto them, patients have learned to hold onto themselves. These patterns of traumatic attaching are the methods by which they survived the worst of situations; it is how they have endured and continue to endure. Although these patterns of constriction and limitation were necessary and crucial assistances in an earlier relational environment, they function far less well in the present and do not bode well for future encounters (Laura Perls, personal communication, September 1986). The patient becomes stuck in asking from the other and yet not receiving that other, or the demanding patient who does not accept what is offered yet continues to ask. Or the patient who can be stuck in not asking at all; the one who waits for yet hides from the other, while not expecting to be found: "There is an attunement that cannot be supplied by others and cannot be felt by the patient" (Stolorow 2007, 14). Both kinds of performances exemplify a retreat of *Me* from *You*; a primary symptom in all neurotic behaviors and substantially present in the startling moments of re-traumatizing.

Re-traumatization strangles the sensuousness of fluid contacting. The more reduced the capacity to experience kinesthetic streaming throughout one's body, the more complete the retreat of *Me* from *You*. Though patients come to therapy with the wish to live more fully, their unconscious dedication to maintaining their *false floors,* and the work involved in preserving these constrictions, illustrate the impact of the original pattern of traumatic attaching and states a kind of loyalty to an earlier relational field. Patients' identities are deeply embedded in these patterns; to begin to untangle them brings forward insufferable, anxiously held feelings. Remembering that the emergence of re-traumatizing occurrences in therapy is a bi-directional happening, the therapist can take as much responsibility as patients for their presence. It is not solely a constriction *within* the patient, nor *within* the therapist, but a constriction surfacing within the situation—a movement of the field. Therapists need to be curious as to what they did or said, or did not do or say, to provoke the re-traumatizing of the patient, and to wonder whether their own subverbal or verbal expressions were in habitual *reaction* to the patient rather than in spontaneous, creative *response*. When both patient and therapist grow dynamically sensitive to each other, the ground for open dialogue takes shape. Responsivity replaces reactivity.

Discovering their own *false floors* and understanding the relational theme that is anxiously held within them, therapists help patients discover their own fixations, as they emerge in session and magnify in moments of re-traumatization. It is not useful to have patients at first relax these places of holding because, in doing so, the information held within them may not surface. But if the isometric contractions are slowly explored, their life-saving nature can be unmasked; the importance of the fixations realized and appreciated. Patients are invited to find the qualities or feelings that are expressed within these held areas: clutching in my chest, holding around my eyes, heaviness in my abdomen, hardening in my jaw. If patients are unable to name a quality, it is possible to find a metaphor: tornado in my head, whirling dervish in my torso, heavy weights in the palms of my hands. Patients may also use gestures to illustrate feelings that cannot be expressed with words alone; for example, hands may firmly grasp, shake, flop, or the spine may abruptly lengthen and harden or shorten and crumble. At this point, there is no story *about* what is happening, only the experience *of* the happening. Staying with pure experience rather than the evaluation of themselves, patients' long-held creativity of their suffering springs forward. Once patients feel anguish moving through their bodies, they recognize these feelings as their own rather than some invader that they must vanquish. Their feelings become a valued part of themselves. The depth of the grief and heartache, a symptom of earlier inadequate attunement, is no longer held onto but shared with, since the elements that have created the symptom now have been explored in relation. Just as therapists are here with patients, patients also are here with themselves. Compassion develops on both sides of the equation as therapists and patients find themselves and each other. Now there is no retreat of *Me* from *You*; there is a forming *We* as one finds a belonging with the other—a home. A fresh narrative develops along with novel bodily formations. When we open to our *false floors/fixed gestalts/ isometric contractions*, we open to the kinesthetic resonating that is always already there. This is a slow ongoing process as patients move back-and-forth between the more vulnerable open position and the more familiar closed position. Just as a fawn stands on its feet for the first time, there is wobbling (L. Perls 1992).

Case Vignette

The following session was recorded via the internet and during the first year of the Covid 19 pandemic. At the time of this session, Sally and I had worked together for several years and in-person. Just before I click on the icon to admit Sally into our meeting, I orient myself to the room. To prepare for the abrupt appearance of the other on the screen, I take time to experience phenomenal space; the space in front, to the sides, above, below, and even behind me. This will give me a sense of the literal depth of my experience, such that my focus will not be central and *stuck* to the screen, which would flatten the connecting between me and my patient. Instead, with a greater sense of the surrounding space, I can take a more peripheral focus. Long hours working online can be exhausting and finding lived space allows greater breathing room.

Sally, in her mid-thirties, now joins me on the screen. In general, Sally's vocal tone is of such low intensity that it is as if her words never quite reach me but softly appear and then quickly disappear, dropping into her lap. Her face is narrowed, and her brows furrow when she is struggling with a feeling or attempting to figure herself out. This puzzled look is heightened by the tilt of her head, notably leaning to her right. Sally's spine is lengthened, her upper chest open and wide at the collarbones. Though I cannot see the whole of her body on the screen, I notice my breath slightly held on the inhale in the first moments of our meeting. This leads me to wonder whether Sally is sitting back in her chair or holding herself up and away from it, or if the soles of her feet are touching the floor.

We begin and Sally lunges forward to grab some tissues placed on the table in front of her and immediately wipes her eyes. I ask: "Did you start tearing?" Sally is quick to respond and laughs: "Yeah, I'm crying already." She places both hands on her chest, grasps-onto her fingers, and appears to hold back a deeper sob. Nodding her head up and down, Sally inhales more deeply, as if trying to pull air into her lungs. With a choked voice she says: "I feel so relieved to have you with me for the moment." Her vocal tone grows softer, without much intensity. I question: "Can you tell me more about what is relieving for you?" Sally pauses for a while and then says: "I'm sitting with that question, trying to find the answer." After another substantial pause, she states: "I think it's about having you see me. I want you to see me." Sally nods to herself as if in agreement with what she has just figured out. Fresh tears arrive. Sally struggles to hold them back, which creates a holding on inhalation, and almost simultaneously she attempts to take in more air. At this moment, it appears as if something wants to come out while something wants to be held back.

A softening arises in my chest. I say: "I feel how important it is for me to see you," and I slightly lean toward the screen, my hands resting on my thighs and gently grasping-onto my knees. Sally replies: "I feel at odds because I have to keep reminding myself that I know you're there. I have to do this intellectual work to know that. To know you are there and that you see me." Sally narrows her forehead and purses her lips as if working on this problem. Her head is tilted in the familiar position, and her eyes are cast downward. After a few moments, she gradually looks up and toward me. She straightens her head, and with a soft and open gaze her eyes reach-for me. I wait a few moments and then respond: "And now? How do you experience me now?" With the same light quality to her voice Sally continues: "I think I feel you more." Her voice rises at the end of the sentence as if her statement is more like a question. She goes on: "I can see your eyes. I'm noticing your eyes." Sally's forehead is now smooth, and her mouth slightly opens. Noticing the gap between me and Sally's onscreen image, I say: "I'm going to move my computer closer." Sally immediately retorts: "Is it hard to hear me?" I add: "No, I can hear you. I noticed my computer was at some distance from me. I wanted to move it closer so that you could better see and feel me." I pull my computer, which sits in the middle of my deep desk, closer to my face. Sally says: "I noticed that when you said you were moving closer, I wanted to move closer as well." As she tells me this, she slides her chair closer to her screen, sits back, and exhales more completely.

Sally and I take some time to be in this new relational configuration. I remark: "I wonder how the back of the chair and the seat feel to you now?" This is a reminder for Sally as we have been working with attending to her kinetic-kinesthetic experiences since the beginning of our in-person therapy some years prior. She comments: "Well, I can feel both the back and the seat of the chair, but it starts to become difficult at the same time." For further clarification, I say: "You say that you can feel the back and seat of the chair, but it starts to become difficult. Can you say more about that? I'm not sure what you mean when you say it becomes difficult for you." "Well," she responds, "that is a bit complicated. I recently noticed that I always have my right hip up when I stand or sit. And when I begin to feel the seat, my hip releases down, and my body begins to relax." As Sally shares this, she raises and lowers her right hip to demonstrate the move. Tears begin to form as she continues: "And then I anticipate this twitch will happen. It's a kind of startle/twitch." Sally demonstrates the reaction and abruptly jumps in her chair, slightly torquing and rounding her body to the right side, while simultaneously raising her arms, grasping-onto her hands, and placing them closer to her chest. She begins to cry, and yet holds back her tears at the same time. To further clarify, I wonder: "You anticipate something will happen if you relax into the chair and that startles you?" In a hushed voice, Sally answers: "Well, yes. I anticipate something, but I don't know what. I feel a knot in my gut when I say this." Sally's eyebrows knit together as she reprises her startle/twitch movement several times. I ask: "What do you imagine that particular movement is saying?" Repeating the movement, she responds: "It's as if I'm saying, 'get off me.'" As she says these words, she quickly and forcefully pushes against the imaginary someone or something in front of her with both hands. Surprisingly, her vocal tone matches the intensity and abruptness of her pushing-against movement. Sally states: "I'm not sure if I'm manufacturing this startle or it happens on its own. It's so easy to make it happen." After a rather long pause, I ask: "Has your startle happened since we have been together this morning?" "No," Sally says with certainty, "I anticipated that it could start when I felt the chair underneath me and I could relax."

I suggest: "You might take a risk and find the seat of your chair underneath you. You can find your more relaxed position and see what happens. See whether your startle/twitch will come as a result." Sally waits for a moment and then acknowledges: "Yeah, I'm already anticipating it because I get this feeling in my thigh. I don't know how to describe it, but it's some kind of activation in my thigh, a charged feeling. I'm feeling that now and if I stay with it, I usually startle/twitch." I comment "You could stay with this feeling and see what you're preparing yourself for." After a long pause, Sally's startle/twitch movement returns: "Oh, there it is. And I didn't make that happen." Sally's tears flow, and she attempts to hold them back. "It's hard to show you that," she says. I ask: "What do you imagine my response could be?" Immediately, and with some shaking in her voice, Sally states: "Well, maybe you can see that I have a lot of problems. Maybe more than you thought. And maybe other people can see that I have a lot of problems." Sally says this with a wrinkled forehead. I repeat: "So you have a lot of problems. That is what your startle/twitch means for you, and you imagine that this is what it means for me as well as for others." Sally pauses. With pursed lips, she looks down at her lap for some time and then toward my image on the screen. I wait with Sally and I add: "It seems you are letting me see something about you that I haven't seen before." Sally affirms: "Yes, this is something new that I'm showing you." I say: "It took some courage to let yourself show your startle/twitch to me." Sally continues to tear, and her exhale deepens and slows. With a soft voice she says: "I think you understand." She exhales fully several times, and I feel my body settle into my chair. I let Sally know: "Some people may feel your startle/twitch is a problem. Others not. Some people may feel your tears are a problem. Others not. That depends on how these people are living in their worlds. How we regard ourselves is generally how we regard others."

Sally looks down at her lap for some moments and then looks up at me. "When you say that," Sally resolutely states, "I feel stronger somehow." Listening to her, I experience the base of my pelvis firmly push-against my chair and my spine lengthen. I tell Sally: "I would like to hear more about your stronger feelings?" Sally replies: "If my startle is a problem for them, it's their problem. I don't want to make myself the problem anymore." With her head upright, hand on chest, and not a tear in sight, Sally continues: "I am *not* the problem." Her vocal tone has a steady, higher intensity as she pronounces each word slowly and with solidity. I suggest: "Sally, would you like to try this sentence, '*I am not the problem, you* are.'" Sally laughs and exhales deeply. She takes some time to think about this and wonders: "Am I saying this to you? Because I don't know if it really pertains to you." I suggest: "Well, I am here, and you are startling with me. You can experiment and see what it might feel like to say that directly to me."

Without much hesitation and without a wrinkle in her forehead, Sally tells me directly: "*I* am not the problem. *You* are the problem." Her tone remains solid and clear. Growing more animated, Sally repeats the statement, "*I'm* not the problem, *you* are." Then she adds laughingly: "If you think it's *my* problem, that's *your* problem." Her last statement now has both of us laughing, an indication that we are breathing more fully. Sally repeats the phrase several more times and then waits. "Well, it just occurred to me. I mean, I'm wondering if my startle-twitch is really an attempt to push someone off. To push off that person who thinks I'm a problem." Now Sally extends each arm to either side with flexed wrists as if pushing-against someone. I respond: "You did say, 'Get off me,' when you first explored that statement." I mirror a similar movement as I say this. "Yes!" Sally more powerfully exclaims. Matching her excitement, I say: "Did you hear the sound of your voice?" Again, Sally exclaims: "Yes," in a similar declarative tone.

Repeating the pushing-against movement, Sally announces several more times and directly to me: "I am not the problem, you are. It's not me, it's you." Seemingly satisfied with her lively pronouncements, Sally goes on: "My startle/twitch is my attempt to be free." I nod my head and ask: "Now, how do you experience the back and seat of your chair and the floor under foot?" Sally waits for a while to attend to these potential supports and says: "I feel my right hip connecting with the chair, and that vague charged sensation in my thigh is not present. And I feel the floor is more there... more under my feet." Sally smiles and nods as she says this. I, too, feel my chair more palpably behind my back and under both my pelvis and the thighs of my crossed legs, as my breathing deepens.

Taking my cue from this experience, I propose the next step to our experiment and state: "Sally, I am curious if you would like to do this moving-feeling exploration standing up?" Instantly, Sally responds and is already rising from her chair, "Yes, yes. I like that idea." I add: "Play with the movement and the phrase and see what they become. Go wherever you wish in your room. You don't need to stay in view of your computer's camera." I also rise with Sally as she shares: "I'm not sure what I'm doing now. I need another sort of orienting." I say: "What would you like to do? It's your exploration. Only for you." Sally finds sufficient space to move around in her room and begins pushing in a variety of directions. I assert: "I see you know what to do." Sally's movements are firm and well-animated. Sometimes the words accompany the movement, and sometimes the movement speaks for itself. She asks, "Can you see me?" I firmly state: "Yes, I do see you, and I feel my excitement as I see you moving." Sally pushes-against the air and the imagined other with her whole body; her hips move side-to-side, her pelvis moves forward-and-back, and even her head and buttocks get into the pushing-against act. Sally takes her time in this novel exploration. Then she begins to jump up-and-down while she continues pushing her hands in varied directions.

Sally stops to breathe and places the palms of both hands flat against her chest. "Wow," she pronounces with a wide and open smile, her head erect: "I really like that." I ask: "Do you feel your hands placed on your chest?" "Yes," she says. I state: "I would like to add one more element to this experiment you created. See if it fits for you." I place my hands over my chest and say to Sally: "I am over here." Then I move my hands outward, wrists flexed and pushing-against her image on the screen and say: "And you are over there." I return my hands to my chest, palms pushed-against it, and slowly repeat, "I am here," and pause to feel the experience. I again push-against Sally's image on the screen and say, "And you are there," and I pause again. I suggest: "If you choose to make this move, you might try it with those exact words." Trying the experiment and with both hands on her chest, Sally says: "I am over here." She waits in this position and then, pushing-against my image on the screen, she states: "You are over there." Sally explores these movements and the phrases that accompany them as she moves closer or farther away from the screen. "I like moving around: I can be in different places, and you are still over there." After some time passes, Sally's exploration ends. "I feel finished now. I want to come back and sit closer to you." Sally returns to her chair: "It's not difficult to feel the chair behind me and underneath me now. I feel quite open. And I feel the floor." I agree: "Yes!" Sally shares: "And I can wiggle my hips side-to-side. Usually, I feel locked in my hips, but now I feel free." I say: "Yes, and free with me. You have let me see all the ways you can move and with some excitement." Sally smiles and laughs as she wiggles in the chair, and I join her in the act. Her breathing is deep and steady, as is mine. At session's end, Sally and I pause for a while to linger in this more intimate experience of our being together.

Psychodynamics

The session began with tears flowing down Sally's cheeks, which simultaneously seemed to express the hope of my seeing/being with her and the dreaded possibility of my not. To avoid the worrisome and hovering anticipated lack of support, Sally worked to convince herself that I was there. Although she grew more open as our dialogue continued, there remained a holding back. I dually observed this in her breathing patterns and felt it in my lived bodily experience of the unfolding situation.

The responsivity of our body to the behaviors of significant others in our past shapes how we open to the world and how we encounter it. The story of what *was* early on haunted Sally and obscured the reality of what now *could be* between us, what I might offer her. Just as she had difficulty trusting she could give over to the ground beneath, expressed in her difficulty in "relaxing" on the chair, Sally had similar difficulty with relaxing to the ground of our relationship, giving to and receiving from me.

Sally's natural desire to live as part of a harmonious world, where she would be welcomed and received, was difficult to conceive. She had to hold herself together in a way she imagined no one else could or would. The ongoing and often unfelt maintaining of her lifted right hip signified the isometric contraction/false floor that had inadvertently formed early on. This was an attempt to provide some sense of cohering. These are areas of secondary responses with their psychological equivalent: "If you will not be *there* and with me, I will not be *here* and with you." This statement, made in relation to chronic situations of potential danger and frustration, exemplifies adjustments necessary to find certainty within a discordant world (Perls et al. 1990, 260–261). It signals a way of going on.

When Sally took the risk to release her pelvis onto the chair, her anticipation of its lack of support quickly and anxiously rushed in, and she was startled. Sally inadvertently re-traumatized herself. It was not as if this movement and its accompanying affect was willfully produced, as it concerned her: rather, it simply happened. Bearing witness to her own difficulty, Sally thought others would see her startle/twitch as evidence of her being "a problem." Her wish to meet with a welcoming other was rapidly replaced by her fear of being rebuffed. The narrative, forged many years prior, inhabited her everyday experience. Its accompanying anxious meanings were well concealed within the secondary patterns, or the structured isometric constrictions/false floors.

The form Sally's difficulty took, an inability to give herself over to her experience with me, was co-created in the situation we together lived. Remembering Sally's spontaneous statement, "Get off me," I suggested she say: "You are the problem, not me," to further the process of disclosure and bring what was background to the fore. This enabled her firmly to push-against the other rather than to push-against herself in a hardened way, which would create psychophysical constrictions. As Sally discovered the significance of her startle-twitch, and explored the meaning of the movement, the authenticity of her lived bodily experience replaced familiar and mechanized constricted behaviors. Whatever happens next is always implied and anticipated in this passing present moment. Feeling the next step in her exploration,

I invited Sally to continue the movement while standing. This would lend more bodily support to her freely developing experience. Moving in diverse directions and with her mantra, "I am not the problem, you are," Sally found the support of the earth. Once found, she could reach for the world.

When Sally felt finished with her improvised gambol, I took the risk of adding another element to her experiment. With my invitation for her to push-against her chest with both hands, Sally could discover a novel kind of containing, one necessary for developing a more solid and core sense of self. The push-against my onscreen image accomplished the psychophysical investigation of differentiation: "I reach for you there as I move here." It is a necessary differentiation that forms the ground of all fluid contact. In the performing of those acts, the cohering of person and world is completed.

Concluding Remarks

It is crucial for the therapist to be with the other in a way that demonstrably appreciates that person's unique and individual experience of the world. That is, one must respect the manner in which the world comes to be for the patient and not attempt to make it different based on an ethical judgment of what is acceptable or unacceptable, what is normal or abnormal behavior. It is one's internally experience lived body, a subjective experience, that is what is normal for that person.

Bringing the patient's kinetic-kinesthetic experiences to the fore unfolds the many layers of pre-reflective happenings and illustrates the essentials of what it means to be human. This process includes psychic realms that are integrated within particular ancient and evolutionary physiological states that suddenly come into being and cut through our conscious and voluntary movements. This is the experience of the Startle Response. In describing such experiences, one transforms and the transforming leads to further describing, which leads to further transformation, and so on. In becoming a partner on this journey, the therapist must intrude just enough to be acknowledged but, at the same time, not intrude so much that the patient loses a burgeoning experience of freedom, where the novelty of "I can" replaces the habitual "I cannot."

References

Aristotle. 2011. *De Anima*. Translated by Mark Shiffman. Newburyport, MA: Focus Publishing/R. Pullins Company (original work published 350 BC).

Aristotle. 2018. *Physics*. Translated by Charles D.C. Reeve. Indianapolis: Hackett Publishing Company.

Baumgarten, Alexander Gottlieb. 1988. *Esthétique: Précédée des Méditations philosophiques sur quelques sujets se rapportant à l'essence du poème, et de la Métaphysique*. Translated by Jean-Yves Pranchère. Paris: L'Herne.

Behnke, Elizabeth A. 1997. "Ghost Gestures: Phenomenological Investigations of Bodily Micromovements and Their Intercorporeal Implications." *Human Studies* 20, no. 2: 181–201.

Behnke, Elizabeth A. 2012. "Enduring: A Phenomenological Investigation." In *Body Memory, Metaphor and Movement*, edited by Sabine Koch, Thomas Fuchs, Michela Summa, and Cornelia Muller, 83–103. Philadelphia: John Benjamins Publishing Company.

Benjamin, Walter. 2010. *The Work of Art in the Age of Mechanical Reproduction*. Scottsdale, Arizona: Prism Key Press (original work published 1935).

Bergson, Henri. 1992. *The Creative Mind*. Translated by Mabelle L. Anison. New York: The Citadel Press (original work published 1934).

Bergson, Henri. 2010. *Matter and Memory*, trans. Nancy Margaret Paul, W. Scott Palmer. Lawrence, KS: Neeland Media LLC.

Bloom, Dan. 2005. "A Centennial Celebration of Laura Perls: The Aesthetics of Commitment." *British Gestalt Journal* 14, no. 2: 81–90.

Bloom, Dan. 2016. "The Relational Function of Self: Self Functioning in the Most Human Plane." In *Self: A Polyphony of Contemporary Gestalt Therapists*, edited by Jean-Marie Robine, 65–84. Saint Romaine Virvée, France: L'Exprimerie.

Bloom, Dan. 2019. "Neither from the 'Inside' Looking 'Out' nor from the 'Outside' Looking 'In.'" In *Psychopathology and Atmospheres, Neither Inside nor Outside*, edited by Gianni Francesetti and Tonino Griffero, 178–190. Cambridge Scholars Publishing.

Bloom, Lois. 1993. *The Transition from Infancy to Language: Acquiring the Power of Expression*. Cambridge, MA: Cambridge University Press.

Bornemark, Jonna. 2016. "Life beyond Individuality: A-subjective Experience in Pregnancy." In *Phenomenology of Pregnancy*, edited by Jonna Bornemark and Nicholas Smith, 251–278. Stockholm: Södertörns högskola.

Bowlby, John. 1982. *Attachment and Loss. Vol. 1, Attachment.* New York: Basic Books (original work published 1969).

Brazelton, Barnnard. 1990. *Touch: The Foundation of Experience.* Madison, CT: International Universities Press.

Brothers, Doris. 2008. *Toward a Psychology of Uncertainty: Trauma-centered Psychoanalysis.* New York: The Analytic Press.

Bruner, Jerome. 1990. *Acts of Meaning: Four Lectures on Mind and Culture.* Cambridge, MA: Harvard University Press.

Campos, Joseph, and Eric Walle. 2014. "Infant Language Development Is Related to the Acquisition of Walking." *Developmental Psychology* 5, no. 2: 336–348.

Casey, Edward. 2000. *Remembering: A Phenomenological Study.* Bloomington: University of Indiana Press.

de Vries, Jip, Gerald H.A. Visser, and Heniz F.R. Prechtl. 1984. "Fetal Motility in the First Half of Pregnancy." In *Continuity of Neural Functions from Prenatal to Postnatal Life,* edited by Heniz F.R. Prechtl, 46–64. London: Mac Keith Press.

Dewey, James. 1896. "The Reflex Arc Concept in Psychology." *Psychological Review* 3: 357–370.

Epstein, Mark. 2001. *Going on Being.* Somerville, MA: Wisdom Publications.

Epstein, Mark. 2014. *The Trauma of Everyday Life.* New York: Penguin Books.

Fiedler, Fred E. 1950. "A Comparison of Therapeutic Relationships in Psychoanalytic, Nondirective and Adlerian Therapy." *Journal of Consulting Psychology* 14, no. 6: 436–445.

Finlay, Linda. 2011. *Phenomenology for Therapists: Researching the Lived World.* Chichester, West Sussex, UK: Wiley-Blackwell.

Fogel, Alan. 1993. *Developing through Relationships: Origins of Communication, Self and Culture.* Chicago: University of Chicago Press.

Frank, Ruella. 2001. *Body of Awareness: A Somatic and Developmental Approach to Psychotherapy.* Cambridge, MA: GestaltPress.

Frank, Ruella. 2005. "Developmental Somatic Psychotherapy: Developmental Process Embodied within the Clinical Moment." In *New Dimensions in Body Psychotherapy,* edited by Nick Totten, 115–127. Berkshire, UK: Open University Press.

Frank, Ruella. 2013. *Introduction to Developmental Somatic Psychotherapy.* New York: Center for Somatic Studies Production. DVD.

Frank, Ruella. 2016. "Self in Motion." In *Self: A Polyphony of Contemporary Gestalt Therapists,* edited by Jean-Marie Robine, 371–386. Saint-Romain-la-Virvée: L'Exprimerie.

Frank, Ruella. 2021. "The Lived-body: A Moving-Feeling Experience." *Gestalt Review* 25, no. 1: 11–30.

Frank, Ruella, and Frances La Barre. 2011. *The First Year and the Rest of Your Life: Movement, Development and Psychotherapeutic Change.* New York: Routledge.

Franscesetti, Gianni, Michela Gecele, and Jan Roubal, eds. 2007. *Gestalt Therapy Approach to Psychopathology. Gestalt Therapy in Clinical Practice: From Psychopathology to the Aesthetics of Contact.* Milan: Franco Angeli.

Fuchs, Thomas. 2005. *Corporealized and Disembodied Minds: A Phenomenological View of the Body in Melancholia and Schizophrenia.* Baltimore: John Hopkins University Press.

Fuchs, Thomas. 2007. "Psychotherapy of the Lived Space: A Phenomenological and Ecological Concept." *American Journal of Psychotherapy* 61, no. 4: 423–439.

Fuchs, Thomas. 2010. "Phenomenology and Psychopathology." In *Handbook of Phenomenology and Cognitive Science*, edited by Daniel Schmicking and Shaun Gallagher, 546–573. London: Springer.

Fuchs, Thomas. 2013. "The Phenomenology of Body Memory." In *Body Memory, Metaphor and Movement*, edited by Sabine C. Koch, Thomas Fuchs, Michela Summa, and Cornelia Muller, 9–22. Philadelphia: John Benjamins Publishing Company.

Fuchs, Thomas. 2013. "The Phenomenology of Affectivity." In *The Oxford Handbook of Philosophy and Psychiatry*, edited by K.W.M. Fulford, Martin Davies, Richard Gipps, George Graham, John Sadler, Giovanni Stanghellini, and Tim Thorton, 612–631. Oxford, UK: Oxford University Press.

Fuchs, Thomas. 2017. "Intercorporeality and Interaffectivity." *Phenomenology and Mind* 11: 194–209.

Fuchs, Thomas. 2019. "The Interactive Phenomenal Field and the Life Space: A Sketch of an Ecological Concept of Psychotherapy." *Psychopathology* 62, no. 2: 63–70.

Fuchs, Thomas, and Sabine C. Koch. 2014 (June 6). "Embodied Affectivity: On Moving and Being Moved." *Frontiers in Psychology*. Accessed March 20, 2020. 10.3389/fpsyg.2014.00508.

Fuchs, Thomas, and Jann E. Schlimme. 2009. "Embodiment and Psychopathology: A Phenomenological Perspective." *Current Opinion in Psychiatry* 22, no. 6: 570–575.

Fulkerson, Matthew. 2014. *The First Sense*. Cambridge, MA: MIT Press.

Gallagher, Shaun. 2020. *Action and Interaction*. Oxford: Oxford University Press.

Gendlin, Eugene. 1992. "The Primacy of the Body, Not the Primacy of Perception." *Man and World* 25, no. 3–4: 34–53.

Gendlin, Eugene. 1997. *Experiencing and the Creation of Meaning: A Philosophical and Psychological Approach to the Subjective*. Glencoe, IL: The Free Press (original work published 1962).

Gibson, James. 1979. *The Ecological Approach to Visual Perception*. Boston: Houghton Mifflin.

Gibson, James, and Eleanor Gibson. 1977. "The Theory of Affordances." *Perceiving Acting and Knowing: Toward and Ecological Psychology*, edited by Robert Shaw and John Bransford, 67–82. Hillsdale, NJ: Lawrence Erlbaum.

Hanna, Thomas. 1988. *Somatics: Reawakening the Mind's Control of Movement, Flexibility, and Health*. New York: Addison-Wesley.

Hermans, Hubert, and Agnieszka Hermans-Konopka. 2010. *Dialogical Self Theory: Positioning and Counter-Positioning in a Globalizing Society*. New York: Cambridge University Press.

Husserl, Edmund. 1964. *The Phenomenology of Internal Time Consciousness*. Translated by James Churchill. Bloomington: Indiana University Press (original work published 1928).

Husserl, Edmund. 1973. *Cartesian Meditations*. Translated by Dorion Cairns. The Hague: Martinus Nijhoff.

Husserl, Edmund. 1989. *Ideas Pertaining to a Pure Phenomenology and to a Phenomenological Philosophy: Second book: Studies in the Phenomenology of Constitution*. Translated by Richard Rojcewicz and André Schuwer. Dordrecht, The Netherlands: Kluwer Academic.

Jacobs, Lynne. 2009. "Relationality: Foundational Assumptions." In *Co-creating the Field: Intention and Practice in the Age of Complexity*, edited by Deborah Ullman and Gordon Wheeler, 41–66. New York: Gestalt Press/Routledge.

Jacobs, Lynne. 2017. "Hopes, Fears and Enduring Relational Themes." *British Gestalt Journal* 26, no.1: 7–16.

Jeannerod, Marc. 2006. *Motor Cognition: What Actions Tell the Self*. Oxford: Oxford University Press.

Kelso, J.A. Scott, and Thomas Fuchs. 2016. "The Coordination Dynamics of Mobile Conjugate Reinforcement" *Biological Cybernetics* 110, no. 1: 41–53.

Krueger, Joel. 2018. "Intentionality." In *The Oxford Handbook of Phenomenological Psychopathology*, edited by Giovanni Stanghellini, Matthew Broome, Andrea Raballo, Anthony Vincent Fernandez, Paolo Fusar-Poli, and René Rosfort. Oxford, UK: Oxford University Press. Accessed March 1, 2020. https://philarchive.org/archive/KRUI-4

Landis, Carney and William A. Hunt. 1968. *The Startle Pattern*. New York:Farrar & Rinehart (original work published 1939).

Maratos, Olga. 1998. "Neonatal, Early and Later Imitation: Same Order Phenomena." In *The Development of Sensory, Motor and Cognitive Capacities in Early Infancy: From Perception to Cognition*, edited by Francesca Simion and George Butterworth, 146–158. Hove, East Sussex, UK: Psychology Press.

Mead, George H. 1938. *The Philosophy of the Act*. Chicago: University of Chicago Press.

Meltzoff, Andrew N. 1985. "The Roots of Social and Cognitive Development: Models of Man's Original Nature." In *Social Perception in Infants*, edited by Tiffany Field and Nathan Fox, 1–30. Norwood, NJ: Ablex.

Meltzoff, Andrew N., and Richard W. Borton. 1979. "Intermodal Matching by Human Neonates." *Nature* 282: 403–404.

Meltzoff, Andrew N., and Keith M. Moore. 1977. "Imitation of Facial and Manual Gestures by Human Neonates." *Science* 198: 75–78.

Merleau-Ponty, Maurice. 1968. *The Visible and the Invisible*. Translated by Alphonso Lingis. Evanston, IL: Northwestern University Press.

Merleau-Ponty, Maurice. 2012. *Phenomenology of Perception*. Translated by Donald A. Landes. New York: Psychology Press (original work published 1945).

Miller, Michael Vincent. 2011. *Teaching a Paranoid to Flirt: The Poetics of Gestalt Therapy*. Gouldsboro, ME: The Gestalt Journal Press.

Mühlhoff, Rainer. 2019. "Affective Disposition." In *Affective Societies: Key Concepts*, edited by Jan Slaby and Christian von Scheve, 119–130. New York: Routledge.

Noland, Carrie J. 2009. *Agency and Embodiment: Performing Gestures/Producing Culture*. Cambridge, MA: Harvard University Press.

Orange, Donna M. 2009. "Intersubjective Systems Theory: A Fallibilist's journey." *Self and Systems: Annals of the New York Academy of Sciences* 1159: 237–248.

Paterson, Mark. 2012. "Movement for Movement's Sake? On the Relationship between Kinaesthesia and Aesthetics." *Essays in Philosophy* 13, no. 2: 471–497.

Perls, Frederick S., Ralph Hefferline, and Paul Goodman. 1990. *Gestalt Therapy: Excitement and Growth in the Human Personality*. London: Souvenir Press (original work published 1951).

Perls, Laura. 1992. *Living at the Boundary*. Gouldsboro, ME: The Gestalt Journal Press.

Piontelli, Alessandra. 1992. *From Fetus to Child: An Observational and Psychoanalytic Study*. London: Routledge.

Piontelli, Allesandra. 2010. *Development of Normal Fetal Movements*. Milan: Springer-Verlag Italia.

Plato, and Benjamin Jowett. 1990. *Theaetetus*. New York: C. Scribner's Sons.

Prechtl, Heinz F.R. 1984. "Continuity and Change in Early Neural Development." In *Continuity of Neural Functions from Prenatal to Postnatal Life*, edited by Heinz F.R. Prechtl. London: Mac Keith Press.

Prechtl, Heinz F. R. 1989. "Fetal Behaviour." In *Fetal Neurology*, edited by Alan Hill and Joseph J. Volpe. New York: Raven Press.

Rank, Otto. 1932. *Art and the Artist: Creative Urge and Personality Development*. New York: Alfred A. Knopf.

Richardson, Keith. 2000. *Developmental Psychology: How Nature and Nurture Interact*. Mahway, NJ: Lawrence Erlbaum Associates.

Robine, Jean-Marie. 2013. "Psychotherapy as a Situation and Contacting as its Aesthetic Focus." Lecture presented at the conference, Psychology and the Other, Cambridge, MA, October 6.

Robine, Jean-Marie. 2015. *Social Change Begins with Two*. Milano: Istituto di Gestalt HCC Italy.

Robine, Jean-Marie. 2011. *On Occasion of the Other*. Gouldsboro, ME: The Gestalt Journal Therapy Press, Inc.

Rochat, Philippe. 2009. *Others in Mind: Social Origins of Self-Consciousness*. New York: Cambridge University Press.

Rochat, Philippe. 2011. "What Is It Like to Be a Newborn?" In *The Oxford Handbook of the Self*, edited by Shaun Gallagher, 57–79. Oxford: Oxford University Press.

Rosa, Hartmut. 2019. *Resonance: A Sociology of Our Relationship to the World*. Translated by James C. Wagner. Medford, MA: Polity Press (original work published 2016).

Rovee, Caroline Kent, and David T. Rovee. 1969. "Conjugate Reinforcement of Infant Exploratory Behavior." *Journal of Experimental Child Psychology* 8, no. 1: 33–39.

Russell, Matheson. 2006. *Husserl: A Guide for the Perplexed*. London: Continuum.

Sheets-Johnstone, Maxine. 1999. *The Primacy of Movement*. Philadelphia: John Benjamins Publishing Company.

Sheets-Johnstone, Maxine. 2010. "Why is Movement Therapeutic?" *American Journal of Dance Therapy* 32, 2–15.

Sheets-Johnstone, Maxine. 2012. "Kinesthetic Memory: Further Critical Reflections and Constructive Analysis." In *Body Memory, Metaphor and Movement*, edited by Sabine Koch, Thomas Fuchs, Michela Summa, and Cornelia Muller, 51–72. Philadelphia: John Benjamins Publishing Company.

Sheets-Johnstone, Maxine. 2014. "Animation: Analyses, Elaborations, and Implications." *Husserl Studies* 30: 247–268.

Sheets-Johnstone, Maxine. 2016. *Insides and Outsides: Interdisciplinary Perspectives on Animate Nature*. La Vergne, TN: Ingram Book Company.

Sheets-Johnstone, Maxine. 2017. "Agency: Phenomenological Insights and Dynamic Complementarities." *The Humanistic Psychologist* 45, no. 1: 1–22.

Sheets-Johnstone, Maxine. 2019. "Kinesthesia: An Extended Critical Overview and a Beginning Phenomenology of Learning." *Continental Philosophy Review* 52, no. 2: 143–169.

Sheets-Johnstone, Maxine. 2020. "The Lived Body." *The Humanistic Psychologist* 48, no. 1: 1–26.

Smith, Nicholas. 2016. "Phenomenology of Pregnancy: A Cure for Philosophy?" In *The Phenomenology of Pregnancy, Sodertorn Philosophical Studies* 18, edited by Jonna Bornemark and Nicholas Smith, 15–49. Stockholm: Elanders.

Socraides, Daphne, and Robert D. Stolorow. 1984/1985. "Affects and Self Objects." *The Annual of Psychoanalysis*, 12/13: 105–119.

Spagnuolo-Lobb, Margherita. 2013a. "From the Need for Aggression to the Need for Rootedness: A Gestalt Postmodern Clinical and Social Perspective on Conflict." *British Gestalt Journal* 22, no. 1: 32–39.

Spagnuolo-Lobb, Margherita. 2013b. *The Now-for-Next in Psychotherapy: Gestalt Therapy Recounted in Post-Modern Society*. Siracusa: Istituto di Gestalt HCC Italy.

Spagnuolo-Lobb, Margherita. 2018. "Aesthetic Relational Knowing of the Field: A Revised Concept of Awareness in Gestalt Therapy and Contemporary Psychiatry." *Gestalt Review* 22, no. 1: 50–68.

Sparling, Joyce W. 1993. *Concepts in Fetal Movement Research*. Binghamton, New York: The Haworth Press.

Stanghellini, Giovanni, and Matthew R. Broome. 2014. "Psychopathology as the Basic Science of Psychiatry." *The British Journal of Psychiatry* 205, no. 3, 169–170.

Stern, Daniel. 1985. *The Interpersonal World of the Human Infant: A View from Psychoanalysis and Developmental Psychology*. New York: Basic Books.

Stern, Donnel B. 2003. *Unformulated Experience: From Disassociation to Imagination in Psychoanalysis*. New York: Routledge.

Stolorow, Robert D. 2007. *Trauma and Human Existence*. New York: Analytic Press.

Stone, Sarah A., Ilse DeKoeyer-Laros, and Alan Fogel. 2012 (September). "Self and Other Dialogue in Infancy: Normal Versus Compromised Developmental Pathways." In *Applications of Dialogical Self Theory. New Directions for Child and Adolescent Development,* 137, edited by Hubert J.M. Hermans, 23–38. Wiley Periodicals.

Taipale, Joona. 2014. *Phenomenology of Embodiment: : Husserl and the Constitution of Subjectivity*. Evanston, IL: Northwestern University Press.

Thelen, Esther. 1995. "Motor Development: A New Synthesis." *American Psychologist: Journal of the American Psychological Association* 50, no. 2: 79–94.

Thelen, Esther, and Linda Smith. 1994. *A Dynamic Systems Approach to the Development of Cognition and Action*. Cambridge, MA: MIT Press.

Trevarthen, Colwyn, and Kenneth Aitken 2001. "Infant Intersubjectivity: Research, Theory, and Clinical Applications." *Journal of Child Psychology and Psychiatry* 42, no. 1: 3–48.

Tronick, Edward. 2007. *The Neurobehavioral and Social-emotional Development of Infants and Children*. New York: W.W. Norton.

Wachtel, Paul L. 2007. "Carl Rogers and the Larger Context of Therapeutic Thought." *Psychotherapy: Theory, Research, Practice, Training* 44, no. 3: 279–284.

Waldenfels, Bernhard. 2011. *Phenomenology of the Alien: Basic Concepts in Phenomenology*. Evanston, Il: Northwestern University Press.

Welsh, Talia. 2013. *The Child as Natural Phenomenologist: Primal and Primary Experience in Merleau-Ponty's Psychology*. Evanston, IL: Northwestern University Press.

Wynn, Francine. 2002. "The Early Relationship of Mother and Pre-infant: Merleau-Ponty and Pregnancy." *Nursing Philosophy: International Journal for Healthcare Professionals* 3, no. 1: 4–14.

Yontef, Gary. 2009. "The Relational Attitude in Gestalt Therapy and Practice." In *Relational Approaches in Gestalt Therapy*, edited by Lynne Jacobs and Rich Hycner, 37–59. Santa Cruz, CA.: GestaltPress.

Zhao, Guoping. 2020. *Subjectivity and Infinity*. Cham, Switzerland: Palgrave MacMillan.

Index

For Product Safety Concerns and Information please contact our EU
representative GPSR@taylorandfrancis.com
Taylor & Francis Verlag GmbH, Kaufingerstraße 24, 80331 München, Germany